CONFRONTATION IN KOSOVA

THE ALBANIAN–SERB STRUGGLE, 1969–1999

BY
PETER R. PRIFTI

EAST EUROPEAN MONOGRAPHS, BOULDER
DISTRIBUTED BY COLUMBIA UNIVERSITY PRESS, NEW YORK

1999

EAST EUROPEAN MONOGRAPHS, NO. DXXXVII

To President Bill Clinton and
America's NATO allies, in recognition
of their compassionate support of the
Kosovars' aspiration for liberty and
justice

Table of Contents

Acknowledgment

In the making of this book, I am indebted first of all to Naum Prifti, distinguished Albanian author of short stories, plays and humor. He worked tirelessly to put the manuscript together, and I benefited at every step along the way from his considerable experience as an editor both in Albania and America. I also benefited from the close cooperation of Sokol Kondi, and I thank him for his assistance. Ela Kondi was enthusiastic from the start about this enterprise, and I thank her for her encouragement. Thanks also are due to Julika Prifti for her consistent support, and to her teenage son, Eric, who showed commendable self-discipline in the chore of typing the manuscript.

It has been a pleasure to work on this project with Prof. Stephen Fischer-Galati, the erudite and affable editor of the *East European Quarterly*, who has done so much to further knowledge through the institution of the *East European Monographs* series.

I express my gratitude to all the publications in which the contents of this book first appeared. These include the *Albanian-American Catholic Bulletin, Balkanistica, Dielli,* the *South Slav Journal,* and *Illyria.*

Author's Note

This book owes its existence primarily to the violence that wracked the province of Kosova, through most of 1998. The violence, although not new to the region, intensified dramatically with Serbia's massive military crackdown on the restive Albanians in late February of 1998.

I have been preoccupied with the problem of Kosova for some 30 years, since the Albanian demonstrations there in autumn of 1968. Over the years I have published studies and articles on Kosova in a variety of publications, with a view to providing information on the subject, and hoping at the same time to contribute to the search for a solution to a conflict that has been a festering wound in the Balkans for over a century. This volume is a collection of a substantial portion of such studies and articles

Not infrequently with books of collected materials, there is an unevenness about the contents, owing to changing circumstances over the span of time in which they were written, as well as other factors. The contents of this book illustrate that fact. A few of the articles are strictly "scholarly," i.e., detached, dispassionate and analytical. A larger number, written over a ten-year period (1982-1992), are essentially reportage, intended to give a detailed history of the events of the period, as they were occurring. They have the merit, I believe, of recreating the "feel" or political atmosphere of the time, as well as providing a considerable quantity of data for researchers. A number of other articles are "partisan" in character, in the sense that they reflect openly the Albanian viewpoint on the Kosova question. Prompted by the events of the moment, they are more akin to political tracts than to standard academic discourse. The tone of urgency and spirit of militancy in them, is especially marked in the material in Part II, "Correspondence.".

In writing the articles that comprise this work, I was careful to observe, as best as I could, the basic criteria of scholarship: adherence to facts, respect for truth, reasonable interpretation of data. But in terms of style and aim, most of this book is a departure from other writings of mine in the field of Albanian studies. Unlike such writings, in this particular work I have not hesitated to be both objective and subjective, combining reason with feeling and intellect with passion in the interpretation of the data. In this sense, this work is a departure as well from my characteristic temperament which, I am told, is rather mild and tranquil, not easily ruffled or unsettled by circumstances.

The Serbian-Albanian conflict, however, being a matter of great urgency, affecting the lives and fortunes of two million Kosovars (i. e., the Albanians of Kosova), it was not possible to remain "neutral" and emotionally uninvolved. I make no secret of the fact that, in this conflict, I plead in effect the case of the victims, namely the Albanians. Accordingly, I have sought to articulate, as clearly as I could, their plight in the Republic of Serbia. Nor have I shied away from using strong language, at times, to criticize the policies of Serbia in Kosova, which over the past decade created a crisis situation that portended tragic consequences for both Albanians and Serbs. Having lived in the time-frame of the events discussed in this volume, and experienced their impact, I make no apology for showing anger and dismay in many instances over the injustice done to the Kosovars. Indeed, in view of what has happened in Kosova since February 1998, I would not have been out of place if I had used even more emotive language. I rather wish the text of this book were imbued with the spirit and fire of a Patrick Henry or a Tom Paine. It would be much more compelling to the reader. If, nonetheless, some readers find the harsh criticism of the Serbs objectionable, I answer that the vivid language is far less offensive and painful than the humiliation and abuse to which ethnic Albanians in Kosova have been subjected for decades.

While granting that this volume is, in good part, "partisan" in character, the underlying message of the text is broader, non-partisan and non-confrontational. Explicitly and implicitly, I have argued that it is necessary to forswear the politics of ethnic hatred and oppression, and supplant it with the politics of accommodation and coexistence and a novel, future-oriented agenda. I have intimated that both parties to the dispute need to foster productive inter-ethnic relations, and break the cycle of violence to which they have been hostage for generations.

The contents of the book have been printed as originally published, except that a few of the articles have been abbreviated to avoid repetition of material that was basically similar in substance. Stylistic changes were made here and there, where that seemed advisable to clarify the meaning of the text, or improve the language. A single article, "Position Paper on Kosova (1988)," is published here for the first time. The materials are arranged and presented in chronological order, in accordance with the date of publication. The letters in the Correspondence section include a few replies from the recipients.

Two different spellings are given for the province: "Kosovo" and "Kosova", in keeping with the usage of the term in the original texts. "Kosova" (Ko-SO-vah) is the name by which the province is known to its Albanian inhabitants, who make up more than 90 percent of the population, and it seemed proper to include their spelling of the term, alongside the other, more widely known version.

Lastly, a large number of books have been published—especially since the death of Tito—which give the Serbian version of the conflict in Kosova. By comparison, books presenting the Albanian thesis have been relatively few in number. An imbalance has been created, which ought to be redressed. My awareness of this fact was a major motive in my decision to publish this book. It is my hope that its publication will prompt other writers to follow suit.

San Diego
November 1998

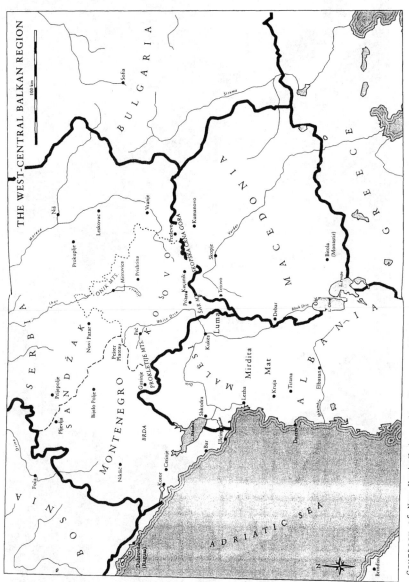

THE WEST-CENTRAL BALKAN REGION

100 km

BULGARIA

Sofia

SERBIA

Niš

Leskovac

Vranje

Morava

Prokuplje

Preševo

Mitrovica

Prishtina

Kumanovo

KOSOVO

ŠKOPSKA CRNA GORA

Skopje

Vardar

Tetovo

MACEDONIA

Bitola (Monastir)

SANDŽAK

Novi Pazar

Peć

Pešter Plateau

PROKLETIJE MTS.

Prizren

Kačanik

SAR MTS.

White Drin

Debar

Black Drin

GREECE

Struma

Ibar

Prijepolje

Pljevlja

Bijelo Polje

MONTENEGRO

BRDA

Gusinje

Kukës

Luma

MALES

Mirdita

Mat

Tirana

Elbasan

ALBANIA

Foča

Nikšić

Cetinje

Shkodra

Lezha

Kruja

Drin

Bar

Ulcinj

Durrës

BOSNIA

Kotor

Dubrovnik (Ragusa)

N

ADRIATIC SEA

Brindisi

Courtesy of New York University Press, publisher of Noel Malcolm, Kosovo – A Short History, 1998.

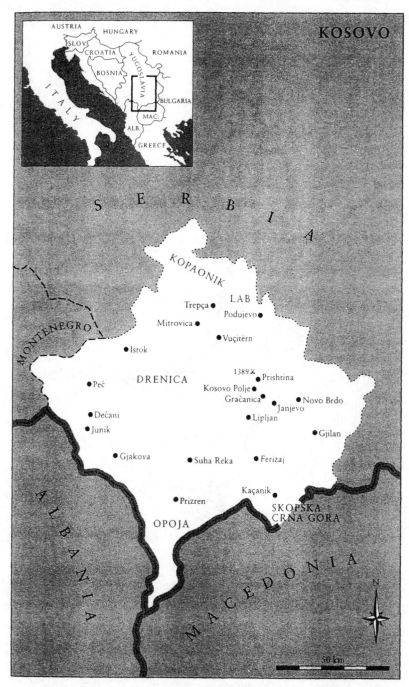

Courtesy of New York University Press, publisher of Noel Malcolm, <u>Kosovo - A Short History</u>, 1998.

I.
Studies, Articles, and Commentaries

Chapter 1:

*Kosova in Ferment**

    1968 might well be called the Year of the Student. Caught in a circle of increasing violence by campus militants and repressive response, the American press has emphasized domestic explanations—middle class alienation, the demoralizing impact of Vietnam, frustrated impotence when the "children's crusade" for MacCarthy ended in defeat. Yet recent student unrest has not been limited to the United States or to highly technical, industrialized societies. It has cut across boundaries of technology and ideology, for similar and sometimes even more violent student demonstrations have swept Japan, Western Europe, Mexico, and Brazil. Indeed even the Kosova, the least developed area of Yugoslavia, has been affected by student militancy interacting with long-suppressed, latent Albanian nationalism.

    The events, occurring in three different phases and spaced about a month apart, each one more serious than the one that preceded it, took place in the predominantly Albanian-populated areas of Yugoslavia that lie close to the border of Albania. The first two demonstrations, occurring in late October and late November of 1968, took place in Kosova, one of two autonomous provinces in federated Yugoslavia; the third erupted in late December in Tetovo (Tetova),[1] principal town in the Republic of Macedonia.

---

* Source: A monograph published under the title "Kosovo in Ferment" by the Center for International Studies, M.I.T. (Massachusetts Institute of Technology), Cambridge, Mass., USA, June 1969, 37 pages.

They brought again to the fore Yugoslavia's nationality question, [2] and focused attention on Yugoslav- Albanian relations over the most sensitive, concrete issue between the two countries—the issue of Kosovo (Kosova). [3] The following analysis of these demonstrations has three purposes: 1) to untangle—when possible—conflicting reports of what actually happened, 2) to show the implications for Belgrade's nationality policy, and 3) to evaluate the repercussions in Albanian-Yugoslav relations.

The study utilizes three sources: publications of the Albanian minority in Yugoslavia, official Belgrade reports, and publications of an Albanian émigré group based in Istanbul, Turkey. An examination of the data show that these sources gave different accounts and interpretations of the demonstrations, the result apparently of their particular biases, self-interest and goals. In general, the leadership of the Albanian minority became secretive and did its best to withhold information on the true extent and intensity of the disturbances. The émigré group, on the other hand, took the opposite position: it emphasized the dramatic and violent aspects of the demonstrations and placed the responsibility for them on Yugoslavia's repressive policy toward its Albanian nationals. For its part, official Belgrade, seeking to allay any suspicions that its policy on nationalities, and toward Albanians in particular, may be unsound or perhaps even unjust, attributed the upheavals to international intrigue, most of it originating from Tirana, capital of Albania. Their contrasting positions suggest the complexity of the Kosova problem and its ramifications for Yugoslav-Albanian relations.

The riots, by and large, caught Yugoslav authorities off guard. The November demonstrations in particular, although expected by "the better informed" people in the area, nevertheless came as "a great surprise" [4] to the wider Yugoslav public, caused serious concern among local, state and federal authorities, and attracted widespread publicity abroad.

The surprised reaction of the Yugoslav public appears to have been due in part to unfamiliarity with Kosova, and in part to the persistent and intense efforts of the government to sell, as it were, its policy on nationalities to the public. Formulated in 1945, the two chief pillars of that policy have been: "cultural autonomy" within each nationality group, and "unity and fraternity" (Bratsvo-Jedinstvo) among the various nationalities. It was apparently believed that such a policy was best adapted to promoting the economic and social development of the country, while containing dissent and defusing international rivalry; thereby preserving the political unity of the federated state. The liberalization and decentralization campaigns, especially since the fall of Aleksandar Rankovic in the summer of 1966,were seen as instrumental in carrying out the nationality policy.

As a corollary, the progress achieved by the various nationality groups was emphasized, while manifestations of political unrest and rivalry among them were played down. Actually, liberalization came late to Kosova, by comparison with other regions in Yugoslavia, and presumably resentment generated by this delay contributed to the tensions that exploded into violence in the fall of 1968. But a more important point perhaps is to ask whether a gradualist, middle-of the-road nationality policy, such as the one currently practiced by Yugoslavia—at least in Kosova—can succeed. In other words, can a nationality policy that is not based on complete suppression of a minority group achieve its objectives short of granting that minority total and unconditional autonomy? In the light of the demonstrations by the Albanian minority in Yugoslavia last autumn, the question is at least debatable.

However, such speculation requires some background knowledge of the Kosova so that the events can be understood in context.

Some Data on Kosova

This region lies in the southern part of the Republic of Serbia, and covers an area of 4,127 square miles, two-thirds of which is mountainous terrain. It was established as an Autonomous Province in 1945 in recognition of the fact that the area was populated predominantly by Albanians. Kosova is "in fact primarily an ethnic region." [5]

Estimates of its population vary. However, the latest report given at the Sixth Congress of the League of Communists of Serbia last November lists the population of Kosova as 1,200,000, of whom about 840,000 (70 percent) are Albanians, 288,000 (24 percent) Serbs, and the rest a mixture of Montenegrins, Turks and others. [6] One speaker at the Congress, Kadri Reufi, Vice-Chairman of the Provincial Assembly, was quoted by *Politika* (November 23, 1968) as saying that "the Albanians nationality accounts for nearly 80 percent of the population of Kosovo-Metohija," which would raise the Albanian figure to nearly one million. [7] Kosova is the most densely populated region in Yugoslavia, with 104 inhabitants per sq. km. as against the Yugoslav average of about 73, and it has the highest rate of population increase—40 births per 1,000 inhabitants as against the national average of 20.

There are two languages for administrative purposes, Serbo-Croatian and Albanian, the former employing the Cyrillic alphabet, the latter the Roman. The two main religions in the province are Islam, the faith of the Albanian population, and the Eastern Orthodox, the faith of the Serbs.

In terms of land resources, Kosova is poor in agriculture but potentially rich in industry. Owing to its varied terrain, only a small part of the cultivable surface is suited to modern farming methods, including irrigation and mechanization, and the greater part of the farming population engages in primitive subsistence farming. The area, however, abounds in largely un-exploited mineral wealth, such as lead, zinc, chrome, and lignite. Its lignite deposits account for nearly half the total known coal reserves of Yugoslavia, and its lead mine at Trepça is the largest in Europe. [8]

Kosova is a land of great scenic beauty, particularly the area around the old city of Prizren, and has often been described as the most colorful region in all of Yugoslavia. At the same time, all accounts agree that it is by far the most backward and primitive section in the country [9]—a fact that contributed to a large degree to the demonstrations of last fall.

A Closer Look at the Demonstrations: The October Events

On October 25, 1968, the Pristina daily *Rilindja* [10] wrote that "in recent days" there had been demonstrations in three Kosova communities, Prizren, Pec, (Pejë), and Suva Reka (Suharekë). (See map.) It ascribed the demonstrations to certain people who had "deceived a few tens of pupils and set them marching behind the national (Albanian) flag." [11] It divided the "trouble-making elements" into two rival groups: Albanian nationalists on the one hand and Serb chauvinists, including followers of the fallen Rankovic, on the other. It noted that the two groups had a common denominator—they were opposed to the decisions of the Fourth (Brioni) LCY Plenum, which shattered Rankovic's power and put new emphasis on solving the national question in Yugoslavia. It condemned the demonstrations and warned that necessary measures would be taken to deal with the "provocateurs." It also said that on October 24 Tito had received in Belgrade a delegation of Kosova leaders, with whom he had "a long discussion... about certain current questions regarding the autonomous province."

These themes were expanded and elaborated upon in later issues of *Rilindja,* and in the two national dailies, *Borba* and *Politika.* There were lengthy reports on numerous mass meetings of workers, educators, party and government organizations throughout the province, condemning the demonstrations, demanding "severe punishment" of the guilty, and reaffirming their dedication to the principles of unity and brotherhood of all the peoples of Yugoslavia. Charges were made that the individuals responsible for the outbursts sought to discredit the self-management system of Yugoslavia and the League of Communists. What is more, they had been "inspired by certain foreign intelligence services" and aimed at "weakening the country's defenses" [12] —a grave charge at a time when Yugoslavia was especially concerned about her national security and defense posture as a consequence of the invasion of Czechoslovakia by the Warsaw Pact countries two months earlier.

These charges went considerably beyond the first appraisals of the demonstrations and transformed them from a local to a national and potentially even international issue. The officials now took the position that the demonstrations were the work of an organized conspiracy with foreign connections. While there was no direct reference to Albania in this accusation, it is probable that Tirana was suspected of being involved in some way. Belgrade's reluctance openly to implicate Tirana may be ascribed in part to the fact that the Albanian leadership had ceased its attacks on Yugoslavia since late August 1968, following the Czech invasion , but even more on account of a deliberate policy of Yugoslavia, adopted some three years previously, not to engage in polemics with Albania, in the hope that this would lead finally to an improvement of relations with the Hoxha regime.

The sensitivity of the Kosova leaders to the demonstrations, their concern over the causes and likely consequences of the turmoil, and most of all their desire to find a solution to the problems at hand was underlined by the meeting they had with President Tito on October 24. The meeting, requested by the Kosova officials, was the third encounter between them and their chief of state in two years. It will be treated in detail in the section on the implications of the riots for Yugoslav nationality policy.

In retrospect, the demonstrations in Prizren, Pec, and Suva Reka were but a prelude to outbursts of greater scope and intensity which struck Pristina and several other towns in Kosova on November 27, 1968, the eve of Albania's national day. Apparently the momentum toward civic disorder and violence among the Albanians, set in motion by the October events and fed by deep-seated discontent and rising expectations, was too strong to be checked by Tito's offer of help and by the vigorous efforts of local officials to persuade them that the best means of obtaining a fuller measure of their national rights lay in moderation, unity, and fraternity with other nationals in the Province. Other, more anthropological factors may have contributed as well. The celebration of Albania's national day has traditionally tended to bring Albanian - Serb rivalry to a head and on two other occasions, in 1945 and 1956, caused incidents in Pristina (Prishtinë), capital of the autonomous province of Kosova. Moreover, Albanian social and family life in Kosova is to a considerable degree still primitive and tribal. Consequently many Kosova Albanians are inclined to view government and government authorities with suspicion and mistrust and to feel especially hostile towards them when any members of the group—such as those who demonstrated in Peç, Prizren, and Suva Reka—are rebuked, condemned or punished for their actions. The reaction of the authorities to the demonstrators may well have stirred a tribal instinct of revenge among Albanians and contributed to the climate of rebellion that led to the larger and more serious demonstrations in Pristina and other communities.

It is possible, too, that the martial and heroic spirit characteristic of societies like Kosova played their part in the developments of last fall. In Kosova today the oral tradition lives on, along with myth, legend, and epic, and news of the demonstrations probably had an electrifying effect among people and was embellished and dramatized to a point where the demonstrators emerged as heroes, whose example other members of the group must follow and if possible surpass.

Such, in brief, was the general picture in Kosova on the eve of the November disturbances.

The Pristina Explosion

On November 28, 1968, *Rilindja* came out with a special issue in honor of Yugoslavia's national day (November 29), crammed with statistics showing the progress achieved in Kosova over the past decade in the fields of education, medicine, transportation and other areas. The issue was marred, however, by a report which told of renewed demonstrations in the Province. Following is a slightly abbreviated text of the report:

> Yesterday, at about 4 p.m., organized demonstrations took place in Pristina, of a clearly hostile character, aimed against self-management

socialism and the constituted order of the FSRY (Federated Socialist Republic of Yugoslavia).

Several hundred took part in the demonstrations, which set off from the Faculty of Philosophy building.

During the demonstrations, which lasted many hours, the participant caused disorder, smashing shop windows and overturning cars... Casualties also occurred.

Similar demonstrations, but on a much smaller scale and without disorder, occurred in Ferizaj, Gnjilane (Gilan) and Podujevo (Podujevë). This shows that the demonstrations were organized and synchronized.[13]

The *Rilindja* account of the riots concealed as much information as it revealed, an indication that the local authorities were reluctant to make known the true magnitude of the disturbances, for fear perhaps of unduly alarming the public and, it may be, official Belgrade as well. However, information on "the gravest disturbances in a quarter-century" in Pristina could not long be kept under the lid and news of the explosion soon made headlines in the world press.[14]

Two days later the local daily gave a fuller account of the riots. It said that the demonstrators marched to the main square in town, carrying Albanian flags and shouting slogans, which were at first in favor of Tito and LCY, but later turned hostile. Then "someone from the mob shot a firearm," and this led to a clash with the police, who "resorted to physical force in self-defense." The demonstrators returned to the Faculty of Philosophy—their starting point—but soon set off again, this time heading toward the Regional Secretariat for Internal Affairs. More shots rang out from the crowd, which was turned back by the police using "chemical bombs and tear gas." The demonstrators returned once again to the Faculty of Philosophy building, where they dispersed around 9 o'clock in the evening.[15]

Rilindja then listed the casualties as follows: one demonstrator killed, 41 men injured, including 10 policemen, 4 firemen, and 27 demonstrators. Eleven of the injured were hospitalized. Twenty-one persons were arrested.

The Belgrade version of the demonstrations added a number of significant details. It said that the demonstrators shouted "the most extreme nationalist-chauvinist slogans" as they marched through the main street in town, Marshal Tito Boulevard, and at one point read a proclamation signed by a Committee of Demonstrations. The proclamation called for the "promulgation of the Province into a republic," the right of self-determination, and the right of the people of Kosova to live under their own constitution.[16]

The most somber report by far on the Pristina explosion appeared in Le Monde. In a dispatch from Belgrade, the French daily's Yugoslav correspondent said that the demonstrators had "acclaimed the head of the Albanian party, Mr. Enver Hoxha, and booed Mr. Veli Deva..." [17] He noted that they had attacked shops bearing signs in Serbo-Croat and had wrecked the office of the Serb journal, *Jedinstvo* (Unity), and the city's main hotel. In a subsequent dispatch the following day, he wrote of "irredentist Albanian demonstrations" which so alarmed the authorities that they moved several army units into Pristina to preserve order. The military units, it was learned later, included tank contingents. [18] The report that demonstrators had called for the union of Kosova with Albania was confirmed by official sources. In an article on the meeting of the provincial Conference in Pristina on December 1, 1968, *Rilindja* said that sworn enemies of Yugoslavia had shouted "reactionary, irredentist, and separatist slogans." [19]

There was some contradiction in Yugoslav sources on the number of participants in the Pristina riots. First official reports spoke of "several hundred" demonstrators, later the number was upgraded to 500, and still later to 1,000. Yankovitch of *Le Monde* put the number at between two and two three thousand, while the Albanians in Istanbul estimated the crowd at four thousand.

The accounts of the November 27 demonstrations given so far are based on sources from within Yugoslavia. Tirana for its part withheld comment on the events. However, an Albanian version of what happened, which differs markedly from the Yugoslav story, was given by the Albanian group in Istanbul which publishes *Besa* (The Pledge). [20]

According to *Besa*, the demonstrators had requested, and were given a verbal authorization by the authorities to hold "a peaceful demonstration," yet when they began to march the militia intervened and ordered them to disperse. Disregarding the order and rifle-butt attacks by the militia, the demonstrators marched to the heart of the city, on the way shouting such slogans as: "We want a Republic of Kosova," "Down with the policy of Colonization of Kosova." [21] "We want a National University," [22] "We want the rights promised us during the war." [23] They called Veli Deva a "traitor," and referred to him contemptuously as "Velimir Deviç." According to *Besa,* the demonstrators were orderly until someone, a Serb, fired a revolver at them from the Hotel Avala, at which point they reacted by destroying property. Upon returning to the Faculty of the Philosophy building, they were quickly surrounded "by a large military force, armed with tanks and machine guns," brought in hurriedly from Nis, Novisad, Kursumlija, and Prokuple, and estimated at ten thousand men.

The *Besa* report claims that five students lost their lives as a result of gun shot wounds or beatings by the police and 400 demonstrators were arrested, fifteen of whom are expected to be sentenced to long prison terms on charges of organizing the demonstration.

The reaction of Communist officials to the demonstrations was marked by alarm, some confusion, suspicion of treason, and a determination to deal firmly with the unruly elements of the population. Contrary to the Istanbul Albanians' position, they viewed the demonstrations not as a legitimate protest on the part of the Albanian population seeking a redress of grievance within the local community but as a dangerous plot by an organized group acting in opposition to the highest interests of the state. Thus Veli Deva, top Communist official in Kosova, called the riots the act of "a hostile group consisting of sworn enemies of our order..., the ideological and political platform of the league of Communists of Yugoslavia, and the fraternity and unity of our people." He said they were "agents in the service of foreign powers." [24] A *Borba* editorial said that the riots were "the joint action of political opponents of all colors, from foreign agents to adversaries...of LCY." [25] The most bitter reaction by far in the national press appeared in *Communist* (Belgrade) (December 5, 1968), which denounced the demonstrators as "sterile and spiritually wretched" individuals, "helpless, spiteful people," whose mob action only revealed their "impotence and baseness." One high Communist official in Kosova identified these hostile enemies and forces as ex-Chetniks, clericals, the petit bourgeoisie, chauvinists, nationalists, pro-Rankovic and pro-Mao elements, ex-Ballisti people, etc. [26]

The Tetovo Incident

On the surface of it, the outbreak of violence in Tetovo last December seemed spontaneous, but the seeds of conflict between Albanians and Macedonian Slavs were sown long ago. In 1958, for example, the Albanian government daily accused Yugoslavia of practicing a policy of genocide against the Albanian minority, and in an attempt to document the accusation said that in the fall of 1944, "…as many as 10,000 persons were arrested in Tetovo, 1,200 of whom were killed without trial and many more met their death in filthy prisons." [27]

Regardless of the truth of Tirana's accusations, the political atmosphere in Tetovo late last year was charged with old resentments and current grievances, a situation reflected in public discussions, the local press, and even, it seems, in the poetry of the Albanian minority in Macedonia. Barely a month before the Tetovo incident, there appeared in the local Albanian press the following lines, taken from a poem by an Albanian national:

> I am on the right road, from which there is no turning,
> on the road of freedom which makes men brothers.
> There, where the innocent Albanian also—wretched captive—
> will emerge from darkness into the light of May—in Freedom.. [28]

The lines above are marked by an angry, aggressive tone. Another poem by an Albanian national, published in the same issue, is pervaded by despair, frustration, and hatred but also by a certain underlying aggressiveness:

> Without the last goodbye the travelers departed,
> On paths that lead to distant time,
> And, stunned, we await
> The rebirth and festival of spring,
> That will come to us one day.
> Oh, long we have waited
> And have told the last tale
> Of the travelers treading lengthy roads.
> We have hated the darkness that has fallen
> On our heads... [29]

Even allowing for a certain amount of the pessimism characteristic of Yugoslav and Balkan literature, the mood and sentiment of these poems appear to be politically significant, especially in the light of subsequent events in Tetovo. It is likely, too, that the "catastrophic rainstorms" which hit the Tetovo district in May of 1968, together with the October and November demonstrations in Kosova, added to existing economic and political tensions in the city and increased the potentiality for violence between Albanian and Macedonian nationals. [30] By late December these tensions had reached dangerous proportions and required but a spark to set off an explosion. The spark came on December 23, the day the Moslem Albanian minority was celebrating Bairam, a major Moslem holiday.

According to *Politika,* the trouble started over a "seemingly unimportant incident"—the removal of the Albanian flag by a Macedonian photographer, Srecko Janevski, from the shop of Ismail Ejupi, an Albanian tailor. The incident provoked a violent demonstration on the part of "several hundred Albanian reactionary and nationalist elements," who proceeded to demolish the hotel where Janevski sought shelter, as well as several shops in the center of town, several passenger cars, a truck and a police car. They also attacked the Commercial Bank building which houses the headquarters of the Opstina (Regional) Committee of the Macedonian League of Communists, the Socialist Alliance, and the Trade Union Council, and planted large Albanian flags on the windows of the party's headquarters. The paper reported that four militiamen were injured in clashes with the demonstrators, some of whom carried firearms.[31]

The next day the Belgrade daily reported on the most significant and disturbing element in the Tetovo incident. It said:

> The demonstrators called for a civil war and propagated the idea of the annexation of this part of Macedonia to the province of Kosova.[32]

The paper blamed the upheaval on "resurrected Ballisti," i.e. nationalists of Albania, now in exile, who desire the creation of an ethnic, non-Communist Albanian nation that would include all Albanian-populated territories in Yugoslavia.

In a report on the Tetovo demonstration Yankovitch estimated the number of demonstrators at "about three thousand," most of them youth and secondary school students. The demonstrators, he said, "acclaimed…Enver Hoxha and demanded a federated Albanian republic." [33]

Besa of Istanbul called the demonstrations "a true rebellion," described the Macedonian photographer who sparked the violence as "the brother of a UDB (the Yugoslav Security Service) agent," and noted that hundreds of the demonstrators were jailed, among them many professionals, including educators and 10-15 doctors. The paper added that many demonstrators were wounded, and a number of them were tortured to death by the secret police. [34] Another Albanian source said that about two dozen Albanian students from Pristina had joined the Tetovo demonstrators.[35]

Implications for Yugoslav Nationality Policy

Tito's meeting with Kosova officials on October 24 indicated the extent of official concern. This session was widely publicized and focused national attention on the problems of the region.

Led by Veli Deva, Chairman of the League of Communists for the Kosova Province, [36] the Kosova delegation laid the cards on the table.

They gave Tito a grim report on the economic situation in the province. They said that there was widespread unemployment and inadequate social services in the region, especially in the fields of education and health. They pointed out that "the gap in the rate of development between the province and the other regions" of Yugoslavia was growing instead of narrowing, and frankly admitted that the province "is not in a position to resolve a number of serious problems... that demand a solution." Although they gave a generally positive account of the political situation, the Kosova leaders stressed two major socio-political problems: one in connection with those elements of the population which favored the status quo, the other in connection with those who were calling for republican status for Kosova, i.e. they briefed him on the continuing rivalry between chauvinist Serb elements and extreme Albanian nationalists, especially over the growing demands of the Albanians for their national rights.

Despite reports that Tito listened to the Communist leadership of Kosova with sympathy, [37] his reaction to the demonstrations in the province was direct, uncompromising, and severe. He said:

> We need greater unity than ever before...the internal and external enemy desires our disunity. He will do everything to divide us. Therefore, we must deal a fatal blow to the internal as well as the external enemies, be they Rankovic elements, Albanian reactionaries, or enemies of other colors. Our struggle against these backward forces must be primarily ideological and political, but if need be it ought to embrace administrative measures as well. [38]

The President's offer to help Kosova achieve her economic and political objectives was apparently designed to build up support for Yugoslavia's policy on Kosova, by encouraging the moderate elements in the province, while his remarks on fomenters of disunity served as a warning to extremist in both the Albanian and Serb camps. Tito's reference to "external enemies" could be taken as a veiled warning to Albania and other foreign powers not to interfere in Yugoslavia's domestic affairs. Moreover, the meeting with Tito was an important political gain for the Veli Deva delegation. It meant that Belgrade endorsed, at least outwardly, the Kosova leadership and its handling of the October events.

In response to Tito's suggestions, Communist officials of Kosova sought to restore calm and order in the province by using the double tactic of threatening the extremists, while enticing the moderates by an appeal to reason and to their best interests. Speaking at Lipljan, Fadil Hodza pleaded with the Albanians not to abuse their right to "fly their national flag and to respect their historical personalities." [39]

References to the Albanian flag and Albanian historical personalities—especially Scanderbeg, Albania's national hero—appeared frequently in public discussions and the press in Kosova both before and after the October demonstrations. The use or misuse of the Albanian flag by Albanian nationals seems to have been a chief issue in the demonstrations. Certain Serb and Montenegrin elements in the province blamed the outbursts on the government's decision of October 5, 1968 to allow the Albanian minority to display its national flag during national festivals and other occasions. [40] Such a move, they felt, would only embolden the Albanians to press for more concessions at the expense of the Serb and Montenegrin interests. The authorities, however, justified the move as a concrete element of the Yugoslav policy on national equality, based on "the principles approved by the Brioni Plenum." [41] One report called the decision "the greatest political concession Belgrade has so far made to the Albanians in Yugoslavia." [42] Interestingly enough, Tito's subsequent comments on the November disturbances were comparatively mild and seemed designed to play down the significance of the event. He said that things had been "overly dramatized" since "nothing tragic has happened there (in Kosovo)." [43] Implying that only "a minor segment of the youth and students" [44] had been involved, he denied that police had used force to quell the rioters and praised the "leading organs" in Kosova, thus reaffirming once again Belgrade's continued faith in the local officials of the province, despite the disorders.

Neither the Pristina explosion nor the increased tension with Tirana were strong enough to shake Yugoslavia's faith in its basic policy on Kosova: to press on with the liberalization and to further national equality in the province. The policy was reaffirmed by the Eleventh Plenum of the LCY CC, which

> gave its full support to the activity of the Communists of the autonomous province of Kosova... for the affirmation of equal rights to the Albanian (and other) nationals living in this region. [45]

The decision of the plenum marked a defeat for the pro-Rankovic and other regressive forces in the region, which had hoped for a halt to the liberalization policy if not a roll-back to Rankovic's era. It also assured the Kosova leadership that no political heads would roll as a result of the demonstrations and the deterioration of the political situation in the area.

On December 9, 1968, the Third Plenum of the Kosova Communist League met in Pristina to review the situation produced by the November 27 demonstrations and concluded that the demonstrations had failed of their purpose. The plenum took note, however, of "certain negative consequences" resulting in the region, the emergence of "a certain mistrust and insecurity" among the people, and the development of a more favorable climate for the regressive forces to operate in.

While the Kosova leadership was evaluating recent events in Pristina and other tense spots in the province, another explosive situation was simmering in the city of Tetovo, Macedonia. It burst with violent force late in December, and for the moment at least caused a shift in attention from the Albanians of Kosova to the Albanians in Macedonia.

As in the case of the October and November disturbances, the official reaction to the Tetovo incident followed customary lines: on the one hand Belgrade viewed the eruption as an organized affair rather than as a spontaneous activity of indignant Albanian nationals; on the other hand, it reaffirmed the correctness of Yugoslavia's policy on nationalities.

A communiqué issued by the Socialist Alliance of Macedonia on December 27, 1968 characterized the demonstrations as a "separatist manifestation" and condemned them as:

a grave, direct and premeditated act aimed against... socialist construction, against the fraternity and unity of our people..., and against the sovereignty and integrity of the Socialist Republic of Macedonia and the SFRY. [46]

The cry of "separatism" and "irredentism" became a refrain in official statements on the riots. Thus in a speech in Tetovo on December 28, 1968, Angel Cmerski, Secretary of the LC of Macedonia, called the riots "nationalist, chauvinist and irredentist" and concluded that "there is a tie between the events in Tetovo and those in Kosovo." [47] Radio Belgrade also spoke of the demonstrations as having "separatist goals."

These cries illustrate the alarm and anxiety of the authorities over the developments in Tetovo and explain to some degree the strong measures taken by them to deal with the crisis, measures much stronger than those taken in Kosova. [48] These measures included firing of several elementary school teachers, investigation of civil service workers and educators of Albanian nationality, punishment of "all workers who left their job and joined the demonstrators," [49] withdrawal of financial aid to students who participated in the demonstration, and calls for punitive action against certain members of the medical profession, including physicians, on similar charges. Later, an Albanian publicist, Ali Hoxha, was tried in Skopje and sentenced to five years in prison for "fomenting hatred and intolerance" [50] between Albanians and Macedonians during the Tetovo disturbances.

The demands of irredentism and separatism first heard during the Kosova demonstrations were considerably strengthened by similar but more aggressive cries voiced in Tetovo and apparently induced a correspondingly stronger reaction on the part of the officials. Beyond that, Communist officials in Macedonia and Belgrade have been acutely sensitive as a matter of course to calls or movements by the Albanian minority for a republic of their own, either a Republic of Kosova or an Albanian republic that would include Kosova and Albanian-populated parts of Macedonia and Montenegro. In the eyes of Macedonian leaders, any changes in the boundaries of the republic would almost certainly revive and aggravate territorial claims on Macedonia by Bulgaria and Greece. That in turn could lead to demands for boundary changes within the other republics, which could pose a threat to the territorial integrity and even the sovereignty of Yugoslavia itself.

Importance for Yugoslav-Albanian Relations

At the time of the November demonstration, Tito once again alluded to "interference from abroad" in Kosova. His suggestion of foreign interference was picked up and amplified by his subordinates. In a speech to the regional Socialist Alliance the following day, Iliaz Kurtesi openly pointed the finger at Albania:

> There is no doubt that these events were influenced by foreign propaganda, especially that from neighboring Albania, which lately had begun a planned and very intensive assault on the basic achievements of our people and their system. [51]

In Yugoslavia this represents a long-standing fear. It certainly was not the first time leaders in Belgrade have directly accused Albania of nurturing irredentist aims towards their country, just as Tirana has contended that Yugoslavia seeks to annex Albania. In 1964, for example, Ali Sukrija (Shukriu), member of the Federal Executive Council, made the charge that the Albanian leadership had been pursuing "nationalist, chauvinist and irredentist" aims towards Yugoslavia since 1948, the year of the Belgrade-Tirana break. [52] Belgrade's past deep concern over political unrest among the Albanian minority and the possible loss of Albanian-populated areas to Albania has been reflected in various trials and arrests, over the past twenty years, of Albanian nationals on charges of chauvinism, subversion, irredentism, and the like. One such trial, according to Tirana, took place as recently as March 1968 in the town of Monastir, Macedonia, when several Albanian peasants were accused of conspiring to unite Kosova and part of Macedonia with Albania. [53] In an attempt to document the claim that Tirana has irredentist designs on

Yugoslavia, a Macedonian Communist leader stated recently that: "In Albania there are maps which include parts of Yugoslavia."[54]

Certainly the timing of the Pristina disturbances did nothing to reassure the Yugoslavs about Tirana's intentions. Albania had resumed its attacks on Yugoslavia early in November. In a page-long editorial, the leading party organ wrote about "the miserable condition of the Albanians of Kosovo, Macedonia and Montenegro..." [55] These attacks continued in the days that followed, culminating in an especially inflammatory assault on November 24, 1968, only three days before the Pristina demonstrations. This came in the form of another editorial in *Zëri i Popullit* entitled, "The Albanians of Kosova and the National Flag." The paper charged that back in 1943 Tito and his partisans adopted a resolution proclaiming "the equality of all nationalities and their right of self-determination including the right of secession."

The article suggested that the Albanians of Kosova have the right not only to a republic of their own but even to detach themselves from Yugoslavia if they so choose. The article thus touched on an extremely delicate point in Albanian-Yugoslav relations over Kosova—the possible union of Kosova with Albania—and aroused deeply-rooted fears for Yugoslavia's territorial integrity on the part of Yugoslav authorities. It prompted Marko Nikezic, President of the League of Communists of Serbia, to declare:"We will defend the integrity (of Yugoslavia) by every means,"[56] and that the separation of Kosova "was out of the question." [57]

Apparently these considerations, i.e. the violence and political implications of the *Zëri i Popullit* editorial, coupled with the November 27 outbursts, finally shattered Yugoslavia's long-standing policy of stoic silence in the face of Albanian attacks, and led to the decision in Belgrade to resume polemics with Tirana, at least to a degree.

Conclusion

In a search for the underlying causes of last fall's demonstrations in Kosova, Yugoslav authorities said that there had been delays, inconsistencies, and deviations in carrying out the LCY programs. In part responsibility for this situation was laid at the door of "Greater Serbia" proponents. They spoke, too, of a lack of social equality in the region. In addition, poor relations with Albania contributed to the "stagnation" of conditions in the area.

In general, however, the authorities attributed the demonstrations not to negative conditions and the general backwardness in the region but to the very progress it was making in overcoming its backwardness and socio-political problems. They spoke of the "positive evolution" of the situation in Kosova which "caused dissatisfaction" among Greater Serbia elements and "awakened the appetites" of Albanian nationalists. This evolution encompasses both a growing climate of freedom and democracy and the rapid economic, cultural and political development of Kosova society which, taken together, alarmed and activated the regressive and radical forces in the province and produced an explosive effect. [58]

Looking at the question from the Albanian minority's side, it would seem that the demonstrations were mainly a reaction against condition created in the worst days of Rankovic's power, when Albanians were economically neglected, socially discriminated, politically oppressed, and even personally persecuted, at times on deliberately trumped-up charges, as Yugoslav officials admitted following the Brioni Plenum. Unfortunately, many of those conditions still continued to exist in Kosova, especially in matters of economics and social relations. Taking advantage of the freer political climate of the last two years, Albanians began to air their grievances and demands for full national equality with growing persistence.

Several developments that occurred in 1968 seem to have contributed to the demonstrations. One of these was the commemoration in Pristina, during the month of May, of the 500th anniversary of the death of Scanderbeg—Albania's national hero—which seems to have reinforced the nationalist feelings of the Albanians and enhanced the ethnic differences between them and the Serbs. [59]

Student demonstrations in Yugoslavia last June, which also spread to Pristina, probably influenced the students and youth who led last fall's demonstrations in Kosova and Tetovo. Albanian students and youth are a force to be reckoned with in Kosova today. Progress in education has reduced illiteracy in the region from 90 percent at the end of World War Two to about 40 percent at present, with the result that tens of thousands of Albanian youth are now attending school, including several institutions of higher learning, chief of which is the University of Prishtina. Conscious of their strength, indignant over inadequate educational facilities and living conditions, resentful above all of Serb domination, they may well have felt they had much more reason to take to the streets than students in many other parts of the world.

Finally, the granting last October of the right to fly the Albanian flag, a right won after long agitation, apparently persuaded the more radical Albanian elements that the most effective way to press their demands is through forceful and dramatic public action.

However, the single most important factor which impelled the Albanians to demonstrate appears to have been their aspiration for a Republic of Kosova. They contend that full autonomy is the best and indeed the only solution at present to the problems of unemployment, low standard of living, inadequate education, poor social services, language inequality, cultural underdevelopment, and incomplete juridical and civic rights. It is the solution, in short, to the burdensome legacy of the Rankovic era, which currently manifests itself through continuing "Serbian control and interference" [60] in their lives.

In the light of these considerations, the Tetovo incident emerges as a grave political event which very likely will affect in some measure the course of future relations between Yugoslavia and Albania.

Part of the explanation why the Tetovo incident was more severe than its antecedents may, perhaps, be found in the difference in the political situation and overall condition of the Albanians of Macedonia and those of Kosova. The latter are more advanced politically, since they at least are recognized as a political entity and exercise some measure of control over their own affairs. In addition, they are in a more favorable position in matters of culture, including education, publications, radio communication, and the arts in general.

By contrast, the Albanians of Macedonia are almost completely subordinated, as an ethnic and national group, to the Macedonians and seem to be keenly conscious of their relative lack of political and cultural identity. It is likely that such awareness was responsible for much of the frustration and bitterness and destructive violence that manifested itself during the Tetovo eruption. It seems to account, too, for their insistent call for a Republic of Albania consisting of Kosova and the Albanian parts of Macedonia. Nevertheless, it is not Macedonia but Kosova that remains the focal point in Albanian-Yugoslav relations, insofar as the question of the Albanian minority in Yugoslavia is concerned. That is so by virtue of Kosova's autonomous status and, hence, greater political reality, the great number of Albanians who live there, the growing interest in the final outcome of the region's movement to obtain republican status, and its inherent potentiality for becoming either a bridge of understanding and cooperation or a political battlefield between the Tito and Hoxha leaderships.

The net effects and significance of the demonstrations might be summarized as follows:

1. The Albanians of Yugoslavia are not satisfied with Belgrade's gradualist policy in granting them their national rights. Rather, they want full autonomy now, within the framework of Yugoslavia's constitution and system of self-administration.
2. The demonstrations were an embarrassment to Yugoslavia domestically and internationally, for they tended to cast doubt on the oft-repeated claim of the Tito leadership that Yugoslavia has solved the nationality question.
3. If the aim of the demonstrators was to further the goal of autonomy for the Albanian minority, they achieved the opposite effect. Belgrade's position on the Albanians' demands has hardened. [61]

The irony of last fall's demonstrations in Kosova and Macedonia is that they came at a time when the Albanian nationals were enjoying more rights than at any time during the past two decades [62], and seemed to be on the road to achieving a still greater measure of the rights to which they are entitled.

In short, the demonstrations of last fall seem to have borne out Dr. William E. Griffith's doubts whether Belgrade's liberalization moves could "surmount the extreme ethnic nationalism (of a) rapidly developing but still relatively primitive area like the Kosmet." [63] The liberalization policy failed, at least for the moment, on two counts: it did not halt the movement of Albanian nationals for the creation of an Albanian Republic similar to the other republics of Yugoslavia; and it did not lead to an improvement of relations with Albania.

The demonstrations tested Yugoslavia's three-year old policy to explore all possible avenues—such as trade, tourism, cultural and educational exchanges—leading to a rapprochement with Albania and showed that the policy rested on fragile ground.

Indeed, Kosova has served as a kind of barometer of Yugoslav-Albanian relations ever since Josef Broz Tito and Enver Hoxha took power in their respective countries at the end of World War Two. In times of détente—and these have been infrequent, brief, and more apparent than real—Kosova has tended to retreat into the background or even been used as a bridge to further understanding and cooperation between Yugoslavs and Albanians. Examples of détente are the period between the Twentieth C.P.S.U. Congress and the Hungarian revolution in 1956 and the months immediately preceding Khrushchev's visit to Albania in May of 1959. In times of stress, the two Communist countries have utilized Kosova, at best, as a ready-made propaganda device for hurling incentives at each other and at worst as a fertile ground for promoting espionage and subversion. Such a time of stress was the period following the Stalin-Tito break in 1948; another relates to events connected with the Seventh Congress of the League of Communists of Yugoslavia (LCY) in May 1958.

Conversely, the Yugoslav-Albanian controversy over Kosova has occasionally assumed such proportions that it has burst its national and ethnic confines and become a part of the ideological conflict that has beset the socialist world. For example, a HSINHUA corespondent who had toured Kosova in March 1959 painted a grim picture of the living conditions of the Albanian population and mocked Yugoslav claims to have solved the nationality question. [64] In September 1962 Albania made a violent attack on the Kremlin leadership for its alleged support of Tito on the question of Kosova. In a long editorial, the Albanian party organ wrote:

> When our party and our people rightly condemn the Greater Serbia inhuman chauvinistic policy of the Belgrade band of revisionists, which it practices against more than a million Albanian brothers in Kosova, Montenegro, and Macedonia, when we unmask with facts the policy of discrimination, the crimes of genocide, the judicial regressions, the administrative deportations, and the massive annihilation of our brothers by the Belgrade clique, N. Khrushchev's, group does not hesitate to accuse us of being 'nationalist,' thus approving the inhuman anti-Albania actions of the renegade Belgrade group. [65]

It appears that events in Kosova are influenced by internal developments in Yugoslavia, by relations between Belgrade and Tirana, and indirectly even by what happens in the larger Communist world, above all by the Sino-Soviet conflict, owing to its impact on the foreign policies of the various socialist countries. On occasion Albania has sought to involve the socialist camp—at least ideologically—in the question of Kosova, by linking its Kosova policy with the principles and interests of the world Communist movement and proletarian internationalism. In short, as an area of study Kosova reflects in miniature form the play of forces and movements that reach far beyond the narrow confines of its rugged land. For whether the movement toward autonomy will eventually succeed, and thereby justify the violence and turmoil caused by the demonstrations, will probably depend not so much on what happens within Kosova itself as on what happens between Yugoslavia and Albania, since developments in Kosova are largely determined by the relations between those two proud and passionately nationalistic Balkan nations.

Notes

[1] Names of town or persons in parentheses represent the name in Albanian.

[2] Viktor Meier has called Yugoslavia's nationality question "the problem that contains the most future dynamite for the regime." See William E. Griffith, ed., *Communism in Europe*, Vol. 1 (Cambridge, Mass,: The M.I.T. Press, 1964) , p. 76

[3] Formerly known as the Autonomous Province of Kosovo and Metohija (Kosmet) , the region was renamed last December and is now officially called the Autonomous Socialist Province of Kosovo. See *Rilindja*, December 13, 1968; *Le Monde*, December 20, 1968.

[4] *Borba*, December 1, 1968; Jonathan Randal, "Yugoslavia Worried by Albanian Minority's Rioting for Greater Autonomy," *The New York Times*, Dec. 6, 1968. Randal called the November eruptions "the gravest disturbance in a quarter-century in Pristina" (Prishtina), center of the demonstrations.

[5] Organization for the Economic Cooperation and Development (OECD), *Regional Project of Kosovo-Metohija*, Paris, 1968, p. 15.

[6] *Rilindja*, November 23, 1968.

[7] Apart from Kosovo, there are some 183,000 Albanians in Macedonia, 35,000 in Montenegro, and between ten and fifteen thousand in Belgrade, making a conservative total of 1,068,000 for the entire Albanian minority in the country. These figures have been consistently disputed by Albania, which claims that the total Albanian population in Yugoslavia is at least 50 percent higher than the total given by Yugoslav sources.

[8] These data are based mostly on the OECD report, *Regional Project of Kosovo-Metohija*, Paris, 1968.

[9] For an interesting though somewhat dated analysis of Kosovo, see Dennison J. Rusinow "The Other Albanians," *American Unisversities Field Staff*, Southeast Europe Series, Vol. XII, No. 2 (November 1965) , pp. 1-24.

[10] *Rilindja*, (Rebirth), the Albanian – language daily, is the organ of the Socialist Alliance of the Working People of Kosovo.

[11] A report on the demonstration in Pec, published a few days later, placed the number of demonstrators at 100-150 students, all of them from the Ali Kelmendi (Kelmendi) Teacher's College. See *Borba*, October 31, 1968. This leads to the supposition that the total number of demonstrators in the three cities was probably several hundred rather than "a few tens" of pupils.

[12] *Le Monde*, October 29, 1986.

[13] *Rilindja*, November, 28, 29, 30, 1968. *Borba*, December 1, 1968, said the demonstrations occurred in Pristina, Gnjilane, Podujevo, and Urosevac. *Besa*, (February 7, 1969) agreed with the *Rilindja* version but added that manifestations took place also in the town of Kaçanik.

[14] *The New York Times*, November 28, 1968, December 6, 1968; *Le Monde*, November 29, 1968, November 30, 1968; *The Ecomist*, December 7 – 13, 1968. For a later but very good analysis of the situation in Kosovo, in the light of the November demonstrations, see Johann Georg Reissmüller, "Die albanischen Leiden-schaften in Kosovo," *Frankfurter Allgemeine Zeitung*, December 28, 1968. For the best coverage, however, on last fall's demonstrations and current developments in Kosovo, see the articles by Paul Yankovitch in *Le Monde*.

---

[15] *Rilindja,* November 30, 1968.

[16] *Borba,* December 1, 1968. Unlike the six republics of Yugoslavia, the two autonomous provinces of Kosovo and Voivodina do not have their own constitutions, but are governed under a set of statutes.

[17] Paul Yankovitch, "Des manifestations d' Albanais du Kosmet provoquent de sérieux incidents," *Le Monde,* November 29, 1968.

[18] *The New York Times,* December 6, 1968.

[19] *Rilindja,* December 2, 1968.

[20] *Besa,* (organ of the Albanian Democratic-Independent Group in Turkey) February 7, 1969. Although this was probably exaggerated, the Yugoslav versions probably minimized the disturbances.

[21] The charge of "colonization" is one frequently made by Albania, which claims that Belgrade exploits Kosovo for its natural resources.

[22] At present, the Pristina University is bi-lingual. Presumably the demonstrators were asking for a university in which all instruction would be in the Albanian language, and the course content would be heavily weighed in favor of Albanian studies.

[23] The reference is to the rights of Liberty, Equality and Self-Determination "even to the point of secession" which Tito and his partisans reportedly promised to the Albanian minority during the Second World War. See Nicholas C. Pano, *The People's Republic of Albania,* (Baltimore, Md.; John Hopkins Press, 1968) , p. 40; *Zëri i Popullit,* November 24, 1968.

[24] *Rilindja,* November 30, 1968.

[25] *Borba,* December 1, 1968.

[26] Smail (Ismail) Bajra, in *Rilindja,* December 10, 1968. The term "ballisti" refer to the nationalist front (Balli Kombëtar) which opposed the the Communist Party in Albania during the Second World War and insisted on the union of Kosovo with Albania.

[27] *Bashkimi,* September 9, 1958.

[28] Esad Mekuli, "In the Street," *Flaka e Vëllazërimit,* November 29, 1968, a weekly published in Skopje (Shkup) , organ of the Socialist Alliance of the Working People of Macedonia.

[29] Jonuz Fetahaj, "Late Return," *Ibid.*

[30] Outwardly, Tetovo last year presented a picture of prosperity. An interview with Dzemal Veseli (Xhemal Veseli) , member of the LC-CC of Macedonia, revelead that the Tetovo comune had the best road system in the country, and that everyone of its 92 villages had electricity and its own school. *Politika,* December 25, 1968.

[31] *Politika,* December 24, 1968.

[32] *Ibid.,.* December 25, 1968.

[33] *Le Monde,* December 25, 1968.

[34] *Besa,* February 7, 1969.

[35] *Dielli,* Boston, MA., February 5, 1969.

[36] For a lengthy report on the meeting, see *Rilindja,* November 4, 1968. Other members of the delegation were Fadil Hodza (Hoxha) , President of the Provincial Assemby and member of LCY Presidium, Ilijaz Kurtesi (Kurteshi) , President of the Socialist Alliance of the

Working People (SAWP) of Kosovo, and Ilija Vakiq, President of the Kosovo Executive Council.

[37] He said: " I fully approve and support all the ideas you have expressed here," and granted that " the problem of Kosovo and Metohija are great and serious." He said that "many political, social and natinonality problems (in Kosovo) have their source in the uneven development of the province."

[38] *Rilindja*, November 4, 1968.

[39] *Politika*, October 28, 1968.

[40] For details on the government's decision, see *Rilindja*, October 6, 1968; *Flaka e vellazerimit*, October 5, 1968.

[41] *Rilindja*, October 5, 1968.

[42] Dr. Drago Matkovic, "Belgrad Schwierigkeiten mit der albanischen Minderheit," *Deutsche Welle Dokumentation*, November 19, 1968, pp. 1-7.

[43] Tito's press conference in Jajce, *Borba*, December 1, 1968.

[44] The official position that only students and youth had taken part in the demonstration was contradicted somewhat by an article in *Rilindja*, (December 3, 1968) which said that some workers had "attempted" to join the students, an indication that discontent in the province ran deeper than what might be supposed from official party reports.

[45] *Rilindja*, December 3, 1968; *Le Monde*, December 4, 1968.

[46] *Flaka e Vëllazërimit*, January 2, 1969.

[47] *Ibid.*

[48] See *The Economist*, January 11, 1969; *The Christian Science Monitor*, January 16, 1969.

[49] *Flaka e Vëllazërimit*, December 26, 1968.

[50] *Frankfurter Allgemeine Zeitung*, March 21, 1969; *East Europe*, Vol. 18, No. 5 (May 1968) , p. 37.

[51] *Borba*, December 2, 1968.

[52] *Rilindja*, November 28, 1964. The fact that Sukrija used language that is identical with that of Angel Cmerski last December seems to show that Yugoslav reaction to Albanian irredentist cries has become a kind of reflex action, over the course of two decades.

[53] *Zëri i Popullit*, April 17, 1968.

[54] Zdenko Antic, *RFE Research*, February 7, 1969.

[55] "Denial of Facts and Distortions of History Cannot Erase the Titoite Betrayal," *Zëri i Popullit*, Nov. 5, 1965.

[56] *Le Monde*, March 25, 1969.

[57] *Besa*, February 7, 1969, quoting Radio Belgrade, December 1, 1968.

[58] *Borba*, December 2. 1968; *Rilindja*, December 10, 1968.

[59] For a report on rising tensions between Serbs and Albanians over the approaching Scanderbeg festival, see L[ouis] Z[enga] , *RFE Research*, November 20, 1967.

[60] *The Economist*, December 7-13, 1968, p. 38.

[61] The Twelfth LCY Plenum which met in Belgrade on February 5, 1969 rejected the notion of a federated republic for the Albanian living in Kosovo. *Politika*, February 5, 1969; *Le Monde*, February 7, 1969.

[62] For an outstanding report on the current condition of the Albanians in Kosovo, see Paul Yankovitch, "Lettre de Prichtina," *Le Monde,* March 25, 1969.

[63] William E. Griffith, *Albania and the Sino-Soviet Rift,* (Cambridge, Mass., The M.I.T. Press, 1963), p.171.

[64] *Zëri i Popullit,* May 28, 1959.

[65] "Modern Revisionism to the Aid of the Basic Strategy of American Imperialism," *Zëri i Popullit,* September 19-20, 1962. For text, see William E. Griffith, *Albania and the Sino-Soviet Rift,* op. cit., Doc. No. 31, pp. 364-387 at p. 384.

Chapter 2:
*The Albanians in Yugoslavia**

Postwar Yugoslavia is a country of unusual interest to students of international affairs and other scholars for its foreign as well as its domestic affairs. Among the major points of interest in foreign policy has been Yugoslavia's doctrine of nonalignment, including its opposition to bloc policies of both East and West and its experiment in building communism independently from Moscow—indeed, often in strong opposition to Soviet policies. Domestically, Yugoslavia has attracted attention first of all, because of its institution of Self-Management, but also for its policy of nation-building based on the unity and fraternity of many diverse national groups. This very diversity is also at the root of "the national question" in the country.

The national question is in fact the major domestic issue in Yugoslavia at present. It is a complex issue involving questions of political power, as well as economics, language, culture, and history. It is a question of reconciling the yearnings for self-affirmation of the various ethnic groups that make up Yugoslavia with loyalty to the larger Yugoslav community, and support of the common goals and interests of the nation.

* *Source: Balkanistica*, organ of the American Association for Southeast Europian Studies, Slavica Publishers, Columbus, Ohio, USA, No. 11 (1975) , pp. 7 – 18. The article is based on a speech given by the author at the annual meeting of the American Association for South Slavic Studies, held in New York on December 29, 1974. The author wishes to thank Dr. Robin Remington of the University of Missouri at Columbia who suggested the idea for this paper.

The Albanian minority in Yugoslavia is part of the problem of ethnic groups, along with the Croats, the Macedonians, the Hungarians, the Serbs, the Slovenes, and others. The term "minority," however, needs to be clarified somewhat as it can be misleading in discussions of the national question in Yugoslavia. The Albanians in the Autonomous Province of Kosovo object to the term for they see themselves not as a minority but as a majority within the province—indeed, "an absolute majority." [1] The Yugoslav government itself does not use the term "minority." Instead, it uses the term "peoples" to refer to the populations of the six republics within the federated state, and the term "nationalities" to refer to the populations of the two autonomous provinces of Kosovo and Vojvodina, and other ethnics, such as Turks, Bulgarians, and Italians, whose co-nationals reside in other countries. For the purpose of this study, however, I think we can use the term "Albanian minority" without risking intellectual confusion or leaving ourselves open to the charge, say, of indulging in linguistic adventurism.

The predominantly Albanian-populated province of Kosovo is an important region of Yugoslavia for a number of reasons, including its size and population, its economic and social conditions, and the politics of the area—taken in the narrow sense of that word. In size, Kosovo is 10,882 sq. km. (4,127 square miles), or bigger than the states of Delaware and Rhode Island combined (3,271 square miles). In population, it numbers 1,245,000—according to the 1971 national Yugoslav census—a figure two and a half times larger than that of the neighboring Republic of Montenegro. Of this number, approximately three-fourths (74%), or slightly under one million (920,000) are Albanians; 18 % (230,000) are Serbs; and the rest a scattering of Turks, Montenegrins and others.

But these are not all the Albanians there are in Yugoslavia. There are in addition some 280,000 Albanian nationals in the Republic of Macedonia, where they make up 23% of the population, and 35,000 in Montenegro, where they account for 7% of the population. We thus have a total of 1,310,000 Albanians in Yugoslavia, as against a total of 510,000 Montenegrin nationals, and 1,195,000 Macedonian nationals. In other words, the Albanian minority is the largest ethnic group in Yugoslavia, apart from the Serbs, the Croats, the Slovenes, and the Bosnian Moslems.

Statistics also show that the Albanian minority has the biggest population growth rate in Yugoslavia, compared with the other ethnic groups, and that Kosovo is the most densely populated region in the country. [2] The province is notable, too, for its low standard of living, high unemployment, high illiteracy, and a legacy of backward social customs. In brief, the large population of Kosovo, together with its great economic and social backwardness, aggravates the national question in the area.

The national question is a matter of particular concern to the inhabitants of Kosovo, to the Republic of Serbia, to the national leadership of Yugoslavia, to the Albanian government, and to Albanian émigrés from Kosovo and Albania at the end of World War II. The main political question currently, with respect to the Albanian minority, seems to be: Should Kosovo be granted republic status, thereby becoming the seventh republic of Yugoslavia? In other words, are the Albanians in Yugoslavia to have complete national affirmation, like the Montenegrins and the Macedonians, or are they to continue, organizationally and as a geographical entity, to be a part of, and therefore subordinate to, the Republic of Serbia?

Historical Roots of the Problem

In order to better appreciate the nature of the problem and the intensity of emotions of Albanian and Slav nationals regarding Kosovo, it is useful, I think, to consider briefly the historical background of the region.

From the Slavic viewpoint, Kosovo is the heartland of the original Slav nation and State. It was there that the Medieval Serbian kings were crowned. The great Tsar Stefan Dusan established the seat of his empire in the town of Prizren, in Kosovo. It was in Kosovo that in 1389 the

Serbs and their allies fought the famous Battle of Kosovo against the Ottoman Turks. A monument stands in Pristina, capital of Kosovo, in memory of the martyrs of that decisive battle. Subsequently, that battle inspired the renowned Yugoslav epic, *Kosovo Polje.*

Kosovo is also closely associated in the Yugoslav consciousness with the history of the Serbian Orthodox Church. It was there, in the town of Pec, that the Serbian Patriarchate was founded in the year 1346—an action that made the Serbian Church independent of the Patriarch of Constantinople. The region was the center of Serbian religious life, as well as art and culture, in the Middle Ages.

For the reasons given above, Kosovo is "sacred ground" for the Serbs, who make pilgrimages there from all parts of Yugoslavia. From the Slavic viewpoint, the Albanians are a late arrival in the area. They are said to have come there in the seventeenth and eighteenth centuries by virtue of the favor which they enjoyed under the Turks as a result of sharing with them the same religious faith. The pressure of these "Albanian colonizers," it is said, forced the migration of tens of thousands of Serbs from the region, a development which in time left the Albanians in the majority there. In support of this argument, Slav historians refer to the ordeal of the Serbian Patriarch, Arsen Carnojevic, who in 1690 migrated to Hungary, along with some 30,000 Serbian families.[3]

The idea that Kosovo might some day be separated from Serbia causes, in large part, what one observer has described as "an irrational emotional reaction" among the Serbs.[4]

The viewpoint of the Albanians on Kosovo may be stated as follows: Kosovo, they note, was originally inhabited by the Illyrians, their ancient ancestors. In the seventh century, AD., however, the Illyrians were largely displaced from the area by the Slavs, as these moved into the Balkan Peninsula from the hinterland of Europe. The Albanians, therefore, claim that they are native to the land of Kosovo, and that there has been a continuous Albanian presence there from ancient times down to the present era. In support of this claim, they refer to documentary evidence in the form of reports by Catholic missionaries in the region during the Middle Ages, the accounts of Turkish chroniclers, and the writings of Western European travelers, all of which show that there has always been a strong, if not always dominant, Albanian presence in Kosovo.[5]

The Albanians point out, too, the importance of Kosovo for the modern Albanian nation. It was there that the League of Prizren was established in 1878, marking the beginning of the Albanian national awakening that culminated in the winning of independence from the Turks in 1912, and the founding of the modern Albanian state. Moreover, the armed revolts against the Turks immediately prior to independence (1909-12) were mostly the work of Kosovo Albanians.

If Kosovo then is sacred ground to the Serbs, because of past associations with the Medieval Serbian church and state, the region is equally significant to the Albanians, not only as the home of their Illyrian ancestors, but as the land that sparked the drive for freedom and national independence after nearly five centuries of Turkish domination.

In sum, both the Yugoslavs and the Albanians claim original title to Kosovo: 1) by virtue of possession and 2), because of the historical associations which the region has for both sides.

Kosovo became a problem in Yugoslav-Albanian relations at first in 1878, when the Congress of Berlin awarded parts of the region to Serbia and Montenegro. Then, in 1913, the London Conference—which was convened to arrange peace term, between a defeated Turkey and its Balkan adversaries (Bulgaria, Greece, Montenegro, and Serbia)—ceded the entire region to Serbia. The loss of these Albanian-populated territories amounted to well over one half of present-day Albania.

Following World War I, the Albanian minority in royalist Yugoslavia did not fare well. As a national group, it was a nonentity in the eyes of the Belgrade government. The use of the Albanian language in the schools was forbidden. Indeed, it was dangerous for Albanian nationals to possess Albanian-language books and literature. Belgrade's policy of repression of the Albanian language and of other national rights pertaining to the Albanian minority, led a high ranking Albanian official in Kosovo to remark years later that Kosovo was the only province in royalist Yugoslavia which "had more prisons and police stations than schools." [6]

Kosovo in Socialist Yugoslavia

Following the establishment of the Federated State of Yugoslavia in 1945, two major changes occurred in the situation of Albanian nationals. First, they were granted recognition as a distinct national group, living in a distinct geographical territory, namely the "province of Kosovo." Second, the Albanian language was recognized as "one of the official languages" of Kosovo; in other words, it was granted legal equality with Serbo-Croatian. Accordingly, Albanian schools were opened in the province and the opportunity was given to the Albanians to strive for their cultural development and national affirmation. These events marked a definite improvement in the status of the Albanian minority in Yugoslavia compared with its lot before the war.

But despite these considerable gains by the Albanians, obstacles arose in the way of achieving full equality with other nationals in Yugoslavia. One major obstacle was the Rankovic police-state rule in Kosovo. Another was the ideological polemics which broke out between Yugoslavia and Albania in 1948, following Stalin's expulsion of Tito from the Cominform.

Aleksandar Rankovic, Vice President of Yugoslavia and heir-designate of Tito, nourished a particular enmity toward Albanian nationals. He had a deep distrust of them, believing them to be politically disloyal and "potentially subversive" of the interests of the Yugoslav state. Consequently, he resorted to persecution of the Albanian minority, including illegal imprisonment, torture, and other measures, all in violation of the Yugoslav constitution and the minority rights of a national group. The result was an aggravation of ethnic rivalries between Albanians and Serbs in the province and the creation of a tense political climate there.

The situation was worsened by the polemical war between Albania and Yugoslavia. On the one hand, Tirana mounted vehement attacks on "revisionist Yugoslavia" and Tito's "renegade clique" for carrying out a policy of "denationalization" of the Albanian minority and for repeated attempts to "exterminate" the Albanian nationals. Tirana further accused the Yugoslavs of turning Kosovo into a center of subversion against Albania, using for this purpose escapees from Albania, including war criminals. On the other hand, Belgrade accused the Hoxha leadership in Tirana of pursuing an adventurist policy of irredentism with regard to Kosovo, interfering in the internal affairs of Yugoslavia, and seeking to incite rebellion among Albanian nationals against LCY and the Yugoslav government. In the meantime, the population of Kosovo huddled in the crossfire of this war of words which lasted for nearly two decades.

A reversal of this bitter climate of hostilities began in 1966 with the fall of Rankovic. The excesses of Rankovic's authority came to light in the proceedings of the 4th LCY Plenum, known as the Brioni Plenum, which was held in July of 1966. The demolition of Rankovic's police apparatus in the Kosovo province was a heavy moral and psychological blow to the "Greater Serbia" mentality of his supporters, who had worked actively to maintain Serbian supremacy in the province. Following Rankovic's demise, there was a revival of efforts by Belgrade to grant equal rights to Albanian nationals, in conformity with the provisions of the federal constitution, and to improve the economic condition of the region.

At about the same time, a movement began among the Albanian minority aimed at achieving full national affirmation, including republican status for Kosovo. The movement gathered momentum over the next two years and, in the fall of 1968, exploded into a series of violent demonstrations in at least nine cities with large concentrations of Albanians, among them Pristina, and Tetovo (Macedonia.) [7] The demonstrations were harshly denounced by the Yugoslav authorities; yet, they induced Belgrade to grant still more rights to Albanian nationals, including the fulfillment of their demand for the establishment of a "national university" in Pristina. These measures had the effect of lowering ethnic tensions in the province, and giving time to the leaderships in Pristina and Belgrade to implement more fully Yugoslavia's official policy of "unity and brotherhood" *(Bratstvo i Jedinstvo)* among Albanian and Slav ethnics in Kosovo.

The climate of détente in the province accelerated in the aftermath of the invasion of Czechoslovakia in 1968. The assault on the Czechs led to a tacit alliance between Albania and Yugoslavia—owing mostly to fears of a Soviet attack on them—and a diminution of their polemical struggle. It marked the beginning of an improvement of relations between the two neighboring countries, which culminated in the establishment of full diplomatic relations between them in February, 1971. As a result, Kosovo was converted from a political and ideological battleground to a bridge—however weak—for furthering understanding and cooperation between Belgrade and Tirana.

The most fruitful example of cooperation so far has been in the field of cultural exchanges, covering such areas as education, art, entertainment, communications, tourism, and sports. These exchanges have been particularly intense between the University of Tirana and the University of Pristina. Kosovo educators have obtained a variety of teaching aids, supplies, and textbooks from Albania, while a growing number of professors from Albania have taught courses in the University of Pristina in recent years. Kosovo writers of Albanian nationality have been published in *Nëntori*, organ of the League of Writers and Artists of Albania. Kosovo song and dance ensembles have given performances in towns throughout Albania, and dramatic groups from the province have staged plays in Tirana on a number of occasions. In addition, Kosovo scholars have participated in all of the major academic seminars and conferences that have been held in Tirana since 1968. The same is true of Albanian writers, artists, scholars, entertainers, and athletes with respect to traveling to Kosovo.

Since the mid-1960, Albanian nationals in Yugoslavia have made greater gains than ever before: in obtaining political power in the provincial government and at the federal level, in attaining language equality, in moving to positions of responsibility and power in industry and commerce, in the development of their national culture and educational system, and in the training of technical cadres to help modernize the region's economy. For example, Albanian ethnics are said to occupy the most important posts in the provincial party organization and government. Moreover, an Albanian from Kosovo, Fadil Hoxha—a long-time member of the LCY Presidium—has been designated as a candidate to the nine-member State Presidency, which will become operative when Tito dies. Hoxha is in fact "the only non-slav member in the supreme state collective leadership." [8]

Yet, the basic problems of the region remain unsolved. Economic backwardness is a disquieting reality and a potential source of new ethnic conflicts, for Kosovo is by far the poorest region in Yugoslavia. It has the highest rate of unemployment and the lowest per capita income in the country. Social backwardness, too, continues to shackle the province. Kosovo has the highest rate of illiteracy (41%) in the nation, although great progress has been made in this area since World War II, when roughly 90% of the population of the province could not read or write. The tradition of blood feuds continues, though at a lower level of violence than before the war. These conditions seem to be aggravated by the very high birth rate among Albanian nationals in Kosovo.

Economic and social problems, in turn, add fuel to the tensions in the area. Latinka Perovic, former Secretary of the Serbian League of Communists, has rightly observed, I think, that: "As long as the per capita national product in Slovenia is $1,150 and a mere $ 150 in Kosovo, every economic question ... is turned into a national problem."[9] The national question in Kosovo involves above all two groups: On one side, there are the Serbian and Montenegrin conservatives who bewail the erosion of their former power and influence in the province, and who are fearful of the growing power of the Albanian element. Some of these reportedly have migrated from Kosovo because of pressures exerted by the Albanian minority. On the other side, there are the Albanian nationalists, plus a few extremists, who are dissatisfied with the current rate of progress in attaining their national rights, and who feel frustrated over the economic deprivations they are experiencing.

In short, the national question of the Albanian minority in Kosovo has not been solved. On the contrary, it seems to have worsened lately, in part because of the rising national ferment in all of Yugoslavia, especially since the Croatian crisis in 1971, and also in part because of the greater aspirations and expectations of Albanian ethnics for a better standard of living and greater control over their lives. Kosovo is a problem waiting for a solution.

Current Viewpoints on Kosovo

Over the past 60 years, a number of "solutions" have been tried or envisioned as a means of resolving the national question in Kosovo. The only one, however, that has currency today is the proposal to make Kosovo a republic in which the Albanian minority would have a decisive voice in ordering its affairs and shaping its destiny, instead of being subject to the veto power of the Serbian Republic.

What, then, is the status of the Albanian minority at present, especially in relation to the establishment of a republic of Kosovo? There are four viewpoints, at least, on this question: 1) That of the Albanians of Yugoslavia. 2) That of Serbia and the Yugoslav leadership. 3) That of the Albanian government. 4) That of the Albanian postwar émigrés from Kosovo and Albania.

The Position of Albanian Nationals

The Albanians in Yugoslavia, as might be expected, are in favor of republican status for the province of Kosovo. They feel that the proposal for a republic is supported by the logic of their large and rapidly growing numbers. They ask: Why should half a million Montenegrins have their own republic, and nearly a million Albanians in Kosovo be denied a republic of their own? I think it will be granted that this is a strong argument in favor of their aspirations for a republic. Moreover, by gaining republican status, they would acquire added prestige in the eyes of other nationals in Yugoslavia. Finally, such a development would be the fulfillment of the wartime pledge of Tito's Partisans to grant the right of self-determination to all national groups following the end of the war. [10]

The View from Belgrade

It has been reported that, in early 1968, Tito "considered the idea of making Kosovo the seventh republic of Yugoslavia," but had to abandon it in view of strong opposition on the part of the Serbs. [11] The report is believable, for, to the Serbs, Kosovo is "Stara Srbija"—the renowned soil of Old Serbia. The Serbs feel that there has been an erosion of Serbian strength and authority in postwar Yugoslavia as a consequence of the creation of the republics of Montenegro, Bosnia-Herzegovina, and Macedonia, all of which were formerly under Serbian control. The separation, therefore, of Kosovo from Serbia would mean—from their point of view—a further weakening of the Serbian Republic. Nor is that all. Such a development, they believe, would confront Serbia with the threat of dismemberment since it would inevitably lead to calls for republican status for the other autonomous province of Serbia—the Hungarian-populated Vojvodina.

There is reluctance at the federal level, as well, to making Kosovo a republic, owing to its proximity to Albania. For, assuming that Kosovo were a republic, the Yugoslav leadership fears that the next step might well be the merger of Kosovo with Albania. That is to be avoided, for it would almost certainly trigger a chain reaction among other nationalities in the country, which could end with the disintegration of the Yugoslav Federation. A concrete illustration of Belgrade's fears on this matter appeared in the news recently. Writing from Belgrade, a *New York Times* correspondent reported that four ethnic Albanians had been jailed on charges of advocating "the secession of Kosovo from Yugoslavia so it could be joined to neighboring Albania." [12] Leaving aside the question of the veracity of the charges, the report is nevertheless an indication of the

Yugoslav leaders' continuing suspicion about the political loyalties of the Albanian minority and their consequent reluctance to upgrade the political status of the province to the level of a republic.

The View from Tirana

The main stance of Albania on Kosovo since 1948 has been to pose as the defender of the Albanian minority against discrimination and persecution by the Slavs, and to support the struggle of Albanian ethnics for full national equality. This stance translated itself into support for the proposition to make Kosovo a republic, as well as support for self-determination for Albanian nationals, even to the point of secession from the Yugoslav Federation, if they so chose. At the same time, Albania has not advanced a serious territorial claim on the province, although it has stated from time to time that it is "natural and just" for the Albanians of Yugoslavia to want union with Albania. Since normalizing relations with Yugoslavia, however, the Hoxha leadership has practically ceased polemics regarding the condition of Albanian nationals in Kosovo.

The Position of Albanian Émigrés

Albanian émigrés comprise the fourth party or group that is directly and actively interested in the fate of Kosovo. This group is composed of anti-communist exiles from Kosovo and Albania. The group is small in number and lacks actual political power; yet, it is not insignificant and cannot be ignored or dismissed as of no consequence in a discussion of the Albanian minority in Yugoslavia any more than, let us say, Croatian groups in exile can be ignored in dealing with the Croatian national and separatist movement. For the Albanian émigré group represents the major nationalist currents that competed for power, during the war, against the communist forces of Enver Hoxha in Albania, and Marshal Tito's forces in Yugoslavia.

The émigrés see Kosovo as an enslaved land, suffering under the double yoke of Slavic domination and communist oppression.[13] For them, Kosovo is not merely the province of Kosovo but all Albanian-populated areas in Yugoslavia. They claim that the Albanians of

Yugoslavia number well over two million—a figure roughly equal to the population of Albania. Indeed, they view Kosovo as "the other half of Albania," without which Albania cannot be a viable nation or a stable Balkan state.

The émigrés have two objectives with regard to Kosovo. The first, an intermediary one, calls for an autonomous republic of all Albanian ethnics, within the framework of Federated Yugoslavia. The second objective envisions the union of the Albanian minority with "a free, independent, and democratic Albania," and thus achieve the ethnic integration of the Albanian nation.

Conclusion

In view of the preceding discussion, I think one can say that the Albanian minority in Yugoslavia has been a problem in that country for some 60 years. Over the past decade, Yugoslav officials have made greater efforts than ever before to solve the problem, by creating more equitable conditions of life for Albanian nationals in all spheres of activity: politics, economics, language and education, art and culture. Partly as a result of these efforts, the Albanians of Kosovo have more control over their lives and fortunes at present than ever before. Yet, the "national question" of Albanian ethnics persists. Indeed, the indications are that it has become more acute lately, owing to an increase in national fervor and militancy among Albanian ethnics in recent years.

Looking ahead—to the limited extent that one can indulge in such a risky business – the future course or direction of the Albanian minority in Yugoslavia is likely to be influenced by at least three factors: One, how the national question in Yugoslavia as a whole is resolved. Two, the correlation of forces between Albanian party and government leaders in Kosovo, who strive to implement Yugoslavia's official policy on the national question—namely, the fostering of unity and fraternity of all ethnic groups in the country—and their opponents, the Albanian extremists, who seek the separation of the province from Yugoslavia.

Three, the manner in which relations develop between Yugoslavia and Albania.

Future developments in Kosovo, whether they evolve peacefully in the direction of greater harmony and fraternity between Albanian and Slav ethnics or whether they bring sharper conflicts and perhaps even a renewal of violence in the province, will be one good indication of how successfully Yugoslavia is handling the national question—the major domestic issue, by far, in the country at present.

Notes

[1] 1. z., "Sharp Growth in Kosovo Population," *RFE Research* (Yugoslavia) , May 5, 1971.

[2] According to an OECD study in 1968, the region had 40 births per 1,000 inhabitants, as against the national average of 20; and 104 inhabitants per sq. km., as against 73 for the country as a whole. See OECD report, *Regional Project of Kosovo-Metohija,* Paris, 1968, p. 16.

[3] Thomas Adolph Roth, "Yugoslav (Socialist) Rule in Practise: A survey of Developments in the Kosovo Region." M.A. thesis, University of Oregon, 1970, p. 14.

[4] Zdenko Antic, *RFE Research* (Yugoslavia) , Feb. 7, 1969.

[5] H. Kokalari, *Kosova – Djepi i Shqiptarizmit* (Kosovo – Cradle of Albanian Nationalism) , published by the League of the Kossovars (Rome: APICE Press, 1962) , pp. 41 – 45.

[6] Veli Deva, President of the League of the Communists of Kosovo, in *Rilindja* (Rebirth) , Pristina , Nov. 28-29-30, 1968, p. 6.

[7] For a detailed account of these demonstrations, see Peter R. Prifti, *Kosovo in Ferment* (monograph) , M.I.T. Center for International Studies, Cambridge, Mass. (June, 1969) , 37 pp.

[8] Slobodan Stankovic, *RFE Research* (Yugoslavia) , March 18, 1974.

[9] P. Lendvai, "Yugoslavia in Crisis," *Encounter,* XXXIX, 2 (Aug. 1972) , p. 71.

[10] *Zëri i Popullit,* (The Voice of the People) , Tirana, Nov. 24, 1968; See also Nicholas C. Pano, *The Peoples's Republic of Albania* (Baltimore, Md. : John Hopkins Press, 1968) , p. 40.

[11] Ilija Jukic, "Tito's Legacy," *Survey,* No. 77 (Autumn, 1970) , p. 101.

[12] Malcolm W. Browne, "Yugoslavia Jails 4 Ethnic Albanians," *The new York Times,* Jan. 16, 1975.

[13] For a full exposition of the position of émigrés on Kosovo, see Kokalari, op. cit.; and *The Struggle of the Kosovars,* No. 15, July 10, 1974.

Chapter 3:

*Kosova's Economy: Problems and Prospects**

A popular saying in Yugoslavia these days is: "If the other regions in Yugoslavia walk, then Kosova must run." It's a pointed comment on Kosova's economy. The trouble is that Kosova's economy is not running. It's not even walking. More often than not, it is plodding or even crawling.

Kosova is a land of great natural resources, particularly mineral wealth. It is also a land beset with enormous economic problems.

At present, the province has a population of roughly 1,600,00 or about 7 percent of Yugoslavia's total population of nearly 23 million. It is the most densely populated area in the country, and has the highest birth rate as well. It has also the largest ethnic group in the Yugoslav Federation, the Albanians, who presently account for 77.5 percent of Kosova's population.

The province has been, and continues to be, the poorest and least developed area in the Federated Socialist Republic of Yugoslavia. It's a reality borne out by statistics in all areas of economic activity in Kosova: level of development, productivity, urban-rural ratio of the population, income and wages, education, employment, and standard of living.

* Paper delivered at the International Conference on Kosova, Graduate Center, City University of New York, NY, on November 6, 1982. The paper was published as a chapter (pp. 125 – 165) in *Studies on Kosova*, edited by Arshi Pipa and Sami Repishti, New York, NY 1984. *East European Monographs, Boulder, Distributed by Columbia University Press, New York, 1984*. This chapter is an abbreviated version of the paper.

Although Kosova has about 7 percent of Yugoslavia's population, its share of the total social product of the country is considerably below its proportion of the population—only slightly above 2 percent. The region has the highest illiteracy rate in Yugoslavia, nearly double the national average. The per capita income is about one-seventh that of Slovenia, the most developed republic in the Federation. With an annual inflation rate of over 40 percent, Kosova holds an unenviable first place not only in Yugoslavia, but in all of Europe. In the field of employment, the picture is equally dreary. In 1979, only 107 Kosovars per 1,000 in the active population were employed, compared with 253 for the Yugoslav average, and 427 for Slovenia. Particularly, hard-pressed for jobs is the Albanian population. While one in every five Serbs and Montenegrins in Kosova was employed in 1980, only one in every eleven Albanians held a job.

These statistics translate finally into a low standard of living for Kosova. Figures for 1978 show that less than five houses per 1,000 population were built in Kosova, while the number in Slovenia was nearly eight. The proportion of houses with plumbing facilities was less than fifty percent in Kosova, and practically one hundred percent in Slovenia.

The evidence is conclusive that Kosova is in a very backward condition. Whether one looks at industry, agriculture, foreign trade, investments, or social services, one encounters complex and stubborn problems that at times seem to defy solutions, at least in the short run.

Relative to other regions in Yugoslavia, especially the developed ones, such as Slovenia, Croatia, Serbia, and Vojvodina, Kosova presents a discouraging picture of backwardness. Relative to its own past, however, it has moved forward. In absolute terms, it has made progress since the end of World War II. The province has confronted its general backwardness, and attained some degree of success. It has laid the basis for industrial development, and created a professional and technical body of workers.

The illiteracy rate, which at the end of the war stood at 80 percent, had dropped to 31.5 percent by 1971. There have been advances in the training of medical personnel and in health care for the population. The number of cultural institutions, such as libraries, museums, theaters and cinemas has grown steadily. By 1980 Kosova had a modern radio-television station, and a vigorous publishing industry, which printed scores of books annually, plus over two dozen newspapers and magazines.

Such gains unfortunately are small comfort for the unstable situation of the present. A listing of Kosova's current economic problems reads like a litany of woes: inflation, unemployment, shortages of food and other commodities, housing crisis, illiteracy, high birth rate, a weak infrastructure, poverty. Added to these are problems of deficit spending, foreign trade deficits, an overloading of the economy with taxes and tariffs. Still other problems are so-called subjective weaknesses of the economy which include among others: work inefficiency, growing sick leaves, frequent work stoppages, and waste of funds and materials.

Yet, the most critical problem of the economy is Kosova's lag in development with regard to other regions in Yugoslavia. What makes this lag particularly disturbing is that the gap between Kosova and the republics has been continuously growing rather then narrowing. The result is that at present Yugoslavia as a whole is about four times as developed as Kosova.

How did this situation arise? The reasons are many, but cannot all be dealt with here, since they include not only economic, but political, ethnic, cultural, linguistic and other reasons. Nevertheless, the major responsibility for the condition that developed must be laid, it appears, at the door of the Federal Government. The Federation discriminated against Kosova in its policy for the economic development of the country. It's a charge that has been made repeatedly by Kosovar scholars, economists and the media. According to Milija Kovaceviq, a leading economist in Kosova, for fifteen years following the war Kosova was not included in the category of undeveloped regions, and as such was denied financial grants from the Federation, which at the time were unconditional, as well as help with technicians and specialists that were

were dispatched to regions qualifying for Federal aid. When Kosova was included in the group of undeveloped areas, such as Montenegro, and Bosnia-Herzegovina, it received aid in the form of credits that had to be paid back with interest. This policy of the Federation so burdened the economy of the province that it has never been able to recover fully from its effects.

The province is also reaping the consequences of injudicious economic planning, especially in connection with the so-called unsuitable structure of its economy that has prevailed through three decades. The reference is to an economic policy that was mainly geared to production of raw materials, which were processed in the republics, and which made Kosova dependent on the republics for finished goods—a condition that Michael Kaser, the distinguished British economist, says is not conductive to economic growth. The stress on mining and energy resulted in relative neglect of agriculture and other branches of the economy, and because it was a capital-intensive policy, it had an adverse effect on the employment situation as well.

The acquisition and use of investment funds has been a troublesome problem for Kosova ever since the Federal Government began to allocate developmental funds in the sixties. The leadership and the press in the province have complained loudly and insistently that investment funds, in the form of Federal aid, have been erratic and insufficient to meet the pressing needs of the province. The complaint seems valid. But there is evidence also of mismanagement of funds, such as investing in the wrong projects, in the wrong locations, or yet again spending vast sums of money on projects of prestige.

The human resources or personal problems affecting the economy include a vast army of unemployed, estimated at nearly a quarter of a million, counting both registered and unregistered workers; a lack of qualified cadres; a mobile population of urban workers originating from the villages who have not yet adjusted to the new life in the cities, and who have left in their wake a dislocated countryside; and the emergence of an "academic proletariat" made up of intellectuals, professionals, and newly-graduated students with rising expectations, but with no jobs in which to employ their skills and knowledge.

In addition to the Federal Government's inequitable developmental policy, the problems of Kosova can be attributed to some extent to the dislocations that attend a society in the process of modernization, to the pervasive and very costly bureaucracy of the province, and to the imperfect market system of Yugoslavia's economy which, as Prof. Adi Schnytzer observes in his paper, "has worked to the advantage of the richer regions of the country".

These problems crystallized, as we know, in the violent demonstrations in Kosova in the Spring of last year. How, one might ask, did the leadership in Belgrade respond to the demonstrations, from an economic point of view? The leaders had the objectivity to grant that economic factors were a cause of the rioting. Unfortunately, their analyses of the problems of Kosova's economy was in general defective: polemical rather than dispassionate, superficial rather than rigorous. To their credit, they admitted that not enough was done to develop Kosova, but the reason for this, they said, was not a Federal policy of neglect and discrimination against the province, but rather the war-ravaged economy of Yugoslavia and the "consequences of the Cominform blockade" against Yugoslavia. The obvious retort to that of course, is: Why did not the effects of the war and the Cominform blockade prevent the government also from giving aid and support to the other undeveloped regions of Yugoslavia?

As for the prospects of Kosova's economy in the near future, not much need be said. Some notions about the prospects can be gathered from the province's current Five-Year Plan, for the period 1981-1985. The plan is said to be based 1), on a new structure for the economy, which favors the development of the processing industries; 2) on a linkage of Kosova's economy with the economies of other regions, through joint economic ventures between industries in the province and enterprises in the six republics and Vojvodina; and 3), and a growth rate of Kosova's economy which is 60 percent above the Yugoslav national average.

Ambitious goals, indeed, but almost certainly unrealistic. None of the principal features of the plan are new. They were current in the decade of the seventies, but unhappily none proved to be very effective. Progress reports on the unfolding of the plan during 1981 and the first half of this year were not encouraging. Far from achieving the 60 percent figure in overall productivity, Kosova's social product in 1981 increased only 5.5 percent.

Since the founding of the Yugoslav Federation at the end of the war, Kosova has been subordinated to the Republic of Serbia. Yet, Serbia has not been able to bring Kosova out of its backward state. From an economic point of view, Kosova's special relationship to Serbia; that is, its subordinate status in the Serbian Republic, has not worked, inasmuch as the province remains in a critical state of underdevelopment. There is abundant evidence that the people of Kosova are not content with this relationship.

The consensus of scholars, journalists, and travelers to Kosova is that the economic prospects of the region are grim. It would be surprising if the province does not slide further back by 1985. The stagnation that has gripped the economy, and the resulting malaise that afflicts the Kosovar population is reminiscent of the condition of the province in the early postwar period.

In sum, the problems of Kosova's economy are staggering, and unless there is a basic change in the direction, management or operation of the economy, the prospects for recovery, stability and growth are not promising.

Chapter 4:
*Situation in Kosova One Year after 1981 Riots**

Since the demonstrations in the spring of 1981, Kosova has become the focal point of the Albanian world, the outstanding national issue, and the most urgent problem waiting for a solution.

As we all know, the Kosovar demonstrators called for a Republic of Kosova, so that the region would no longer be subordinate to the Republic of Serbia, but be an equal to it in rank and status, from a constitutional and administrative point of view. We may ask: What is the rationale of the demand of the Kosovars? On what basis do they seek a republic of their own?

An objective and impartial examination of their demand shows, I believe, that it is just and proper, and long overdue. The logic of their numbers, first of all, supports their demand. The Albanians are greater in number that either the Montenegrins or t he Macedonians, both of whom have their own republics, while the Albanians do not. Second, by raising the status of Kosova to a republic, the League of Communists of Yugoslavia would be honoring a commitment made to the Kosovars both before and during the Second World War, with regard to self-determination or self-rule. Thirdly, republican status would give to the Albanians in Kosova a sense of self-esteem that they need, and added prestige in the eyes of other ethnic groups in Yugoslavia, as well as in the eyes of the world abroad. They would then be freed of the stigma of being second or third class citizens in the Federation of Yugoslavia.

---

* Speech delivered at the celebration of Albania's Independence Day, in San Francisco, California, Sunday, November 28, 1982.

By having their own republic, like the other six major ethnic groups or people in Yugoslavia, the Kosovars would feel that they are largely in control of their fate and fortunes, that they are masters in their own home, in their own land. For they are native to the land.

The Yugoslav information services have been telling the world, and convinced many people, even in the academic field, that the Albanians are late comers in Kosova. But this story is being rapidly discredited, not only by scholars in Albania and Kosova, but by reputed scholars and specialists in Europe. Early this month, I attended the International Conference on Kosova that was held at the City University in New York. And one of the speakers at the conference was the French scholar, Prof. Alain Ducellier, a world-renowned authority on the Medieval History of the Balkans. And he said: "Based especially on archeological evidence, it cannot be doubted nowadays that an Illyrian-Albanian presence can be detected, from Ancient times to the Middle Ages, in what are now the Yugoslavian territories of Kosova and Macedonia…" The fact is that the Albanians were in Kosova centuries before the first Slavs set foot in the Balkans.

Another claim of the Yugoslav information services is that the Kosovars are exerting pressure on the Serbs and Montenegrins in Kosova, and causing them to migrate from the region. A feverish campaign has been afoot for months in the Yugoslav press, accusing the Albanians of victimizing the Slavs in the area. To leave one's home and land and to emigrate unwillingly, is certainly one of life's saddest experiences. Nobody is more painfully aware of this truth than the Kosovars, for they have been victims of displacement and expulsions by the Yugoslav government for decades, and in the hundreds of thousands. They were forced to immigrate to Turkey both before and after the war. But as to the migration of the Slavs from Kosova, the primary reason for that is economic, not Albanian pressure. They are moving out because they are not willing to face the economic hardships that confront the inhabitants of Kosova, because educational opportunities in the region are limited, and because their prospects for a more prosperous and comfortable life are better in other parts of Yugoslavia.

Unfortunately, in dealing with the question of Albanian nationals in Kosova, the authorities in Belgrade have been unrealistic and un-statesman-like. Instead of negotiating with the peaceful demonstrators on their reasonable demands, the authorities chose the road of violence and repression. They discarded reason and embraced force. They embarked on a path of harsh political oppression of all Kosovars who favor a republic of Kosova. They have resorted to cruel economic reprisals against the demonstrators and their families, depriving them of the opportunity to earn a living. They have instituted a shortsighted crusade against Albanian culture, barring Albanian literature and textbooks published in Albania, and downgrading the Albanian cultural heritage and Albanian national figures, not excluding even the great Scanderbeg.

This intransigent attitude on the part of the Yugoslav officials is a natural result of their refusal to see and accept realities in Kosova. Their refusal, that is, to recognize the real causes of the grave problems besetting the province. The sources of the grievances of the Kosovars for decades have been economic and social inequality, political discrimination including persecution by the secret police, and denial of their rights as a nationality group in the Federated Republic of Yugoslavia. Yet, instead of addressing these issues directly, the Belgrade authorities have placed the blame for Kosova's problems on Albanian "nationalists and irredentists," on "counter-revolutionaries," on émigré elements including the *Balli Kombetar* (National Front), and on the Albanian government in Tirane.

Experience has shown that such a policy is inevitably self-defeating. The entire history of Kosova bears witness to that truth. The current policy of the Yugoslav leadership on Kosova is bad politics, ruinous economics, and very likely the best means to bring about irreversible instability throughout the Yugoslav Federation. For example, since the riots of last year, Yugoslavia has stationed at least one-fourth of its army in Kosova. Armed police and battle-ready troops patrol the streets of Kosova cities, and stand guard over the Albanian population. An Austrian newspaper, *Kleine Zeitung*, wrote on October 6 of this year that the special army units in Kosova are costing the Yugoslav state treasury 300 million old dinars a day. That amounts to about 67,000 U.S. dollars a day, not a small sum, for a country like Yugoslavia, which is currently some 20 billion dollars in debt to Western countries.

World public opinion, however, is more perceptive than Belgrade gives it credit for. Major West European journals (such as *Corriere della Sera*, Italian; *Die Presse*, Austrian; *Die Welt* and *Frankfurter Allgemeine*, West German; *Neue Züricher Zeitung*, Switzerland; as well as such noted magazines as the *Economist* of London and *L'Express* of Paris) have, in general, placed the responsibility for the troubles in Kosova on the Yugoslav government, rather than on the Kosovars or on foreign elements.

Indeed, voices have been raised even in Yugoslavia itself against the official policy on Kosova. There has been criticism by a number of government officials, students, as well as some newspapers. Perhaps the best example of disagreement with official policy came in October of 1981, when 119 students from the universities of Belgrade, Zagreb, and Ljubljana addressed a petition to the Presidency of the Federation on the issue of arrests and trials in Kosova. The petition attacked the harshness of the sentences handed down to the defendants and accused the judiciary of arbitrary actions motivated by political interests.

One would think that such developments in Yugoslavia and Western Europe would influence and shape American policy toward Yugoslavia as well, with regard to the Kosova issue. Unfortunately that has not been the case up to the present. The United States has been curiously silent on Yugoslavia's callous persecution of the Kosovars, in clear violation of international agreements, elemental human rights, and even of its own federal constitution.

It is difficult, for me or any Albanian to criticize the United States of America. For we know how much we are indebted to America for its aid and services to the country of our origin. We know that President Wilson did more than anyone to prevent the partition of Albania in 1920. We know of America's pioneering efforts in education in Albania, through such institutions as the Kennedy School for girls in Korchë, the

American Technical School in Tirane, and Dr. C.T. Erickson's Agricultural School in Kavajë. Nor can we forget that America opened its doors to us, to our parents and grandparents, to come here and earn a decent living, and enjoy the fruits of our labor in peace and freedom.

But at the same time, as Albanians we cannot ignore the sufferings of our brothers and sisters in Kosova. And as free citizens of this great country, we feel it's our duty to urge our government to speak out on the violation of human rights in Kosova. Our government officials speak out almost daily on human rights violations in Poland, in Iran, in any part of the world. It is time for America to come out in support of the national rights of the Kosovars, and their demand for a republic of their own, within the Yugoslav Federation.

We can confidently expect a number of positive results, once Kosova is granted republican status. Such an action on the part of Belgrade will first of all bolster Yugoslavia's political stability, which currently is shaky and fragile. It will go a long way toward solving the national question in Yugoslavia, which has been and still is that country's number one internal problem. Once the Kosovars assume greater control of their economic life, the economy of the region and that of Yugoslavia as well should see a distinct improvement. Furthermore, an up-grading of Kosova's political status is bound to improve Yugoslav-Albanian relations, and that in turn cannot but contribute to peace and security in the Balkans.

There is a slogan in Kosova these days which says: "Kosova Republikë; Ja me hatër, ja me thikë!" Translated into English, that means: "Kosova will become a republic, either peacefully or violently;" either, that is, with the consent of the authorities, or by the use of the knife, by force. It's a slogan the Yugoslav authorities would do well to take seriously.

Let it be said, however, that the Albanians in Albania and in Kosova wish no harm for Yugoslavia, despite the misgivings and allegations of Belgrade officials. Contrary to the notion some people have abroad, Albanians are not an aggressive and warlike race. They do not lust after their neighbors' lands or possessions. They wish to live in peace with the Serbs and with all their neighbors.

The Kosovars ask of Yugoslavia only what belongs to them, only a recognition of their national rights as an ethnic group. It is in Yugoslavia's national interest to meet them halfway, and with patience and goodwill resolve the problems of the region to the benefit of all the parties concerned.

Chapter 5:
*Kosova Issue Presented in U.S. Senate**

Early in June of this year, the Honorable Senator Jesse Helms of North Carolina gave a speech on the floor of the U.S. Senate, which was subsequently printed in the Congressional Record (June 7, 1983, pp. S7815-S7830) under the title, "The Balkans Today: Yugoslavia and the Prospects of Freeing the Albanian Nation." The record includes the remarks of Sen. Helms himself, plus five articles on Yugoslavia, Kosova, and Albania that have appeared recently in the magazine *Problems of Communism*, and the newspapers *Washington Post* and *Wall Street Journal.*

The Senator discussed the Balkans in the broad context of the East-West conflict, with the emphasis on Soviet aims in the region. He began his address by saying that he was "deeply concerned about the deteriorating situation in the Balkan region and particularly the threat that the Soviet Union poses in the area. It is unfortunate, but true," he said, "that the Balkan region for decades has been misunderstood and too little attention has been placed on the consequences arising from potential instability there."

Referring to Yugoslavia, he noted that it is an "artificial state" in which "the rule of Serbia" has been challenged many times, including attempts by force. The fact, he said, that "the Serbs controlled the majority of the Yugoslav economy and the way they disposed of the

---

funds was resented by the Croatians, the Albanians, the Macedonians, and Montenegrins, the Slovenes, and other minority groups."

Revival of Nationalism in Yugoslavia

The Senator said that in recent times, Yugoslavia has experienced a revival of nationalist feeling. He pointed out that "Early in the 1970's Croatian nationalism became a significant threat to the Yugoslav Federation and it has remained so ever since. Armed clashes were reported in the early 1970's and sabotage continues today." He said that "In spite of Yugoslav attempts to contain and crush Croatian nationalism, other national groups within the Yugoslav Federation, such as the Kosovo region, which is ethnically Albanian, and Macedonia, have also started demanding their national rights."

In an interesting remark about Macedonia, the Senator said: "A number of reports have pointed out that Bulgaria has recently stated that one-third of Macedonia belongs to Albania and the other two thirds to Bulgaria." He said that in Macedonia, "the situation is becoming almost as bad as in Kosova, with both Albanian and Bulgarian inhabitants taking part in armed clashes, riots, and countless incidents of sabotage." Incidents and clashes have been reported in the last few months also in Croatia, Bosnia, Slovenia, and Vojvodina, he added.

These nationalist movements, Sen. Helms said, are explosive enough in themselves. But they become much more destabilizing to the Balkans when they come under the influence, wittingly or unwittingly, of the Soviet Union, which seeks to use them in order to acquire land bases in the region and warm-water ports on the Mediterranean.

Turning his attention to Kosova and the Spring 1981 riots, the Senator said that "armed clashes became very severe in the Drenica and Rugova areas." He rejected official Yugoslav figures on the number of casualties resulting from the rioting, and said that the "actual figure was 1,600 killed," while the number of those imprisoned was "about 5,000". Continuing, he said, "As of July 30, 1982, the Albanians lost over

11,800 people, countless numbers have been wounded and crippled, and between 20,000 and 30,000 are in detention." The Yugoslav Army," he said, "has moved a total of 40,000 troops, including 200 armored vehicles, some helicopter gunships and some ground-attack fighters into the area to try to contain the insurrection within the borders of Kosova."

Echoing the Resolution of the Kosovars in January, 1944, Sen. Helms said that Kosova should be "reintegrated with the parent country Albania." He amplified his statement by saying that "The present situation is unjust, because it denies the right of national self-determination" to the Kosovars.

Comments On Albania

The Senator commented also on the conditions in Albania, including the question of religion in the country, and the death of Premier Mehmet Shehu. He said that since 1967, Albania "by decree became the only atheist country in the world where freedom of religion has been absolutely proscribed to the point where several religious personalities have been executed and all houses of worship closed." With regard to the controversial death of Shehu, Sen. Helms, like many other people, does not believe that Shehu took his own life, but rather that he was killed.

He speculated on what might happen in Albania, following the departure of "ailing dictator, Enver Hoxha." He claims that there are pro-Soviet elements in the country, and noted the "conciliatory moves" toward Albania made by the Soviets, both in a covert and overt manner. "The most overt move was made by Andropov himself," on the occasion of Albania's National Day in November of 1982, he said.

Two of the articles recommended by Sen. Helms are particularly interesting as source materials on Kosova. Both are serious studies, and both appeared in *Problems of Communism*. One of them, "Yugoslavia's National Question," is by Viktor Meier, the well known expert on Yugoslavia, who writes regularly on developments in Kosova in the

German press. The other article entitled "Crisis in Kosova," explores many facets of life in Kosova, and is authored by Mark Baskin. (The articles in the *Wall Street Journal* and *Washington Post* are about Albania, but are impressionistic in style and lacking in substance).

Both Meier and Baskin are in agreement with Sen. Helms that the recent upheavals in the province of Kosova are proof that the old problem of nationalism and ethnicity continues to be a major issue in the multi-national state of Yugoslavia. "Communists in Yugoslavia," says Meier, "have been claiming in their propaganda for years, even decades, that they have solved the nationality problem thanks largely to socialism and socialist self-management. Yet, today they are confronted by national problems that are hardly less serious than those of the inter-war Yugoslav state." In fact, since the death of Tito, the trend toward nationalism has grown in the country, as the republics and various ethnic groups have sought to reassert themselves. This assertiveness has been strongest among the Kosovars, and shows the limitations of Belgrade's policy which aims to integrate the different groups in the country.

Meier notes that the very name "Yugoslavia" signifies the land of the Southern Slavs. But the Albanians are not Slavs. "According to modern scholarship, they are descendents of the ancient Illyrians. This hypothesis is accepted today by all Albanian scholars and by a large number of non-Albanian Balkan specialists."

The last census in Yugoslavia (1981) showed that the Albanians make up about 78 percent of the population of Kosova, as against 13 percent Serbs and 2 percent Montenegrans. Socially however, they have traditionally been looked down upon. Baskin writes that the average Yugoslav sees Albanians as lazy, stupid, cruel and barbaric. The low social status of the Albanians, he says, "might" be exceeded only by the Gypsies. Meier notes that the Serbian press these days is crowded with expressions of low esteem for Albanians. Even their Illyrian ancestry is being denied, because it is seen as a political problem for the country, namely a force that feeds the nationalist feelings of the Kosovars.

Background of Kosova Problem

Both Meier and Baskin devote much space to the background of Kosova, in an effort to place the problem in historical context, and thus illuminate the current situation. Meier points out that the Serb-dominated prewar Yugoslavia "viewed the annexation of Kosova after the first Balkan Wars as a return of places sacred to the Serbian national past." Acting on this premise, they attempted to "push back the Albanians through colonization" of the region with Serbs. It was for this reason that most Kosovars "welcomed the breakup of Yugoslavia by fascist Italy" in 1941, and the union of Kosova to Albania proper.

In 1944, when Tito's Communist Partisans moved to reincorporate Kosova into Yugoslavia, despite pledges that the Kosovars would be allowed to determine their own future, the Albanians took up arms in self-defense. According to Baskin, "as many as 30,000 Albanians in Urosevac, Gnjilane, and Trepca staged an uprising" against Titto's partisans. Overcome by superior strength, they were afterward subjected, says Meier, to "a brutal police regime," symbolized above all by Aleksandar Rankovic, second in command after Tito.

A new phase, called by Baskin the "Albanianization" of Kosova, began only after the fall of Rankovic in 1966 and the second uprising of the Kosovars in 1968. During this phase, which continued through the 1970's, the Kosovars' participation and influence in the administration of the province increased, enrollment in the University of Prishtine grew rapidly, reaching the figure of 35,000 students and beyond, and cultural relations between Kosova and Albania developed as never before.

The third uprising occurred in the Spring of 1981. Baskin notes that Albanians in Prishtine came out with slogans such as "Kosova Republike," "We Are Albanians, Not Yugoslavs" and "We Are Children of Scanderbeg." He says that besides the upheavals in Prishtine, "clashes between demonstrators and police" occurred in the municipalities of Vuchiterne, Mitrovice, Gllogovc, Gjakove, Prizren, Podujeve, and Gjilan in Kosova; as well as Tetove, Gostivar , Diber, Kerchove, Struge, Ohri,

Kumanove, and Shkup in the republic of Macedonia. Baskin observes that in terms of its intensity and duration, the 1981 uprising "surpassed all such disruptions in postwar Yugoslavia."

Despite drastic measures by Belgrade authorities to "settle accounts with Albanian nationalists," the situation in Kosova has not been normalized. The so called "differentiation" campaign—a euphemism for "purges"—mounted against Albanian nationalists has not stamped out dissidence in the region. Baskin reports that two interesting forms of Albanian dissidence have appeared recently. He says that some Albanian-managed firms in Kosova and Macedonia now "conduct business solely in the Albanian language," and Albanians in Prishtine "are refusing to pay taxes".

There is neither political nor economic stability in Kosova. According to Baskin, statistics show that the downward trend in the economy of Kosova "accelerated in 1982". Total industrial production fell by 3.3 percent, losses grew to 10 billion dinars, and the number of unemployed rose by 12.5 percent, from 72,000 to 82,000. Considering that Yugoslavia's own economy is in disarray, an improvement in Kosova's economy in the foreseeable future is not to be expected.

Prospects for Resolving Kosova Issue

What then are the prospects for a resolution of the Kosova Issue? The central fact to take into account, according to Meier, is that Kosovars "feel themselves to be Albanians," and this very feeling tends to make them indifferent to Yugoslavia. In this connection, Baskin remarks that the Belgrade authorities doubt the loyalty of the Kosovars, and are haunted by "the specter of Kosova's possible secession from the federation," if the province is made a Republic. Baskin's reading of developments in Kosova is very pessimistic, as regard the future of the Yugoslav Federation. "One might see the Kosova events," he says, "as signifying the disintegration of the federation into a collection of fiefdoms."

Viktor Meier, on the hand, is less pessimistic. He believes that a political solution to the Kosova question is still possible. He is critical of Belgrade's policy of force now in effect in the province. He notes that because of the specter of separatism, there is reluctance to give Kosova republic status. Yet, postponement of a political solution," he warns, "might necessitate greater concessions in the future," on the part of the Yugoslav state.

At any rate, all this material and more on Kosova, is now a part of the Congressional Record of the United States of America. This is in itself a victory for the Kosovars, especially in view of the fact that the Serbs have done their utmost to make Kosova a "non-issue" in the eyes of the world in general, and the eyes of American officials in particular. Viewed from this angle, the speech of the Honorable Senator Jesse Helms in the U.S. Senate on the Balkans and his open support for the Kosovars, is a step in the right direction, which we trust will be followed by other American public officials. Such expressions of support for the Albanians of Yugoslavia at this critical time would not only serve the cause of justice, but also reaffirm America's traditional role of friendship with the Albanians, a tradition best exemplified by the great idealist and humanitarian, President Woodrow Wilson.

Chapter 6:

International Conference on Kosova Held in New York[*]

According to the 1981 Yugoslav national census, there are 1,732,000 Albanian nationals in Yugoslavia. But according to Albanian exiles or emigrants from Kosova, the Albanian population is far greater, roughly one million more than the official figure. By far, the greatest number of Albanians in Yugoslavia (1,227,000 according to the census) reside in the so-called autonomous province of Kosova, a region adjacent to Albania, but incorporated into the Republic of Serbia since the end of World War II.

The lot of Kosovars (the name used by Albanians to refer to all the Albanians in Yugoslavia) has been a difficult one; indeed, the most difficult of any of the numerous peoples that make up the multi-national state of Yugoslavia. The accumulated tensions and frustrations of many decades erupted into massive demonstrations in the Spring of 1981 in the major towns of Kosova. An estimated 20,000 to 30,000 people, including students and intellectuals, professionals, youths, farmers and factory workers, women and children, joined the demonstrations. The demonstrators voiced a variety of demands to redress economic, social, national, cultural, linguistic, and political grievances. The major demand, however, was that Kosova be made a republic; in other words, that its political status be upgraded from that of an "autonomous province" to that of a Republic of Kosova.

---

[*] Source: *Albanian Catholic Bulletin*, Santa Clara, California, USA, Vol. IV (1983) pp. 62-65.

The demonstrations started peacefully, but turned into a bloody confrontation when the Yugoslav authorities used police and military force to disperse the demonstrators. The action taken by Belgrade provoked cries of indignation by Albanians everywhere: in Albania, Western Europe, Turkey, Australia, and in the Western Hemisphere. In the United States, Albanians and sympathizers held demonstrations in Washington, New York, Chicago, San Francisco, and other towns to denounce Yugoslavia's massacre of Albanian nationals and the subsequent arrest, imprisonment and persecution of thousands of demonstrators and their supporters.

The Kosova crisis caused much concern among the Albanian-Americans. Accordingly, a group of scholars took the initiative to organize a conference to discuss the problem of Kosova as thoroughly and as objectively as possible. The riots were clear evidence of a serious problem in Yugoslavia that could have important consequences for the entire Balkan area, and even beyond. That in itself was an important reason for holding the conference. Another concern of the organizers was the portrayal of events in Kosova by the Western media. Much had been written in European and some American newspapers and magazines about Kosova, but unfortunately many of the reports suffered from inaccuracy, superficiality or sensationalism. A conference on Kosova it was hoped, would help to correct media misconceptions, distortions and errors regarding events in the province. The organizers expected moreover that the conference would benefit the population of Kosova, enhance Albanian and Yugoslav cultures, and contribute to mutual understanding and peace in the Balkans.

Organization of Conference

The chief organizers of the conference were Prof. Arshi Pipa, member of the department of French and Italian at the university of Minnesota, Minneapolis, Minn.; and Prof. Sami Repishti of Adelphi University, New York. Prof. Pipa is widely recognized in the Albanian community as a poet and as the distinguished author of *Trilogia Albanica*, which appeared in 1978. Dr. Repishti has for many years been the leading activist on Kosova among Albanian intellectuals in the United States. The full committee for the conference included: Jani Dilo, Fejzi I. Domni, Gjeke Gjolekaj, Agim Karagjozi, Arshi Pipa, Peter R. Prifti, and Zef Shllaku. Stephanie Kosmo was the conference secretary.

The organizing committee planned a most varied program for the conference, intended to cover all of the major aspects of Kosova, past and present: history, folklore, economy, politics, society, education, language, and culture. The roster of scholars invited to participate in the conference included both Albanians and non-Albanians, from within the United States as well as from abroad. Hence the title, "International Conference on Kosova." The countries represented were: U.S., England, France, West Germany, and Australia.

The conference was sponsored by: The Office of International Programs, University of Minnesota; Albanien-Institut, University of Munich; Istituto di Lingua e Letterature Albanese, University of Palermo; Department of French and Italian, University of Minnesota; The Society for Albanian Studies in the United States; the VATRA Federation; and The Albanian Center in New York.

Funds to meet conference expenses came entirely from members of the Albanian community in America.

After months of preparation and hard work by committee members and others, the conference convened in New York City on Saturday, November 6, 1982. The site of the conference was the Auditorium of the Graduate School and University Center of the City University of New York, 33 West 42nd St., New York City. There was an exhibit also in the auditorium of books and other literature on Albania and Albanians.

The conference, subtitled, "The Question of Kosova: Historical Considerations and Prospects for the Future", was divided into a morning and afternoon session. A total of twenty scholars, ten from the United States and ten from overseas, prepared papers for the convocation. Several of the scholars from abroad, however, were unable to attend in person, in which case abstracts of their papers were read at the conference by Ms. Kosmo, the conference secretary.

The conference was opened by Dr. Repishti with a few brief remarks, welcoming the audience and explaining the purpose and objectives of the conference.

The morning session dealt with "historical perspectives and cultural aspects" regarding Kosova, and was moderated by Prof. Albert B. Lord of Harvard University, who has been in the forefront of American scholars involved with the Albanian community, most notably during the centennial of the late Bishop Noli in May of 1982.

Prof. Safete Juka of Lafayette College was the first speaker. The title of her paper was, "The Albanians in Yugoslavia in the Light of Historical Documents: from Illyrian Times to the Present". She made the claim that there has been an Albanian presence in Kosova from ancient times to the present. Her study also affirmed that the Kosovars historically "have been treated with unbelievable harshness" by the Serbs. The time has come, she suggested, to build a new relationship between the Serbs and the Kosovars based on justice and equality.

The second speaker was Prof. Alain Ducellier of the University of Toulouse-Le-Mirail, France. Prof. Ducellier has won world renown as a scholar of the history of Medieval Balkans. He spoke on the "Genesis and Setback of the Albanian State in the 14th and 15th Centuries." Like Juka, he also argued for the continuity of Albanians in Kosova through the centuries. To quote Prof. Ducellier: "Based especially on archeological evidence, it cannot be doubted nowadays that an Illyrian-Albanian presence can be detected from Ancient times to the Middle Ages in what are now the Yugoslavian territories of Kosova and Macedonia..." He stated also that the medieval Albanian state failed not because Albanians lacked a sense of their national identity – a thesis long propagated by Albania's neighbors – but because Albania "was nothing but a part of economic structures whose command was always in non-Albanian hands."

Ducellier was followed to the podium by Prof. Gerhard Grimm of the University of Munich, who spoke on "The Development of

Ethnographic Maps: Kosova from 1878 to 1913". Prof. Grimm discussed the authorship of such maps, the degree of their accuracy, the criteria used by the cartographers and the technical means at their disposal for map-making, the connection between the publication of the maps and political events in the Balkans and Europe at the time, and the extent to which the maps were used by European governments as a basis for delineating frontiers in the Balkans – decisions which affected Kosova's future. He claimed that the making of such maps was not always dictated by disinterested scholarly concerns, but by intentions to manipulate them for political reasons.

Morning Session Continues

In the absence of Prof. Peter Bartl of the University of Munich, Prof. Grimm read an abstract of his paper entitled, "Kosova in the Light of Pastoral Reports." The paper dealt with reports of Catholic Missions in Kosova from 1610 until 1853. According to Bartl, these reports provide data on the number of Catholics and Moslems in the region, confirm their Albanian origin, tell of the process of Islamization of the population in Kosova and the appearance of Crypto-Christians, and of the movements of the population in the area. They are indispensable historical sources for the study of internal developments in Kosova at the time, as seen not through the eyes of Turkish officials, but from the standpoint of "the little people" living in difficult circumstances.

Prof. Nicholas Pano of Western Illinois University, and President of the Society for Albanian Studies, spoke on the topic, "The Kosova Question in Albanian Politics and Diplomacy: 1912-1939". Prof. Pano considered the origin of the Kosova question, and dwelt at some length on the formation of the "Kosovar Committee" and its efforts to win back Albanian territories lost to Serbia and Montenegro. In pursuit of that goal, the committee established relations with the COMINTERN, believing that the Moscow-based organizations might be helpful to the Albanian cause. Prof. Pano also noted that King Zog's policy on Kosova was in some instances detrimental to the Kosovars and the goal of an ethnic Albanian state.

The question of "The System of Education in Kosova" was explored by Jens Reuter of the Südost-Institut in Munich, and author of *Die Albaner in Jugoslawien* (1982). Reuter said that Kosova made progress in the development of education and culture since 1966. Following the 1981 demonstrations, however, the Yugoslav authorities viewed the University of Prishtine as "a hotbed of Albanian nationalism" and began a purge of Albanian intellectuals and students on charges of nationalism. The purge, he said, "does not seem to be the appropriate measure to win the young Kosovars to Yugoslav ideals". The fact is, Reuter maintained, that Kosovar youth by and large feel and think Albanian, and their support of the demonstrations was a reflection of that truth.

There followed the reading of an abstract of a study of Prof. Martin Camaj, the well-known Albanian scholar and author at the University of Munich. Camaj's topic was "The Typology of Kosova's Dialects". He defended the thesis that the current dialect in Kosova developed independently of the other Gheg dialects, such as those of Dibra and Dukagjin, and at an earlier time as well. Moreover, Albanian folklore in Kosova "reflects events from the region's history," thus suggesting that it is native to the region, rather than a graft or import from outside.

Albanian oral epic folklore was discussed by Prof. Albert Lord and by Prof. Arshi Pipa. Both of them discussed the subject in relation to the Serbo-Croatian folklore of the same genre. More specifically, Prof. Lord spoke on "Albanian and Serbo-Croatian Heroic Songs," beginning with the pre-Turkish period and showing their development during the era of Turkish occupation. Using concrete songs as examples, he claimed that there is an affinity between the two folklores.

In his paper, "Albanian Singers of Tales in Serbo-Croatian: the Frontier Epic Cycle," Prof. Pipa maintained that the cycle "is a bilingual cycle of a special kind of epic songs shared by both South-Slavs and North-Albanians". He emphasized the significance of the Parry-Lord collection at Harvard's Widener Library for the study of the epic folklore of this particular region. The materials in the collection reveal, he said, that the cycle under consideration has three components: Catholic North-Albanian songs sung in Albanian, Moslem Kosovar songs sung in Albanian, and Moslem Bosnian-Albanian songs sung in Serbo-Croatian. Pipa argued also that the epic songs having a legendary character are older than the Bosnian songs. A good example is the "Gjergj Elez Alija" rhapsody which is "one hundred percent Albanian." Thus ended the morning session of the conference.

Afternoon Session Begins

The afternoon session was devoted to discussions of "the economic and political situation" in Kosova, and was moderated by Pipa. It began with the reading by Stephanie Kosmo of an abstract of the paper prepared by Prof. Adi Schnytzer of Griffith University in Australia, entitled "The Economic Situation in Albania and Kosova: Notes on a Comparison." Schnytzer claimed that while available data is of some use in understanding the development of the economy in Kosova and Albania, it is not possible to make an accurate comparison of the two economies. The primary reason for this is that Albania is a sovereign state and is thus able to determine it own economic goals, while Kosova is not. Kosova's economic activity is conditioned by the economic plan drafted in Belgrade for the whole community. The evidence nevertheless seems to show that the economies of Albania and Kosova have developed at roughly the same pace in recent years.

The conference continued with other panelists. [1]

Prof. Paul Shoup of the University of Virginia spoke next. A leading authority on the nationality question in Yugoslavia, Prof. Shoup examined "The political System in Kosova." He said that Kosova has made political gains since the war, and that the granting of republican status to it would be largely a symbolic gesture, but "the symbolic effect of elevation to republican status would be immense." He said that

Belgrade missed an opportunity to make Kosova a republic back in 1946, and again following the riots of 1968. Had that step been taken either in 1946 or 1968, the turmoil of 1981 might have been avoided.

Approximately the same topic was discussed by Prof. Sami Repishti. Speaking on "Constitutional Development in the SFR of Yugoslavia and the Status of Kosova," Repishti discussed briefly the formal aspects of Kosova's political and judicial structure. His comments threw light on the political evolution of the region as shaped by the constitutions of 1946, 1969, and 1974.

The session continued with the reading of another abstract by Ms. Kosmo, this one of a paper by Anton Logoreci, well-known Albanian journalist and author, and a long-time resident of London. In his study, "A Clash Between Two Nationalisms," Logoreci surveyed the history of the problems and conflicts between Albanians and Serbians in relation to Kosova, as they developed from 1913 to 1982.

Roughly the same question engaged the attention of Elez Biberaj, Ph. D. candidate at Columbia University in New York. Taking as his topic "The Management of Ethnic Conflicts in Yugoslavia," Mr. Biberaj explored the roots of the present crisis in Kosova, and Yugoslavia's attempts to deal with the situation. "At the center of this conflict," he said, "stands the struggle between the Serbs—who want to preserve their dominant position and keep Kosova within Serbia's jurisdiction—and the Albanians who are dissatisfied with the status quo and are challenging what they perceive as an unjust political arrangement." He called Belgrade's policies unrealistic, claiming that military repression, trials and purges have only worsened the ethnic confrontation. The alternative, he said, is to initiate a dialogue between Belgrade authorities and the Kosovars.

Afternoon Session Continues

Prof. Robert Sharlet of Union College, Schenectady, NY, continued the discourse on the ethnic question in Kosova, under the topic, "Ethnic Dissent in Yugoslavia." He said "The Kosova crisis is the most recent and possibly the most serious manifestation of ethnic dissent in Yugoslavia in the postwar period." He asserted that "the ethnic question and the economic dilemas together are pushing Yugoslavia towards a general crisis of the system in the post-Tito era."

There followed the reading of an abstract of a paper by Francis Dessart, of the Institut des Hautes Etudes Economiques et Sociales, Brussels. Dessart, it will be recalled, is the author of a study of Albanian ethnic groups in the world. Dealing with the subject, "The Question of Kosova in the Political Context of Europe's Future," Dessart held that the problem of Kosova goes beyond the borders of Albania or Yugoslavia, since its outcome will hold a key to similar situations in Europe. Arguing for the merits of regionalism, Dessart maintained that the Kosovars as a regional group have a right to self-determination. He concluded by calling for "international solidarity in behalf of Albanian communities wherever oppressed."

The political aspect of Kosova was addressed once again, this time by Prof. Patrick F.R. Artisien of the University of Bradford in England, who took as his topic, "Kosova and the Future of Yugoslav-Albanian Relations: a Balkan Perspective." Artisien made the point that while recent events in Kosova aggravated the ideological warfare between Albanian and Yugoslavia, the two countries have maintained—for reasons of national self-interest—NORMAL STATE AND ECONOMIC RELATIONS. Furthermore, they have common strategic interests, as long as they perceive a threat to their security from the Soviet Union. This realization seems to have had a moderating influence on their reactions to the flare-up in Kosova.

Prof. Branka Magas, also of the University of Bradford, spoke on "The Yugoslav Perception of the Situation in Kosova." She said that Yugoslavia believes it has followed a rational and equitable policy in its attempt to solve the nationality problem. The Albanians, she said, are seen as equals and as beneficiaries of all the rights enjoyed by other ethnic groups.

The last speaker at the conference was Mihajlo Mihajlov, the notorious Yugoslav dissident, now teaching at the University of Virginia. His topic was, "Kosova and the Future of Yugoslavia in the Case of Democratization." Prof. Mihajlov views the solution to the Kosova question in terms of the struggle between "democratization and dictatorship." He claimed that if democratization takes place in Yugoslavia, then Kosova will want to remain in the federation. However, should Albania become a democracy, while Yugoslavia continued as a dictatorial state, then nothing can keep Kosova from joining Albania. And if both Yugoslavia and Albania become democracies, then Kosova will no longer be a problem, since the matter will be resolved in accordance with democratic processes.

* * *

There followed a stimulating question-and-answer period, but unfortunately it was all too brief, owing to lack of time. Prof. Pipa then summed up the proceedings of the day-long conference with a few concluding remarks. He said that the Albanians have survived because, having met overcome numerous challenges in the course of their long history, survival has by now become almost a profession with them. He said that the Conference on Kosova "was inspired by a firm belief that efforts must be made by all people concerned, in Yugoslavia as well as elsewhere, to avoid another outburst of violence" such as the one that occurred in the Spring of 1981. He concluded with an appeal to reason as the only way for people of goodwill "to dispel the baneful myths" that cloud the minds of men. Only such an attitude can lead to a just and lasting solution to the problem of Kosova.

As far this writer knows, this was the first conference of its kind ever held in the United States, and perhaps in the world. The organizers of the conference, particularly its two coordinators, Arshi Pipa and Sami Repishti, are to be heartily commended.

Notes

[1] Note - The author of this volume also read a paper at this conference. Titled, "Kosova's Economy: Problems and Prospects," the argument of the paper briefly was as follows: While Kosova is rich in mineral and natural resources, it is in deep trouble economically, owing to the gap between it and the rest of Yugoslavia, which has been widening steadily. The responsibility for this condition rests mainly with the Federal Government, which, according to the record, neglected the development of the province. Serbia also shares responsibility, since it has been unable to arrest the province's backward slide. Accordingly, the prospects for Kosova's economy appear dim.

Chapter 7:
*Kosova Events in the World Press and Academic Forums**

Developments in Kosova, Yugoslavia, since the violent demonstrations that occurred there in the Spring of 1981, have been widely reported in the world press, particularly in Western Europe. The coverage in the press and on the radio extends from the Scandinavian countries to Saudi Arabia, and from Turkey to the Western Hemisphere and beyond to New Zealand. The interest shown by the outside world in Kosova, as reflected by the media, is a clear indication of the magnitude of the developments, as well as of their importance in the eyes of foreign observers.

The average American, however, is not aware of this fact, in large part because the coverage in Kosova has been limited in our country, by comparison with most Western European countries. This article is intended to fill the void, and eliminate as far as possible that information gap. For the most part we shall let the media agents speak for themselves, rather than paraphrase or comment on their reports.

The Kosova question has been prominent especially in the West German and Austrian newspapers, magazines and radio. In Germany numerous articles have appeared in such newspapers as *Die Welt, Suddeutsche Zeitung, Berliner Morgenpost, Frankfurter Allgemeine*, and *Nuremberger Nachrichten.* The internationally known magazine, *Der Spiegel,* also has written on Kosova. There have been commentaries on

* Source: *Albanian Catholic Bulletin*, Santa Clara, CA., USA., Vol. IV (1983), pp. 68 – 73.

the radio as well. Here is what the West Berlin Radio said on Kosova on April 2, 1981:

"These demonstrations and clashes have their own social causes. They were initiated by students at the University of Prishtina on account of unsatisfactory food and living conditions. (Yugoslav authorities) see these actions as manifestations of Albanian chauvinism, but it should be kept in mind that they occur because of the unpleasant social conditions in this autonomous province.... These turbulence are also the result of problems that exist among the different people in this province that is inhabited mostly by Albanians, who nevertheless do not enjoy the same rights and treatment accorded to others. The central administration does not approve of these actions, and therefore it intervenes. The Albanians of Kosova want to develop like all the other nationalities in this province."

Reporting on the martial law imposed by Belgrade in Kosova following the demonstrations on April 1 and 2, 1981, the influential West Germany daily, *Frankfurter Allgemeine*, wrote on April 21: "...the state of emergency, the ban on meetings and on travel outside the province are still in force. The region continues to be out-of-bounds to foreigners. An atmosphere of tension persists in the streets. Eye witnesses report that Albanians are incensed over the brutal actions of the police."

Austrian publications writing on Kosova include *Die Presse, Tagblatt fur Osterreich, Neue Zeit,* and *Kurier*. Contesting the Yugoslav story that 9 people died during the Spring riots, the April 17, 1981 issue of the *Kurier* said: "Eye witnesses from Kosova reject the reports given out by Belgrade, and say that nearly a thousand died." The paper went out to say that the estimate of casualties given by witnesses was "probably reasonable."

On April 25, 1981, the widely-read Swiss newspaper, *Neue Zuricher Zeitung,* noted that "Dissent among Albanians in Kosova is to be found not only among militant groups calling for an Albanian Republic in Kosova, but also among the 300,000 who inhabit Macedonia, and 50,000 others who live in Montenegro."

Italian, French, and British Reaction

Kosova has been much in the news in Italy, France, and Great Britain. Leading publications in all three countries have kept their readers informed about events in Kosova. Among Italian newspapers featuring news on Kosova are *Corriere Della Sera, Republika, L'Umanita,* and *Il Manifesto.* One of the most informative and dramatic accounts of the Spring 1981 events in Kosova was published in the Italian magazine, *Espresso,* by an Italian student at the University of Prishtina. Following are excerpts from his account of the demonstrations in Prishtina.

"On the night of March 11, students at the University of Prishtina decided to organize a demonstration based chiefly on three demands: the right to study, the issue of textbooks, and living conditions.

"At noon on March 12...the students poured into the street shouting, 'bread, bread!' The police, ignoring the pleas of certain professors to remain calm, attacked the demonstrators with tear gas bombs. The students reacted by throwing stones at them. The demonstration broke up, but left young people angry and startled.

"On March 26 several thousand students began a march, carrying with them a huge Albanian flag—which is the same as the flag of Kosova—and shouting, 'Free our comrades in prison,' and 'Long live the Republic of Kosova.' A group of people joined the demonstrators, and together they formed a column, and headed for the center of the city. Suddenly, police contingents dispatched from Belgrade by plane appeared, and began to attack the throng...By evening of March 26, several hundred people lay wounded. Hundreds more were arrested...The inhabitants of Prishtina were filled with hatred for the police.

"On April 1, two hundred construction workers of the 'Dardania' enterprise at the outskirts of Prishtina organized a solidarity march to ask for the release of arrested students...Along the way to the city, ordinary people, passers by and others joined the workers...Seeing that the police had not intervened, women with children and even unescorted children who happened to be in the streets joined the marchers.

"By now the throng of demonstrators reached 15,000. Suddenly the police attacked again with tear gas bombs, wounding many. Nevertheless, the demonstrators remained cool...and continued to march in the street until they took complete possession of it. The number of demonstrators had now grown between 30,000 and 40,000. Presently they turned the demonstration into a sort of revolutionary festival. The higher schools interrupted their afternoon classes, and students descended on the city carrying their professors on their shoulders. In the evening women came with bread and fruit for the hungry demonstrators. At 6:15 the police resumed their attack, leaving many wounded on the ground. The demonstrators dispersed as twilight fell...

"But in the morning of April 2, the streets were filled once again with groups waving Albanian flags. The whole city (of Prishtina) was in the streets. No one went to work. At 11:00 tanks appeared, and four military aircraft flew low over the streets and rooftops to create panic. The demonstrators became indignant. At noon, using bottles filled with benzene, they burned two of the tanks. The police responded with bullets. Eight of the demonstrators including two children, fell dead on the asphalted street.

"More tanks and armored cars were brought in from Macedonia...but the demonstration would not break up. The participants kept regrouping after each assault. Trucks filled with bread rolled in from a bakery near the city to feed the demonstrators who had now turned warriors. Women used strips of fabric and lemons to protect themselves from the tear gas. The throng accepted the challenge (of the police and the army) to make this a test of strength...The blood flowed freely in the streets." The Italian student added that the "revolt" had spread not only to the main cities of Kosova, but even to remote villages in the province.

The French public has read about Kosova in the world-famous *Le Monde*, in *Le Journal, Le Quotidien de Paris, Figaro*—said to the largest daily in Paris—and the magazine *L'Express*. On June 30, 1981, *Figaro* wrote:

"Although Kosova is rich in lignite, nickel, and chrome, the Albanian population occupies the lowest bracket of the national income in the country. That income is ten times smaller than that of Slovenia, five times smaller than that of Croatia, and three and a half times smaller than that of Serbia... There are 70,000 unemployed, and this is the reason why... 40,000 Albanians earn their livelihood in the West."

Among the English publications that have written on Kosova are the renowned *Times* and *Guardian*, and the *Economist* magazine. Writing in the *Economist* on May 7, 1981, correspondent Chris Switch said:

"I think that the greatest dissatisfaction (among the Kosovars) is nationalistic in nature. The Albanians of Yugoslavia, who live mainly within the Republic of Serbia, now want a republic of their own, which would have the same status as the other republics in Yugoslavia. There are many more Albanians than Montenegrans, and yet Montenegrans have their own republic, while the Albanians of Kosova do not."

Coverage in Scandinavia, Greece, Turkey

News on Kosova has been carried by the press in Spain, Portugal, and Ireland. The coverage has been greater in Scandinavia, above all in Sweden, where Kosova has had exposure in *Sundsvalstidning, Aftenbladet, Dages Nyheter, Svenska Dagbladet*, and in the magazine *Tempus*. An article in the Danish paper, *Socialistik Daglad*, dated April 29, 1981, said among other things:

"It is known that in this zone (Kosova) there live 1.5 million Albanians with a strong national identity, and their own tongue and venerable culture. They make up over 80 percent of the population of the province. Large groups of Albanians (numbering half a million) reside in Macedonia and Montenegro..."

"Albanians fought bravely together with the Yugoslav people for the liberation of Yugoslavia... Yet, Kosova was not proclaimed a republic, as happened with the other regions, but a so-called 'autonomous province under Serbian rule'. And the Albanian nationality group was divided among three republics. A fierce campaign was carried out at the end of the fifties to displace the Albanians *en masse* through arrests, imprisonment, and oppression. Discrimination against Albanians continued, depriving them of their political and democratic rights."

Shortly after the demonstrations, Yugoslavia began a campaign of accusations against Albania, blaming Tirana for the unrest, and charging Albanian authorities with interference in the internal affairs of Yugoslavia. But the foreign press generally turned a deaf ear to the Yugoslav charges. The reaction of Swedish paper *Svenska Dagbladet* is typical. On May 22, 1981, the paper wrote: "...official Yugoslav organs are trying, as much as possible, to place the blame for what is happening in Kosova on Albania. But their argument is not convincing."

There was the same reaction on the part of the Greek media to an attempt by Yugoslavia early in June of 1981 to impute to Albania aggressive designs on the territorial integrity of both Yugoslavia and Greece. As evidence for the plot, Yugoslavia pointed to a map of Albania, allegedly prepared and distributed by Tirana, which incorporated large chunks of Yugoslavia and Greece into Albania. Commenting on this incident, the Greek paper *To Vema* wrote on June 21, 1981 as follows:

"The aim of the Yugoslav agency in this action was not only to strengthen the Yugoslav position on Kosova, but to openly influence Greek opinion and try to win the cooperation of the Greek media so as to echo the Yugoslav viewpoint. True, the function of official channels of information is to defend and disseminate the policies of the country where they operate, but in a manner which will not lead to error."

The Turkish media have been among the strongest defenders of the rights of Kosovars, and probably the most eager champions of their demands. An example is the article by Prof. Ahmet Esmer in the Turkish newspaper *Baresh,* dated June 6, 1981.

"The question may rightly be asked: What do the Albanians of Kosova want? They want Kosovo to be declared a republic within the framework of the Yugoslav Federation...But the Serbs have never shown any sympathy for Albanians. Indeed, they have made plans for the displacement of Albanians. According to a report we have at hand...the Serbs aimed to uproot 200,000 Albanians and send them to Turkey. But it is known that the Albanians are the oldest people in the Balkans and in Europe. They are in their own native land."

In fact, Yugoslavia expelled hundreds of thousands of Kosovars to Turkey both before and after World War II.

Articles sympathetic to the Albanians in Kosova have been published by the press in the so-called Third World, including our neighbor to the south, Mexico. On May 21. 1981, the Mexican paper *Uno Mas Uno* wrote:

"The protests in Prishtina are undoubtedly expressions of dissatisfaction with the position of the central government of Yugoslavia on the national aspirations of the Albanian population...But neither a policy of pression, nor draconian actions...are the most appropriate ways for solving problems of national minorities."

View of Kosova in U.S. Press

Reportage on Kosova in America has been limited, but much of what has been printed has been favorable to the Kosovars. Moreover, the reportage has appeared in some of the country's most prominent journals, including the *New York Times,* the *Herald Tribune, the Christian Science Monitor, the Boston Globe*, and the *Chicago Tribune.* On April 20, 1981, the *Herald Tribune* commented on the social status of the Kosovars saying, "Kosova is populated mostly by people of Albanian origin who are on the bottom rung of the social ladder in the country".

The same point was made earlier in an article in the *Christian Science Monitor*, dated April 8, 1981. "Kosova...has experienced a visible decline in living standards. Many Albanian Kosovar youth do not feel themselves to be masters in their own home. Although traditionally they have maintained their national pride, Kosovar Albanians still suffer from an inferiority complex. The Serbs and other large elements in the country often look down on them."

Commenting on the question of a republic of Kosova, the *New York Times* wrote on April 27, 1981: "The federated state of Yugoslavia presently has six republics. What difference would it make if it had another republic? Why should Kosova not be a republic, when 85 percent of its inhabitants, numbering one and a half million, are Albanian ethnics?"

The same basic argument has been echoed time and time again in the world press reports and commentaries on Kosova. In a lengthy article on Kosova on June 18, 1981, the *Boston Globe* wrote:

"Albanians have always been second class citizens in the country of the South Slavs, called Yugoslavia. They are the poorest of the poor...If they leave Kosova in search of work (elsewhere in Yugoslavia), they end up as porters, dishwashers, shoe-shiners...

"For twenty years in succession, the Minister of the Interior, Aleksandar Rankovich, a Serb and second in rank after Tito, used his secret police to suppress the Albanians. For example, in the years 1955-56, a great drive was launched under the pretext of collecting arms from the villagers, during which many Albanians were slain...Kosova is the little Third World of Yugoslavia: poor, proud, insulted and insufferable."

The world press kept up its reportage on developments in Kosova also in 1982 and 1983. But attention now shifted increasingly to the arrests, trials and imprisonment of Kosovars by the Yugoslav authorities, in the wake of the 1981 disturbances. On July 27, 1982, Eric Bourne wrote in the *Christian Science Monitor*:

"...Yugoslav authorities are shaking their political fists at this region in the south. More than sixty Albanians have been jailed this month, with sentences ranging as much as 15 years, because they were allegedly behind secret groups that called for an independent republic of Kosova within Yugoslavia. About 700 persons have been sentenced in more than 55 trials, while many more have lost their jobs. One thousand others have been expelled from the local branch of the Yugoslav Communist Party because they supported the slogan for a 'Republic of Kosova'...

"Belgrade's opposition to granting republican status to Kosova does not seem to be in accord with Tito's old slogan on fraternity and equality. The question arises: How long can his heirs reject such a solution...?"

Pursuing the same theme, the Italian newspaper *La Republika* wrote on July 30, 1982 that among the Albanians sentenced in Kosova, "...278 are university students in the middle schools, and 64 are professors and teachers. Among intellectuals who were given sentences, two hold doctoral degrees in science, seven are lecturers, ten jurists. But there are also workers and peasants. In the meantime, slogans scribbled on walls of buildings (calling for a Republic of Kosova, etc.) are on the increase. Official sources confirm that since the beginning of the demonstrations, some 7,000 slogans have appeared in public places."

The Canadian press also has taken note of events in Kosova. There have been articles in the *People's Canada Daily News,* and in the *Toronto Sun,* whose editor-in-chief, Peter Worthington, observed that Kosova represented "the most recent of mini-holocausts that plague the world".

On April 27, 1983, a Saudi Arabian paper, *Arab News,* carried an article describing the situation of jailed Kosovars. It said that prison conditions were lamentable. "The prisoners are obliged to do hard labor which impairs their health. Dr. Adem Demaci, a writer, has lost his eyesight because of his ordeal in prison. There are more political prisoners in Kosova than in South Africa," the article said.

A Chilling Document of Torture

Reports of mistreatment, persecution and torture of Albanians in Yugoslavia, some of them by Yugoslav dissidents, have appeared in the press from time to time. But few of them can compare, for vivid detail and emotional impact, with a document made public only recently that tells of the fate of imprisoned Kosovars in Yugoslavia. The document was published in the periodical *The Voice of Kosova,* in its March 1983 issue. The periodical is printed in Biel, Switzerland. The document is in the form of a petition, signed by 17 Albanians imprisoned for political reasons, and addressed to the Secretariat of Justice in Zagreb, Republic of Croatia. The petition was sent from their place of detention in Lepoglava, Croatia. Following are excerpts from their petition, covering events from November 1981 to May 1982.

"Unusual cruelties are being perpetrated day after day against us, in the prison of Lepoglava. During our transfer from Kosova to the prison of Gospic (Croatia), a special reception awaited us which cannot be called other than savage and inhuman, worthy of comparison with the terrors of the Nazi camps of Dachau and Mathausen.

"In the district jail of Prishtina, the police forced us to undress completely...not to check for arms or other hidden objects, but, in their own words, to humiliate us. Then, kicking us and hitting us with the butts of their automatic guns, they loaded us into a van with metallic cubicles, two men in each cubicle. Our hands were tied with chains used for beasts of burden, and so tightly that our hands began to swell. The doors of the van closed hermetically, and in a matter of minutes we were breathing hard for lack of air, since the cubicles were air tight, and there were 43 of us in the van...We feared we would burst from lack of oxygen, and in desperation hurled ourselves against the metal doors of the cubicles. But the police paid no attention. Only when half of us passed out did they open the door. Then they withdrew and stood several meters away, unable to withstand the stench of our bodies which were drenched in sweat and steaming from the heat. We were pale like corpses. The van had a ventilator, but they did not turn it on in order to make us suffer as much as possible.

"During the 17-hour-long ride, they gave us no food to eat, except a glass of water when we reached Zagreb. In Belgrade, they let us go to the rest room, two by two, and on the way beat us with a whip, kicked us and hit us in the back with the butt of their automatics...

"We reached the Gospic prison in a state of total exhaustion...But our suffering did not end. After taking our clothes and leaving us naked, they began immediately to beat us up, with the prison guards competing with one another to see who could punish us the most! Our naked bodies were covered all over with blood stains. They opened Nexhmi Balaj's mouth and shoved a whip down his throat. He nearly choked to death. For more than two weeks he was unable to eat. They knocked Abdyl Zymberi down on the floor, and a guard thrust his boot in his mouth and yelled "Lick it!" Halit Osman was beaten so badly with a club that he suffered permanent deformation of the nose and of the body. They tore off nearly all of Shaban Dragusha's moustache. Avdi Liman was hit hard on the chest, causing him a heart condition. Naim Bujupi bears to this day the scars of the wounds he sustained from being beaten with a club.

"The most brutal of all the guards was someone by the name of Gjura, who hit us in our genitals. Other guards followed suit, and when striking Naim (Bujupi) they would scream, 'Never again will you have Albanian children!'

"When the hallway was red with blood, they put us into cells, three to a cell. But nobody dared to sit down, for they gave us strict orders to stand at attention. We stood for two hours...Even the crippled Sadik Sadiku, who had lost one leg, was subjected to this torture. With rare sadism, the guards would strike his remaining leg and threaten him saying, 'We will break this one too, and then you can walk on your hands'...

"Apart from the daily beatings, we had to remain standing for four to five hours straight, without making a move...In short, torture in this hellish hole has become routine. Torture was an inseparable part of our lives.

"We have much more to tell about our horrifying experience in the Gospic prison, and not only there...but we think that we have already said enough to give you an idea about how the law is applied in the

(Yugoslav) penal system, especially when it comes to Albanian political prisoners."

The petition concluded with the cry, "...we hold the perpetrators of these crimes accountable before the judgement of history!"

The Historical Argument on Kosova

Since the events of Spring 1981, the Yugoslav press has generally argued that the disturbances were due not to social and economic and political conditions, but to the machinations of Albanian nationalists and irredentists, plus the instigations of the Albanian government, and the plots and underground activities of reactionary and fascist Albanian groups in exile, as, for example, the *Balli Kombëtar* (National Front). The Yugoslav media have also revived the old thesis that Albanians settled in Kosova only in the last three centuries, after driving out most of the Serb settlers in the region. In recent years, however, more and more views have appeared in the world press which contest this thesis.

The Turkish paper *Cumhuriet* wrote on May 22, 1983:

"It is proper to ask: Who indeed are the nationals and irredentists (in Kosova), the Albanians who with justice demand a republican status for Kosova, or the Serbs who have occupied the lands of autochthonous Albanians? To point an accusing finger at the patriotism and nationalism of the Kosovars, as the Serbs are doing, is none other than blackmail."

A more dispassionate and detailed argument, in opposition to the Yugoslav thesis, was published by the French paper *Le Monde,* on June 2, 1982. Its author was Professor Alain Ducellier, of the University of Toulouse in France. Ducellier said, among other things:

"He who has no ulterior motives can verify easily that the Albanians of Kosova are anything but an immigrant population. With rare exceptions, all at present agree that at least since the second millenium BC., contemporary Albania and Kosova have been part of a large Illyrian community, the cultural unity of which has been brought to light by archeology. Archeology has also shown that the Illyrians are indisputably the ancestors of the Albanians.

"It is not without interest to note that the Slavs...are among the later occupiers (of Kosova). Studies of toponomy, names of persons found in archival texts, particularly the documents of the Republic of Ragusa (now Dubrovnik), and documents of the most distinguished Serbian tsars that make mention of 'Albanian villages' in Kosova, and finally the surveys made by the Turks immediately after occupation (of the Kosova region), all testify clearly that the population of Kosova, in the 14th and 15th centuries, was already predominantly Albanian and Christian. Furthermore, contemporaries such as Western reporters on the Crusades, as well as Byzantine chroniclers agree unanimously on the identity of the population of Kosova and its differentiation from the Slavs."

Ducellier defended this position also in the paper he delivered at the International Conference on Kosova in New York on November 6, 1982. But for the most elaborate presentation of his thesis on the unity and compactness of the Albanian nation, including the Kosovars, the reader is referred to his voluminous and well researched work *La Façade maritime de l'Albanie au moyen age* (The Maritime Façade of Albania in the Middle Ages), published in Salonika in 1981.

Academic Conferences on Kosova

Kosova has become a topical issue not only for the media, but for the scholarly world as well. This is indicated by the interest shown in the region by scholars and academic institutions and publications. The preoccupation of scholars with Kosova has grown considerably since the 1981 riots and their aftermath.

The violent reaction of the Yugoslav authorities to the demands of the demonstrators indicated that they had no intentions of satisfying those demands, and resolving the issue amicably and peacefully. Motivated by a desire to explore and understand the root causes of the

Kosova problem, and with the knowledge and insights thus gained contribute perhaps to the solution of the problem, several academic discussions on Kosova were organized in the recent past in Europe and America.

A seminar, "The Albanians of Kosovo," better known as the London Seminar on Kosova, took place on May 19, 1982 at Russell Square 21, London. The seminar was sponsored by London University's School of Slavonic and East European Studies. The seminar took the form of a round table discussion by Arshi Pipa of the University of Minnesota in Minneapolis, Patrick F.R. Artisien of the University of Bradford in England, Branka Magas, also of Bradford University, and George Schopflin of the London School of Economics and Political Science.

Prof. Pipa opened the discussion with a review of the situation in Kosova since the Spring disturbances in 1981. He said that the continuation of the state emergency in the province, and the heavy jail terms handed out to the Kosovars, were actions that only "add fuel to Albanian discontent and resentment". He likened Kosova to a land "under military occupation," and warned that the situation was fraught with danger. He said that Serbian tutelage left Albanians in a state of political inferiority and an economic condition characterized by higher unemployment and lower standards of living than other regions of Yugoslavia. "The Albanians," he said, "are the proletarians of socialist Yugoslavia."

Pipa affirmed that the situation could be corrected only by granting Kosova the status of a Republic. "Once the Kosovars feel that they are their own masters, they should be able to improve their economy," he claimed. Dependency on aid by the Federal Government of Yugoslavia would then gradually disappear, thus relieving the Federation of a heavy burden. Furthermore, the Kosovars would develop their own Albanian culture without having to rely for assistance on Albania. The double dependency, economic and cultural, will come to an end and the situation will be normalized to the profit of both Yugoslavia and Albania.

Pipa also maintained that Yugoslavia's fears that Kosova would secede from the federation if given republican status were groundless, all the more so since Albanian leaders have shown no inclination to incorporate Kosova, knowing that it would not be in their interest to do so.

Patrick Artisien commented on the economy of Kosova and on the demographic developments in the province and beyond. He said that the last official census (1981) showed that the Albanian population in Yugoslavia had reached 1,732,000, and was now almost as numerous as the population of the Slovenians (1,754,000), the third largest group in the country, after the Serbs and the Croatians. Dr. Artisien observed that, considering their high birth rate, the Albanians will soon be the third largest ethnic group in Yugoslavia. Under these circumstances, he went on, to deny the Kosovars republican status can only invite further trouble.

Branka Magas noted that constitutionally Kosova has advanced steadily since 1946, being upgraded from a "region" to an "autonomous province". However, unlike the six republics, it lacks the fundamental right of secession, even through the 1944 Resolution of the National Liberation Committee for Kosova and Metohia acknowledged "the Albanians' right of self-determination, including secession". She remarked that after the war the Yugoslav Communist Party ignored the resolution. In so doing, it created an anomaly, since the population of Kosova is larger than that of Montenegro and Macedonia, both of which were granted republican status at the end of the war.

Dr. Schöpflin spoke with approval of Yugoslavia's policy on national minorities, and added that he had the impression that a feeling of "go it alone" was emerging in Serbia, a feeling that Serbia would be better off without the two provinces of Kosova and Vojvodina.

There followed a period of discussions. Questions were asked and comments made by Dr. Muriel Heppell, co-author of *Yugoslavia* (1961), Quintin Hoare, co-editor of *Labour Focus on Eastern Europe*, Profesor Michael Kaser of Oxford University, Melanie Anderson of Amnesty

International, and Dr. L. J. D. Collins and Richard Clogg, both of the School of Slavonic and East European Studies at London University.

Panel on Kosova at Chicago Conference

From May 7 to 9, 1982, a conference was held in Chicago by the Midwest Association of Societies for Slavic Studies. The conference included a panel on Albanian ethnics in Yugoslavia. It was the first time, to the knowledge of this reporter, that an entire panel, devoted to Kosova, was featured at an academic gathering in America. The fact that it happened is proof of the interest Kosovo has aroused in the halls of Academia in America, just as it has aroused the interest of the world press and—we may be sure, behind the curtains—that of statesmen and governmental experts on Balkan affairs, as well.

The panel on Kosova included Professor Nicholas Pano of Western Illinois University, Branko Bogunovich of the Yugoslav news agency, TANJUG, in New York, and Howard Tyner, reporter for the *Chicago Tribune* and close observer of developments in Eastern Europe.

The panel was opened by Prof. Pano with a concise presentation of the Kosova question in its historical context, beginning with the Congress of Berlin in 1878 and the Albanian League of Prizren. He noted that as a result of decisions by the Great Powers of Europe, the Kosovars were left out of the boundaries of the Albanian nation and incorporated in what is now the federated state of Yugoslavia. (Other Albanians, the Chams, he added, were separated from the body of the Albanian nation and turned over to Greece.)

Pano remarked that subsequently the Kosovars were subjected to a policy of denationalization and forced assimilation into the Yugoslav society. The Kosovars' rights as a national minority were ignored, in violation of the Treaty on Minorities. Their language was not recognized, and their entire economic needs were neglected. Instead, the Yugoslav government sought to colonize Kosova with Serbs, Montenegrans and Bosnians, and on the other hand put into operation a policy of mass expulsion of Albanians to Turkey. These policies, Pano observed, created friction and deep-rooted animosities between Albanians and Serbs.

Following the Second World War, Prof. Pano continued, the Kosovars gained some rights that had long been denied them, and with the normalization of relations between Yugoslavia and Albania in 1971 there was a further easing of tensions in Kosova. But the freedoms granted the Kosovars did not go far enough. As a result, their frustrations grew and erupted into violence.

Bogunovich of TANJUG not surprisingly had words of praise for Yugoslavia's policy on Kosova, and spoke of the "fair treatment of Albanians in that country". He granted that the Kosovars do not have the right to secede, but noted that they hold many prestigious positions in government, including a seat in the collective presidency of Yugoslavia, in the person of Fadil Hoxha. He argued that secession "would destroy the integrity of the Yugoslav state," and for that reason there was no alternative to the course Yugoslavia is presently pursuing in respect to Kosova.'

Continuing his analysis, Bogunovich blamed the intellectuals of Kosova for the recent riots, as well as the Tirana government which, he charged, supported clandestine groups in the province. He had criticism also for the officials in Kosova and Belgrade for their "lack of vigilance". Toward the end of his discourse, the TANJUG representative expressed the hope that reforms and a new sensitivity would bring about a lowering of tensions in the area.

The third speaker, Howard Tyner of the *Chicago Tribune* was not impressed by the argument presented by Bogunovich, and went on to paint a bleak scenario of the reality in Kosova. He said that the violent outbreaks of the Spring of 1981 had engulfed all the major cities in the province, and involved not just the intellectuals but "a large portion of the population". The resulting casualties and the subsequent purges of Albanian cadres, especially educators and intellectuals in the higher institutions of learning, have given Yugoslavia "a very bad image overseas". It has damaged, he said, the concept abroad of Yugoslavia as a land of harmonious ethnic groups.

Tyner said that the core of the problem in Kosova is the lack of sensitivity on the part of Yugoslavia's leaders to the national feelings of the Albanians. Unless they become aware of this truth, and shape their economic and social programs for Kosova in accordance with it, they are likely to face new demonstrations and disturbances in the future. It is time they realized, Tyner remarked, that "the present status (of Kosova) is not acceptable to the Albanian minority".

In later comments at the panel, Prof. Pano warned that unless there is movement toward a solution of the Kosova problem, Yugoslavia could be exposed to "tremendous internal strains" that would weaken the country, and affect its standing in the international community in an adverse way.

A third and much larger convocation on Kosova was held in November of 1982, in New York, under the aegis of the City University of New York (CUNY). The deliberation of that conference were published as a book, under the title, *Studies on Kosova*, Columbia University Press, New York, 1984.

Notes from the Journal of a Traveler to Kosova

In 1982 and again in the Spring of this year, a Western observer traveled extensively in Kosova and talked with many people. This observer, who has a keen eye for detail and a passion for accuracy and fairness, came back with some noteworthy findings and impressions, all recorded in a journal.

On the first trip, the observer, was struck by the poverty of many Kosovars. They have nothing, he journal said, not even a tiny piece of barren land, and the aid they receive from the government is very little. He noted that hatred is not seen as a vice in Kosova or Yugoslavia, when it is directed against Albanians. The blood feud tradition is still alive in the province, though popular sentiment against it is on the rise.

On the subject of politics, he recorded in the journal that a climate of fear pervades Kosova, that the best educated Albanians are in prison , and that the number of people killed during the Spring 1981 confrontations is thought to be closer to 2,000 than 1,000, though no one knows for certain. Albania is off limits to Albanian ethnics in Yugoslavia. An Albanian woman in Montenegro living close to the Albanian border complained that authorities refuse to allow her to visit her relatives who live across the border. The observer found evidence of suppression of Albanian culture. The journal notes, for example, that no books by Naim Frashëri, Albanian poet of the national Awakening, could be found in bookstores.

On the second trip, the observer found a lessening of the political tensions in the region, but the situation in general was not a happy one. The journal records that this time some Albanian literature, such as Illyrian studies and books by Ismail Kadare and De Rada, was available for purchase.

The economic situation is critical, marked by shortages of consumer goods and widespread unemployment. According to the journal, some Serbs fear to travel to Kosova, while others are leaving that region. The observer asked a number of Serbs what the reason was for their departure, and they answered that there was no work for them in Kosova, though some said it was because they feared Albanians. The journal points out, however, that probably many more Albanians than Serbs are leaving the region, owing to lack of jobs.

The Western observer came away with the impression that Yugoslavia is imbued with colonialist attitudes towards the Albanians. For example Albanians are expected to feel grateful for government aid which other ethnic groups in the country accept as a right to which they are entitled, instead of as a favor.

He notes that despite discrimination and the hardships they are undergoing, the Kosovars' national feelings remain strong. As an illustration, he tells of a young Albanian woman engaged to be married. She showed him the trousseau she had prepared. And at the bottom of the hope chest, she had tucked away an Albanian flag. Just as Albanian women took care to preserve the Flag of Scanderbeg through centuries of domination by the Turks, until Albania regained its freedom and independence.

Chapter 8:
*Crisis Calls for National Unity**

History has shown that at times of national crisis, Albanians have put aside their differences, and united as one body to meet the challenge of the day. Within the last 100 years, there have been three occasions when the times called forth precisely that kind of united effort among Albanians. In 1878, Christian and Moslem Albanians, Ghegs and Tosks, beys and peasants, shopkeepers, writers, craftsmen, and merchants united to form the League of Prizren to resist Big Power plans to dismember their nation. In 1909-1912, they united again to wage a successful armed struggle for Albania's independence from five centuries of Ottoman rule. In 1918-1920, they fought in the diplomatic tribunes of Paris and Geneva, and on the battlefield of Vlorë, to preserve Albania's sovereignty and territorial integrity, in the face of aggressive designs and actions of neighboring states.

Today the critical issue is Kosova. The age-old home of over two million Albanians, Kosova today is bleeding under the spiked boots of Serbian oppressors. The Kosovars are being abused, mocked, vilified, persecuted and slain for being Albanians and wanting to live as Albanians.

But as in the past, so also today, they are facing the savage storm of Serbian repression with characteristic courage and heroism. And they are resolved to win. At the same time they look to Albanians outside of

---

* Source: *Albanian Catholic Bulletin.* Santa Clara, California, USA, Vol. IV (1983), pp. 2-3. Published under the pseudonym "The Horned Helmet." This article was printed as a "Guest Editorial" in the *Bulletin.*

Yugoslavia for support and help. In this time of crisis, they need expressions of solidarity with their struggle by Albanian men and women everywhere. Albanians can differ—if they like, or if they must —over anything else: politics, religion, economics, language, history, literature, etc. But they can no longer afford to differ over the issue of Kosova. For the issue of Kosova is a national issue, and an urgent one. It concerns not only the ethnic rights of over two million Kosovars, but also their honor, their national identity, their lives.

Whether or not to give full support to the cause of the Kosovars is no longer a matter for debate or hesitation. As in the days when the fiery tongued Patrick Henry and Thomas Paine spoke for the cause of American liberty, so also Albanians today need to speak with one voice in support of the demands of the Kosovars.

The oppressors of Kosova leave us no choice. Rather than rely on reason and democratic processes to resolve the issue of Kosova, the Serbs seem determined to maintain their colonial rule there at all costs. Their policies on Kosova are plainly geared to serve that purpose. The policeman's club, the torturer's whip and the soldier's bullet are only the more extreme means they are using to enforce those policies. The arsenal of their weapons includes also a relentless propaganda campaign against the Kosovars, pressure on historians and educators to falsify the history of Kosova to serve Serbian interests, diplomatic efforts to influence leaders of nations in favor of the Serbs and against the Albanians of Yugoslavia and so forth.

In their all-out propaganda drive, they have tried also to enlist the services of religion in Kosova. They got the Serbian Orthodox community to issue a strong denunciation of the Kosovar demonstrations in the spring of 1981. Then they tried to obtain similar declarations by the Muslim and Catholic religious communities in Kosova. But here their hopes and expectations were dashed to the ground. The Muslim and Catholic leaderships refused to condemn the demonstrations. They knew that reason and justice were on the side of the demonstrators. And they stood courageously by them in their hour of need.

Albanian religious communities showed the same courage, and the same concern and loyalty to the Albanian nation not long ago, in response to the October, 1981 resolution of the Bishops of the Greek Orthodox Church, who claimed to defend the religious rights of "four hundred thousand Orthodox Greeks" in southern Albania. All four of the Albanian denominations in America, issued prompt and powerful statements rejecting the Bishops' resolution as a chauvinistic provocation towards Albania.

These are two fine examples that show the patriotic posture of Albanian religious communities in our day. Kosova has need today of the same spirit and will on the part of all Albanians. Unity of mind, unity of feeling, unity of action by Albanians everywhere on this national issue will go a long way to help the Kosovars in these difficult times and hasten the day of their liberation.

Indeed, the demands of the Kosovars are so manifestly just and solid that numerous non-Albanians the world over are giving them support. In our own country, two prominent supporters are Senators Charles Percy of Illinois and Jesse Helms of North Carolina. They feel that to help the Albanians of Yugoslavia is to help the cause of justice and democracy in the world.

Can Albanians, who are tied to the Kosovars by blood and language and history and culture, do less for them than these friends of Kosova are doing? The time has come for all Albanians to unite in support of Kosova, just as they did in those other times of trial for the Albanian nation in 1878, 1912, and 1920.

Chapter 9:
*Struggle for Ethnic Rights**

Events in Kosova over the past year kept up the momentum of the last three years. There was no progress toward granting of ethnic and human rights to the Albanians in Yugoslavia. On the contrary, developments pointed toward a worsening of the situation. One did not have to turn to Yugoslav dissidents or political exiles to learn this. The best evidence for it was the media within Yugoslavia itself, especially the Albanian-language Communist Party daily, *Rilindja* (Rebirth), in Prishtina, capital city of the largely Albanian-populated (about 80%) province of Kosova.

Belgrade's policy of no negotiations with the Kosovars and no concessions to them, was reaffirmed at the session of the Central Committee of the League of Communists of Yugoslavia (LCY), held in December of 1983. The session dealt expressly with Kosova. Once again the Party meeting claimed that the Spring 1981 demonstrations in Kosova were "counter revolutionary," that they were orchestrated by Albanian nationalists and irredentists, and that their aim was the destruction of the "integrity and self-management system of Yugoslavia," in other words, the break up of the Yugoslav Federation. The meeting noted that beside Albanian nationalism, "all other nationalisms have been gaining strength" in Kosova and throughout Yugoslavia—an admission that the national question in the country has gotten worse instead of better. While concentrating its attack on

* Source: *Albanian Catholic Bulletin*. Santa Clara, CA., USA, Vol. V (1984), pp. 67 – 71.
The full title in the original text: *Struggle for Ethnic Rights in Kosova Continues.*

Albanian nationalism, the Party meeting also voiced a warning to Serb nationalists to stop their campaign to spread anti-Albanian feeling in the Federation. Could it be that Yugoslav leaders were not aware that their hard line policies on Kosova fed and inflamed the anti-Albanian feelings of Serb nationalists?

The LCY meeting dismissed the main demand of the Kosovars for a Republic of Kosova as a dangerous slogan of Albanian irredentists, whose ultimate aim is the "annexation" of Kosova to Albania. Judging from pronouncements by Yugoslav leaders, this fear lies at the heart of their opposition to Kosovar demands for national equality, justice, respect, and equal opportunity. Rather than reconsider its position on Kosova, the leadership called for tougher measures to deal with "the enemy." One such measure was the subsequent appointment of a new Party Secretary for Kosova. He is Svetislav Dolasevic, a former officer of UDBA (the notorious Yugoslav secret police agency). Previously he served as Attorney General for the province of Kosova. It's reported, meanwhile, that Mahmud Bakalli, the Party Secretary in Kosova during the 1981 upheavals, has been sentenced to twelve years in prison.

The *Rilindja* paper echoed the conclusions of the December 1983 LCY session throughout 1984. Numerous reports said that nationalism had become a very dangerous ideology. One article (May 20, 1984) called it "an opium" that was afflicting all of Yugoslavia. It was a problem that was preoccupying the whole country to "an extraordinary degree." Curiously, however, the media, like the Yugoslav leadership, failed to see a connection between the repression of the Albanians in Kosova and the rampant spread of nationalism in the rest of the Federation.

In the meantime, the arrests, trial and imprisonment of Albania ethnics continued without letup. There were trials in Prishtinë, Pejë, Gjilan, Prizren, Manastir (Bitola), and numerous smaller towns. The toll of Kosovar political prisoners kept mounting every passing month. The accused were given harsh sentences, even for offenses that in the civilized world are considered minor, or not deserving of punishment at all. A Kosovar from the Ferizaj district was sentenced to three years in prison for calling aloud "Kosova—Republic," and for taping programs broadcast by Radio Tirana. Two students from the district of Pejë, one of them in his teens, were sentenced to six months in prison because, upon returning from a trip to Albania, they had brought with them "a few photographs of Enver Hoxha." Similar sentences were handed out to a farmer and an agronomist from the Rahovec district for possessing tapes that praised Hoxha and the Albanian Party of Labor.

If these cases seem extreme, consider the following: a family man in the Decan district—the father of six children and the "only breadwinner in the family"—was sent to prison for eight months because he attended certain meetings of "a hostile character," and carried a matchbook with the inscription "Kosova Republic" (*Rilindja*, Feb 29, 1984). In Prishtinë, a minor was sentenced to three and a half years and another minor to two years, for belonging to an "illegal organization" called the New Kosova. An item in the *Rilindja* of January 6, 1984 said that the secret police in Gjilan hurriedly confiscated all copies of a 1984 calendar, because the dates April 1 and 2 on it—the days of the massive Kosovar demonstrations in 1981—were marked in red ink. The reader of the Yugoslav press these days may be excused if he or she concludes that the country of Tito is showing symptoms of paranoia, at least where Albanians are concerned.

Albanians were punished not only for "offenses" in Yugoslavia, but for actions abroad, especially for demonstrating in support of the rights of Kosovars. A Kosovar migrant worker who returned from Switzerland was sentenced to fifteen months in prison in May of 1984, because he had taken part in "hostile, anti-Yugoslav demonstrations" in Geneva and Berne back in 1981. As in the times of Ottoman oppression, the Kosovars these days are punished merely for reading or possessing literature that the Yugoslav censors have labeled "dangerous." As a result, there has come into being an "index of forbidden literature." The long list includes magazines such as *Zëri i Kosovës* (The Voice of Kosovars) and *Liria* (Liberty), political tracts, books with titles like *Freedom Songs* and *Hasan Pristina and the Patriotic Movement in Kosova*, and even a volume of memoirs by Ismail Kemal Vlora, the hero

of Albanian independence in 1912. The witch hunt was especially hard
on the intellectual community, headed by the professors and students at
the University of Prishtina. New names of victims were added to the
long list of purged professors and students. The drive was called
"ideological and political differentiation," a euphemism for persecution
of anyone accused of Albanian nationalism.

Threat of Guerrilla Warfare

Since the Yugoslav government would not permit freedom of
expression and assembly for its citizens, Kosovar activists have been
forced to operate underground. They began to form so-called illegal
organizations in the struggle to win rights and freedoms to which all
Yugoslav citizens are entitled by law, under the provisions of the Federal
Constitution. The most prominent organizations of this kind were: The
"Movement for the Albanian Socialist Republic in Yugoslavia," the
"Marxist-Leninist Group of Kosova," and the "New Kosova." An article
in *Rilindja* (March 11, 1984), said that since 1981, a total of 72 illegal
Kosovar organizations and groups had been discovered, with a combined
membership of 1,000. In the same period, the article continued, 658
irredentists had been sentenced, and about 2,000 others were prosecuted
on other charges.

Lately there were ominous signs of increasing radicalization of the
population of Kosova. An editorial in *Rilindja* (June 18, 1984) told of
Kosovars who had organized an "attack brigade" for waging guerrilla
warfare. A June 19, 1984 article in the same paper reported a Kosovar
saying that if Kosova is not proclaimed a republic through negotiations,
then this must be done through armed revolutionary action. Other reports
told of the formation of "underground cells" and a "National-Liberation
Front" in the province. These developments seem to signal the start of a
new and prolonged phase of violence in Kosova, which could rock the
whole Federation.

The migration of Serbs and Montenegrins from Kosova continued to be a major issue, but nearly all press reports in the province contradicted Serb charges that the emigration was due to Albanian pressure. For example, *Rilindja* (July 6, 1984) wrote that "...people leave for reasons of employment, family matters, marriage, or because they want to join other members of the family " living elsewhere in Yugoslavia, etc. Another report in the same paper said that of 24 applicants for migration in one district (Serbice) early in 1984, none mentioned pressure from the Kosovars as the reason for wanting to leave the province. The reasons given were mainly marriage, education, employment and the like. Nonetheless, the Yugoslav press in general was calling for stricter laws to halt the migration of non-Albanians, and even to induce those who have left to return to their former homes. One big reason for leaving Kosova—and this was true of Albanians as well, a fact ignored by the Belgrade press—was the ailing economy in the province. According to statistics in mid-1984, unemployment in Kosova was two and a half times higher than the average for Yugoslavia. Only one in nine in Kosova had a job, compared to one in four in Yugoslavia as a whole. And for every job opening in Kosova, there was 42 applicants, compared to 12 in the country as a whole. There were villages that did not have a single general store to supply the needs of the people, and villages with stores that were short of basic food items and other merchandise. School facilities were lacking in parts of the province. Pupils in a village in the district of Deçan had to walk 12 km. each way to school every day. Government authorities concluded that the critical state of the economy in Kosova was a big stumbling block in efforts to achieve political stability in the region.

There were reports that Serb extremists were pushing a drive to "spread distrust of the Albanian population," not excepting even those who "made a great contribution to the revolution" in Yugoslavia during World War II. A theory was being propagated that the Communist revolution in Yugoslavia was the work solely of the Slavic people, that is, the Serbs, the Montenegrins, etc., with no help from ethnic groups like the Albanians and others. Indeed, such groups were stigmatized as

"Fifth Columns," thus implying that they posed a threat to the security of Yugoslavia (*Rilindja*, July 18, 1984). These same extremist voices viewed those groups as "guests" in Yugoslavia, insinuating that they are not entitled to rights pertaining to the "indigenous" Slav people in that country. There is no need to comment on the grave implications of such ideas for the future of the Yugoslav Federation.

Yugoslavia and the Neighboring States

Belgrade had problems not only with the Kosovars, but also with the neighboring states of Albania, Bulgaria, and Greece. As before, Albania's support of the Kosovar demands was interpreted in Belgrade as gross interference in the internal affairs of Yugoslavia. But recently a new accusation was hurled at Tirana. Albania, said Yugoslav sources, is dreaming of becoming "an empire" (*Rilindja*, July 15, 1984). And the first step, presumably, toward realizing that dream is union with Kosova. Belgrade also charged that Albania has a problem with its Slav (Macedonian) minority, which numbers no less than "100,000" (*Rilindja*, Aug. 4, 1984) Albania scoffed at the charge, and pointed to the 1979 census which showed a total of 4,163 persons of Slavic nationality in the country (*Zëri i Popullit*, Oct. 13, 1984).

Friction continued with Bulgaria over statements by Bulgarian officials which the Yugoslavs interpreted as designs to annex the Macedonian part of Yugoslavia to Bulgaria. A high Macedonian authority, Angel Cemerski, attacked those who deny the reality of Macedonia, and called on Bulgaria, Albania and Greece to "restore" or "ensure" the rights of the Macedonian minorities in those countries (*Yugoslav Information Bulletin*, NO. 5, 1982, p. 20).

Uneasy about its shaky position in Kosova, Yugoslavia reacted sharply to demonstrations in Western Europe and the U.S. in support of the struggle of the Kosovars. The reaction was especially bitter against Albanian demonstrations in Geneva, Switzerland on March 2, 1984, and again in Berne on July 14 ("Bastille Day") in front of the Yugoslav

Embassy in that country. The Yugoslav press labeled the demonstrations "circus shows," and warned that such protests were "against the vital interests of the Albanians in Yugoslavia," meaning, apparently, that there would be reprisals against families of the demonstrators in Kosova. But the Yugoslavs did not stop there. Forgetting that Switzerland , unlike Yugoslavia is a western democratic country, Belgrade protested officially to the Swiss government for allowing the demonstration to take place, and demanded that it should stop such "provocations" against Yugoslavia in the future. It was evident that Belgrade was becoming increasingly worried about the fortunes of its propaganda war abroad over Kosova. In this connection, a July 15, 1984 dispatch from Belgrade noted a step-up in a "campaign against Yugoslavia by certain newspapers in Western Europe and elsewhere," which coincided, it said, with Albanian calls for a Republic of Kosova.

In the meantime, Albania continued to attack Yugoslavia's arrests and imprisonment of Albanian nationals. The Albanian press denounced the unending arrests and trials as a "campaign of terror." An editorial in the Albanian daily, *Zëri i Popullit* (The Voice of the People), dated July 11, 1984 asked: Just what do the Serbs expect to accomplish with their terror and violence in Kosova? The editorial said that the Kosovars were being punished not because they were committing crimes, but solely because they were Albanians. Belgrade, it charged , was pursuing a "racist, colonial, and denationalizing policy" toward the Albanians in Yugoslavia. The editorial warned that the policy of persecution currently in force against the Albanians was also an attack on other ethnic groups in Yugoslavia. What is happening in Kosova today, it said, is but a preview of what will happen in other regions of the Federation, if the Serb extremists are allowed to have their way in Kosova.

Much of Albania's criticism was directed against Belgrade's policy on the cultural life of the Kosovars. According to Albania, the policy has had a crippling effect on education, above all on the teaching programs and enrollment at the University of Prishtinë. Since 1981, the number of Albanian students at the university has been cut down by 17,000, a large number of Albanian professors have been dismissed, and courses in Albanian studies have been steadily reduced in size, while some of them have been eliminated altogether.

The new Yugoslav policy on Albanian education an culture in general prompted severe criticisms at the Third Congress of Albanian Writers and Artists, held in Tiranë in late April of 1984. In a speech to the Congress, Prof. Dhimitër S. Shuteriqi of the University of Tiranë said that the "Serbian fury" against Albanian culture aimed at extinguishing awareness of Albanian history literature and art from the consciousness of the Kosovars. Is this, he asked, what Yugoslavia means by its much-trumpeted motto of "Unity—and—Brotherhood"? He suggested that the remarkable flowering of Albanian culture in Kosova over the past 10-15 years, prior to 1981, surprised and terrified the Great-Serbia chauvinists, who had heretofore looked down on Albanians as an inferior race, lacking in culture. Hence their feverish efforts to contain and stifle Albanian culture. He said that the Serbs were bound to fail in their short-sighted drive to suppress the age-old Albanian cultural heritage. A better alternative, he said, was for Yugoslavia to begin talks with Albania to resume cultural exchanges between the two countries (*Zëri i Popullit,* Apr. 27, 1984). Such exchanges were halted three years ago when Belgrade, in reaction to the Spring 1981 demonstrations, lowered a cultural Iron Curtain between Kosova and Albania.

Last June however, after much polemics over this issue, Yugoslavia and Albania initiated talks in Belgrade in an effort to conclude a cultural agreement. One of the proposals of the Yugoslav negotiators was that Albania agree to have cultural relations not only with Kosova, but also with the six republics of the Federation. The Albanian negotiators accepted the proposal. In October, 1984 the two sides met again in Belgrade and held talks for three days, from October 3 to 6. Unfortunately, the talks ended in failure. Both sides then blamed the other for the failure. Albania charged that the Yugoslavs had insisted that there should be no mention of Kosova in the agreement. The Albanian side objected, on grounds that the Yugoslavs were being unreasonable. But the issue, apparently, that finally wrecked the talks was the Yugoslav demand that Albania pledge to "preserve the cultural identity" of the Slavs in Albania. The Albanian negotiators rejected the demand outright, and with indignation, claiming that there is not and never has been a minority problem with the half dozen villages of Slav nationals in the country. It was obvious, the Albanians charged, that Yugoslavia was attempting to create the impression, mainly for public consumption abroad, that Albania has a minority problem with the slavs, just as Yugoslavia has a problem with the Albanians. Albania called Belgrade's attempt to draw a parallel between the two ethnic groups ridiculous, and said that the scheme was not going to fool anybody (*Zëri i Popullit*, Oct. 9, 1984).

An editorial in *Zëri i Popullit* a few days later (Oct. 13, 1984) elaborated on the failure of the cultural talks, and on the state of Albanian-Yugoslav relations in general. The editorial said that the Yugoslav had not entered the talks with sincere motives, but rather with the intent to exploit them for propaganda purposes. "Their purpose," it said, "is to isolate Kosova from cultural contacts with Albania, cut off the historical roots of its culture, and extinguish the national character of the Albanian population of Kosova." This amounts to "a policy of cultural genocide in Kosova," the editorial said. The same fate, the paper said, awaits the other peoples of Yugoslavia, if the Serb chauvinists are not stopped now. The editorial concluded with an appeal to Belgrade to "abandon its short-sighted anti-Albanian policy," both in Kosova and toward Albania, and seek instead a genuine dialogue that will benefit Albanians and Yugoslavs alike.

Albanians Abroad Support Kosovar Claims

As in the past, Albanians abroad in Western Europe, the United States, Canada and elsewhere continued to publicize the cause of the Kosovars, and to build up support for them. In May of 1983, the Union of the Kosovars presented a memorandum to the Congress of the Federal Union of European Nationalities, held in Brussels, Belgium, which contained a long list of Kosovar political prisoners, including college professors, journalists, students, factory workers, technicians, farmers, housewives, secretaries, waiters, and elementary school pupils. Among school pupils were two children aged 8 and 10. They were sentenced to two years in prison each. In Rome, the newspaper *Flamuri* (The Flag), published much valuable material on Kosova in Albanian, English, and French. Among the articles in the October 30, 1983 issue was one by Abas Ermenji—a leader of the *Balli Kombëtar* (The National Front) organization—entitled, "La verite sur les Albanais de Yougoslavie" (The Truth About the Albanians of Yugoslavia), which said that the Kosovars are not separatists, as Yugoslavia would have the world believe. They have no wish to separate from the Federation, but seek only " equal rights with other nationals in the Yugoslav Federation, which is to say, they want their own autonomous republic". Ermenji said that Albanians will no longer endure to live as "citizens of the lowest class" in Yugoslavia.

The Albanian quarterly in Paris, *Koha e Jone* (Our Time), also continued to give strong support to Kosova.. Commenting on Yugoslavia's drive to emasculate Albanian literature and culture in Kosova, Hiqmet Ndreu said in an article that the Yugoslavs "hope to assimilate a race whose tradition does not allow for assimilation." The Albanians of Yugoslavia, he said, "will defend their culture by every means, because it is their national treasure, the spiritual nourishment which has played the chief role in the awakening of their national consciousness "(*Koha e Jone,* Jan.-Feb.-Mar., 1984, pp. 35, 36). Three other Albanian publications in Europe championing the struggle for justice in Kosova were *Qindresa Shqiptare* (Albanian Resistance), *Republika e Kosovës,* (Republic of Kosova) and *Zëri i Kosovës* (The Voice of Kosova,) organ of the Movement for a Socialist Albanian Republic in Yugoslavia. Based in Switzerland, *Zëri i Kosovës* is published by Kosovar activists in exile who are in the forefront of the struggle for ethnic and human rights in Kosova. Their magazine is by far the most militant Kosovar publication, in or out of Yugoslavia, at present. It is also the publication Yugoslav authorities fear most, in connection with Kosova. Its name came up constantly in Yugoslav press report of arrests and trials of Albanian opponents to Yugoslav policy in the province.

In the United States, too, Albanian organizations pressed the fight to help the Kosovars secure the rights due them. In January 1984 , the group known as the Movement for the Albanian Republic in Yugoslavia, presented a Memorandum to the Secretary General of the United Nations in New York, detailing "the persecution of the Albanian population in Yugoslavia," from 1913 to the present. The memorandum concluded with a 7-point program for ameliorating the situation of Albanian nationals. Heading the list was a recommendation that the "territories inhabited by Albanians in Yugoslavia be constituted into an Albanian republic, within the framework of the SRF of Yugoslavia." Two other points called for the promotion of Albanian education, language, culture and art, and the application of democratic principles in the political life of the region.

On January 16, 1984 Albanians from all parts of the country demonstrated in New York, in front of of the United Nations, to commemorate the second anniversary of the assassination by Yugoslav UDB-a agents of three leading Kosovar activists in West Germany, the brothers Jusuf and Bardhosh Gervalla, and Kadri Zeka. An ad for the planned demonstration appeared in the *New York Times* on January 12, 1984. It was placed by the Committee for the Kosova Republic in Yugoslavia. Stung by the unfavorable publicity, a Yugoslav radio broadcast from Prishtine (Jan. 17, 1984) attacked the demonstrators as "enemies and traitors," and blamed "U.S. reactionary circles" for allowing the demonstration to take place.

As usual, the well known Albanian Kosovar Youth in the Free World continued its publicity campaign on Kosova. It sent out periodic reports to the United Nations, U.S. Government officials in Washington, and other influential people and groups, and appealed to them to use their influence to persuade Yugoslav authorities to change course on Kosova.

Albanian publications in America did their part to enlighten the American public on the true state of affairs in Kosova. Among those were *Dielli* (The Sun) and *Liria* (Liberty) in Boston, *Shqiptari i Lirë* (the Free Albanian) in New York, and the *Albanian Catholic Bulletin* in Santa Clara, California. A strong editorial on Kosova appeared in the Dielli issue on May 16, 1984. The editorial took Yugoslavia to task for "violating the human rights of Albanians," and thus "trampling on the Helsinki accords which it signed with solemnity" and vowed to uphold. The Yugoslav diplomats are laboring in vain, *Dielli* said, in trying to conceal the truth about Kosova and justify "with empty words something that cannot be justified". The editorial appealed to Belgrade to "examine the question of Kosova in a realistic light, and to try to resolve it by peaceful means, with justice, in harmony, and with goodwill".

A part of the pressure on Belgrade to rethink its position on Kosova came from the Albanian intellectual community in America. One powerful weapon in this regard was the publication of the book., *Studies on Kosova* (1984) . In June of 1984, Dr. Sami Repishti gave a talk on Kosova, at a seminar in Boston College that was sponsored by Vatra to commemorate the 75th anniversary of *Dielli*. Entitled "For peace and stability in Kosova" Dr. Repishti's presentation offered a number of thought provoking ideas for a peaceful solution of the complex problem. Another Albanian intellectual submitted a proposal to the National Endowment for Democracy in Washington, for promoting democracy in Yugoslavia. The proposal said in part:

> Kosova represents the most extreme case of the abuse of political authority in Yugoslavia today. Precisely for this reason, it is there, where the need to promote democracy in Yugoslavia is greatest. Failing this, the indications are that Kosova's population will become progressively radicalized, and turn to armed struggle as the only viable alternative for attaining self-affirmation and democratic rule. Such an eventuality is fraught with dangerous consequences for Yugoslavia, and for peace and stability in the Balkans.

In addition, more Albanians in America became involved lately in organizing fund drives to help their needy co-nationals in Yugoslavia. This is likely to become an important new phase in efforts to help the Kosovars attain their God-given rights.

World Press Publicizes Kosova Issue

Contrary to the wishes of Yugoslavia officials, the world press refused to ignore the national question in Kosova. Many newspapers and magazines wrote sympathetically about the demands of the Kosovars. Among such publications were the Swedish newspapers *Ekspressen,* the *Dagen Nyheter,* and the *Sydsvenska Dagblatet.* In an article last Spring, the latter paper wrote that the Albanians in Yugoslavia were asking for "bread, work, and their own Republic." The Danish paper *Information* wrote that about two million Albanians in Yugoslavia were fighting for their political, economic, social, and cultural rights. In an article in the influential West German daily, *Frankfurter Allgemeine Zeitung* (Apr. 4. 1984), Viktor Meier said that the Yugoslav regime was pursuing an unjust and "unrealistic" policy toward Albanian nationals. The Italian magazine, *Europeo,* noted in its April 14, 1984 issue that Yugoslavia's rupture of cultural ties between Kosova and Albania served only to "increase the anger of (Kosovar) intellectuals". Two Arab magazines, the *Crescent International* and *Arabia,* reported regularly on the jailings and harsh punishment of Kosovar dissidents. In its March 16-31, 1984 issue, *Crescent International* said that since 1981 over 1,000 Kosovars had been jailed, with sentences ranging from a few years to as many as 15 years.

In the Western Hemisphere, press reports on Kosova appeared in Mexico, Canada, and the United States. In an article headed, "The Kosovar People Are Demanding Their Rights," the Mexican paper *El Nacion* (Apr. 21,1984) wrote that "only a solution acceptable to the Kosovars" can end the turmoil in that part of Yugoslavia. In Canada, the *Toronto Sun* continued its factual and responsible coverage on Yugoslavia, which have earned for it the respect and the gratitude of the Albanian People.

In our country, Americans read about conditions in Kosova in the *New York Times,* the *Christian Science Monitor,* the *Waterbury Republican,* the *Post-Journal* in Jamestown, NY, the *Detroit News,* the

Chicago Tribune, the *Los Angeles Times* and other publications. Most of the coverage was objective and sympathetic to the Kosovars. After a three-day tour of Kosova , Dan Fisher wrote in the *Los Angeles Times* (Marc. 13, 1984) that the "entire province seems to be on edge" . Writing in the *New York Times* (Dec. 25, 1983), David Binder quoted " a distinguished archeologist" at Belgrade University, Milutin Garasanin, as saying, "Kosova is finished as Serb territory. " A more recent article in the *New York Times* (Oct. 5, 1984), headlined "Yugoslavia's Albanians: Poor, Proud and Prolific," said "Already Albanians represent more than 80 percent" of the people in Kosova. But the *New York Times* article which must have sent shock waves through the Belgrade officialdom was the one that appeared on July 16, 1984. Entitled "Yugoslav Repression," the article said that Yugoslavia is silencing political discussion, and that "the situation has taken a serious turn toward repression". The Albanians, of course, have known this for a long time, but now, as a result of the *Times* exposure, the whole world has become aware of it. Henceforth, it should be easier for the American public and government officials to accept the Albanian side of the story on Kosova.

In the meantime, a number of scholarly studies were published over the past year or so that dealt directly or indirectly with Kosova. Writing on post-Tito Yugoslavia, an American scholar of Croatian origin, Mathew M. Mestrovic, noted that the Albanians are the third largest ethnic group in Yugoslavia (after the Serbs and the Croatians), that they, like the Croatians, are denied basic national and human rights, and that the State Department in Washington should speak out on this issue without further delay (*the new renaissance*, V, 1983). An article by Gabrielle Rebecchi titled, "La Posizione Albanese Rispetto Alla Questione Del Kosovo" (The Albanian Position with Respect of the Kosova Question), appeared in *Oriente Moderno*, II (1983). Dr. Patrick F.R. Artisien of Bradford University in England offered some interesting ideas in "A Note On Kosova and the Future of Yugoslav-Albanian Relations" (*Soviet Studies*, Apr. 1984).Commenting on the issue of migration of the Slavs from Kosova, he said that "the majority of

Serbian and Montenegrin emigrants are the offspring of, or are themselves post-1912 settlers (in Kosova)," following its annexation by Serbia. They are identified, he said, with Serbia's colonisation policy in that region. The East European affairs expert, J. F. Brown , had some noteworthy comments on Kosova, Yugoslavia, and Albania in an incisive study on the Balkans *(The World Today*, June, 1984). Also, the Albanian-American scholar, Elez Biberaj, published a new study on Kosova, this time in the authoritative British quarterly on international affairs, *Survey* (Autumn, 1984 issue). Titled "The Conflict in Kosovo, " Biberaj's study made a strong case for change in the status quo there. Following are some excerpts from the study:

> Demands for the establishment of an Albanian republic within the Yugoslav federation represent a just and viable solution to the problem of Kosovo after more than 70 years of Serbian occupation, repression, domination and exploitation.... Yugoslav rule in Kosovo is based on fear, and popular aspirations have been suppressed by sheer force.... The cost of keeping Kosovo under Serbia's tutelage will rise. The continuation of the current policy could prove more detrimental to Yugoslavia's interests in the long run than granting the Albanians a republic.(pp. 52, 56).

Biberaj concluded with a warning that "until a just solution is found to the Albanian problem, the threat of a larger ethnic confrontation, with potential international complication, will persist".

Croatians and American Republican Group Support Kosovars

As in the past, Croatians in America and abroad made common cause with the Albanians against Serbian domination. Croatian publications carried much valuable material on Kosova. One useful source of information in America was the *CNC Report*, monthly publication of the Croatian National congress, headquartered in New York. In Hamburg , West Germany, the Croatian magazine, *Hrvatska Domovina*, published a monthly English-language supplement called

That's Yugoslavia, devoted mainly to the issue of human rights in Yugoslavia. The plight and the struggle of the Kosovars featured prominently in the pages of the supplement. This publication offers a view of Yugoslavia - the grim view of the oppressed, the destitute, the forgotten- that is rarely, if ever seen in the American press or other media channels. Support for the Albanians also came from an émigré Yugoslav group in Great Britain, known as the Liberation ("Oslobodjenje"). In November, 1983, this group, which has been described as "a prestigious Yugoslav organization, " issued a Statement recognizing the right of the Kosovars to have their own Republic in Yugoslavia.

A significant development in American politics relative to Kosova took place in Washington, D. C. in May of 1984, when the National Republican Heritage Group Council passed a Resolution condemning Yugoslav repression of ethnic Albanians. The Council is an auxiliary of the Republican Party National Committee, hence the importance of the Resolution. We understand that the Resolution- the first of its kind to date, as far as we know, on the American political scene – was introduced by a delegation of the Albanian-American Republican Clubs. After enumerating in clear and forceful language Yugoslavia's "brutal repression" of its Albanian population, the Resolution said that the National Republican Heritage Groups Council:

> Convinced that the continuation of the current Yugoslav repressive policy represents a serious danger to stability and peace in the Balkans:
> Condemns the flagrant and systematic violation of the fundamental human and national rights of ethnic Albanian...;
> Calls upon the Yugoslav government to implement the provisions of the Helsinki Final Act...:
> Appeals to the United States government to urge Yugoslavia to take immediate measures to allow ethnic Albanians to exercise their basic individual rights and fundamental freedoms, in particular: a)grant ethnic Albanians the right to their own republic...; b) immediately release all Albanian political prisoners, and c) take measures to improve the economic situation in the Albanian- inhabited territories.

The well-drafted document could mark the beginning of the long-awaited turnabout in official American policy on Kosova. The Resolution was a major political victory for the Kosovars. We may assume also that it added to the pressure on Yugoslavia (or more exactly Serbia) to abandon its tragic policy toward the Albanian population.

In sum, the situation in Kosova as of this writing is grim and volatile. There are , to be sure, a few signs that offer hope for the future, as we have shown in this account. But whether genuine, essential change will take place, in order to avert further tragedy and even general disaster, depends almost entirely on Yugoslavia, at this point.

Chapter 10:
A Case of Callous Injustice *

Of the thousands of Albanian political prisoners in Yugoslavia at present, the most notorious and revolting is the case of Adem Demaçi, a talented writer and intellectual from the district of Prishtinë, the capital city of the province of Kosova. Now in his late forties, Demaçi has been languishing in Yugoslavia's prisons for nearly a quarter of a century. That means that he has spent most of his life in prison.

Demaçi was first arrested in 1958, and rearrested twice since then, not for any crime he had committed, but for political reasons, because his beliefs were seen as a threat to the Yugoslav Federation. He is one of numerous Albanian political prisoners currently isolated in the penal institutions of Yugoslavia on charges of "nationalism," "chauvinism," "agitation against the state" and similar vague, unsubstantiated accusations.

He has been tortured for his alleged crimes to such an extent that he is now reported to be very feeble and nearly blind. Yet, the Yugoslav authorities, oblivious to his suffering, continue to keep him behind bars.

But despite all efforts by his inquisitors to force or bribe him to plead guilty, Demaçi has stood his ground. He has remained scrupulously faithful to his beliefs and his conscience. His steadfast endurance of the worst pressures designed to break his will, has made a deep impression among the Kosovars. It has strengthened their unity and

---

* Source: *Albanina Catholic Bulletin*, Santa Clara, California, USA, Vol. V (1984) , p. 72. The full title in text: "Yugoslavia's Imprisonment of Adem Demaçi – A Case of Callous Injustice."

heightened their courage. He has become a hero in their eyes and, indeed, in the eyes of Albanians everywhere.

Adem Demaçi has waged a long and painful struggle for justice in Kosova. He has become a symbol of Albanian yearnings for ethnic and human rights in Yugoslavia. He is a symbol, too, of Kosovar resistance to state injustice and violence in the Federation of Yugoslavia. His suffering has raised the national consciousness among the more than two million Albanians in Yugoslavia, and at the same time shocked the conscience of many in the world community who had been led to believe that Yugoslavia is a democratic country.

The cruel punishment inflicted upon Demaçi has aroused Albanians everywhere, and prompted them to rally to his defense. There is hardly an Albanian today who does not speak with sympathy, respect or admiration for him. Many of them have written directly to leaders of Yugoslavia asking for his release from prison. Tow leading Albanian intellectuals in America who had worked to secure his release are Dr. Sami Repishti in Baldwin, N.Y., and Prof. Arshi Pipa in Minneapolis, Minn. Both of them have known long prison sentences (in Albania) for political reasons, and appreciate fully the terrible plight of Demaçi. But the Yugoslav authorities have callously ignored all pleas to set Demaçi free.

In the United States, Demaçi's case has been publicized in the Albanian press, in *Dielli* (The Sun) in Boston, the *Albanian Catholic Bulletin* in Santa Clara, and other publications. In Switzerland, the Albanian magazine *Zëri i Kosovës* (The Voice of Kosova) has written at length about him.

But concern about Demaçi is not limited to the Albanian press, groups, or individuals. Human rights groups have been outraged by Yugoslavia's persecution of him, and pledged to support him. In a pamphlet on Yugoslavia (1982), the U.S. Helsinki Watch Committee documented the cases of some two dozen leading dissenters in Yugoslavia, including two Albanians, Adem Demaçi and economist Skënder Kastrati, whose rights have been violated by the state. Both Demaçi and Kastrati have been adopted by Amnesty International as "prisoners of conscience." Both organizations have called for the release of the two men. Yet, Yugoslavia which parades itself before the world as a staunch defender of human rights, has paid no attention to their appeals.

But efforts to end Belgrade's barbarous treatment of Demaçi continue. Lately, a group of well-known Albanian intellectuals in America, all of them with university affiliations, drafted a petition calling for the release of Demaçi. The petition says among other things:

> We, the undersigned, all members of the Albanian community in America, call upon the Government of Yugoslavia to release Adem Demaçi from prison. We further call upon the intellectual community and the information media in the United States of America to support our effort to uphold the rights and dignity of an innocent man, Adem Demaçi, and bring to an end his suffering by obtaining his release from prison.

The petition will be circulated among associations of students and professors in America, as well as among leading media agencies, including newspapers and magazines and possibly radio and television stations, with a view to enlisting their support in this initiative.

It seems evident that the longer the Yugoslav officials persist in their senseless persecution of Demaçi, the greater will be the anger and opposition of the Kosovars, and the greater as well the loss of Yugoslavia's standing in the eyes of the world.

Chapter 11:
Kosova Stalemate Deepens [*]

Recent developments in Kosova showed no sings of progress toward a solution of the many problems the province is facing. Instead the situation continued to deteriorate, as the problems worsened. The Yugoslav authorities talked much about "stabilizing" the province, but the means they chose to bring about such a result proved counter-productive. Instead of recognizing the demands of the Kosovars as reasonable and legitimate, they responded by taking still harsher measures against them.

A new campaign of repression began in May, 1985 when the Workers Social League of Yugoslavia held a conference in Belgrade. Delegates to the conference demanded that new steps be taken to curb the ethnic rights of the Albanian population. The Kosovar youth became a special target for attacks, on the grounds that they are "indoctrinated" with Albanian nationalist sentiments.

Similar strident voices bordering on hysteria, were heard the same month at a meeting of the Presidency of the Republic of Serbia. There, a member of the Presidency, described by a Yugoslav publication (NIN) as "highly agitated," called (in indirect language) for all-out war on the Albanian population of Kosova, just as Tito's armed forces did in 1945. Bitter anti-Albanian feelings erupted also in the wake of the latest congress of the League of Writers of Yugoslavia, held in 1985. A like atmosphere of anger and resentment of Albanians prevailed at a meeting of the Association of Journalists of Macedonia in October of 1985.

---

[*] Source: *Albanian Catholic Bulletin*, Santa Clara, Calif., Vol. VI (1985) , pp. 82-87.

Such meetings, and the reports they gave rise to in the Yugoslav media intensified and worsened inter-ethnic tensions in Kosova. The Serbian press, in particular, seized on anti-Albanian reports like a desert traveler thirsting for a drop of water. The inevitable result was more hostility towards Albanians, more arrests of Albanian nationals, more trials and more imprisonments.

According to official Yugoslav sources (NIN, June 2, 1985), a total of 3,344 Albanians in Yugoslavia had been sentenced on charges of "counter-revolutionary" activity, from the time of the Spring 1981 demonstrations to the end of 1984. The London *Sunday Times*, however, reported on June 9, 1985 that "35,000 Albanians have been brought before the courts for 'counter revolutionary activities' since 1981" in Yugoslavia. Those activities included membership in illegal Albanian nationalist organizations, contact with exiled Albanian groups abroad and listening to Radio Tirana. The repression of Albanians by Belgrade caused even an official of the Socialist League of Kosova, Ismail Mikulovci, to admit that "Serbian nationalism is creating an anti-Albanian disposition" in Kosova and throughout Yugoslavia (*Zeri i Popullit*, May 30, 1985). Actually, such a "disposition" has been a bitter fact of life in Kosova for generations.

Victims of Yugoslav Repression

An example of repression of Kosovars is that of Miss Aishe Gjonbalaj, an Albanian elementary school teacher from the district of Plave and Gusinje in Montenegro. In 1973 Miss Gjonbalaj took a trip to Albania. Upon her return home, she was dismissed from her job on charges that she had engaged in political activity while in Albania. What was the nature of this activity? Well, she shouted "Long Live Albania!" in Tiranë. Confronted with this "charge," Miss Gjonbalaj did not deny that she wished Albania a long life, but failed to see that she had committed a crime in voicing such a sentiment. But that was not the end of the matter, nor the worst part of it. In March of 1984 she was arrested because she had helped families that had been victimized by the repression that followed the Kosovar demonstrations in 1981. For seven long months she was subjected to cruel interrogations, then sentenced to 13 years in prison. According to the Albanian Kosovar Youth in the Free World, this was the heaviest jail sentence given to an Albanian woman in postwar Yugoslavia.

But as in 1973, so also this time, Miss Gjonbalaj stood her ground and held her head high. She said she was proud and happy to have helped families in need, despite her meager salary.

The campaign of repression against the Kosovars is no respecter of age. Witness the case of an old woman, Hanefia Avdagic, 71. She was arrested and sentenced to five years in prison for blaming Yugoslavia's economic problems on the country's Self-Management system, and for "justifying the demands by Albanian nationalists in Kosovo". Her case was reported in Amnesty International's *1984 Report* (p. 321). the organization adopted her as a "prisoner of conscience".

In Slovenia, Macedonia and other parts of Yugoslavia, the working people use the language of the local population at work, be it a factory, mine, shop or government office. But in the town of Mitrovicë, Kosova, a court sentenced an Albanian engineer, Nazmi Peci, to five years in prison merely because he asked that the Albanian language be used as the medium of communication at a mine where the majority of the workers were Albanian (*Zëri i Popullit*, July 25, 1985).

In early December, 1985 TANJUG (Yugoslav Telegraphic Agency) reported the arrest of fifty Albanians in Kosova, Macedonia and Montenegro. In the same month, just a few days before the New Year, 94 more Albanians, most of them intellectuals and students, were arrested. Sources in Belgrade said they were placed under arrest because they "wanted to change the constitutional order of Yugoslavia" – the government's jargon for the Albanian demand for a Republic of Kosova. The massive arrests offered fresh evidence of the continuing persecution of Albanian nationals.

Rather than permit Albanians to express freely their national and cultural heritage, Yugoslav authorities took new steps to curb such expression. An example of this trend is a letter by an Albanian that was published in the local press in Prishtinë, capital of Kosova. The letter complained that Yugoslav authorities in Macedonia were forcing Albanian ethnics to Slavicize their names. Thus, the writer of the letter, Jetulla Jashari, was obliged to change his last name to Jasharovski. Numerous other Albanians in Macedonia, he said, have had to tag on to their family name the Slavic suffix "ski" or "ov" because of government pressure (*Rilindja*, May 27, 1985).

Reporting on this trend, the Albanian press in Tiranë said that the Academy of Sciences in Macedonia had recommended that henceforth place names in that republic be written according to the spelling rules of Slavic. Already "tens of place names have been changed, including cities, villages, neighborhoods and historic centers," merely because those names had reference to the ethnic origins of the Albanian people. The report added that a movement was underway to change the names of leading Albanian towns in Macedonia such as Dibër, Tetovë, Kërchovë, Shkup, and Kumanovë (*Zëri i Popullit*, November 19, 1985).

Reaction in Albania to Latest Events

The Albanian press and intellectuals reacted with concern and indignation over the latest Yugoslav measures against the Kosovars. The leading Albanian author, Ismail Kadare, deplored the anti-Albanian temper of the 1985 Congress of the League of Writers of Yugoslavia. In an article published in the literary weekly *Drita* (The Light), he defended the Kosovar writers Rexhep Qosja, Hasan Mekuli, and Ibrahim Rugova who had spoken out at the congress against measures that belittle, abuse or restrict Albanian literature and culture in Yugoslavia. He likened Yugoslav attacks on Albanian literature to the ideology and practice of the   Inquisition and lamented that it is especially shameful when chauvinism "affects the men of culture in a country, above all its writers whose duty is to cool the vile passions, and rise above them in the interest of civilization, humanism, and friendship among peoples."

In an editorial entitled, "The Truth Cannot be Hidden By Bluffs and Demagogy," the leading daily in Albania chided Yugoslav leaders for claiming that Albanian nationals enjoy equality with the other peoples in Yugoslavia. "What kind of equality is that," it asked, "when voices call for stopping the teaching of Albanian history at the University of Kosova" because it is supposedly harmful to "coexistence in Yugoslavia?" The paper charged that an "anti-Albanian psychosis is being fostered in Yugoslavia that is akin to racism," and reminiscent of the Nazi meetings in Munich in the 1930s. In support of this charge the editorial noted that stores owned by Albanians in Belgrade, Nish and other cities in Serbia are being assaulted and burned down, and in public gatherings the Yugoslav people are told not to patronize Albanian bakeries nor eat in Albanian restaurants (*Zëri i Popullit*, July 25, 1985).

Another article in the same paper (dated Nov. 19, 1985) denounced the "chauvinist drive" in Macedonia against Albanian nationals. The article said that Macedonian leaders are bent on de-nationalizing the Albanian element. The "Albanian language, including the unified literary language, Scanderbeg, the League of Prizren... and the national identity of Albanians" have all become targets in the de-nationalizing drive, it said. Written by Kristaq Prifti and Xhevat Lloshi, the former a historian and the latter a linguist, this is one of the most eloquent critiques of Yugoslav policy in Kosova to appear in Albania in recent times.

Still another article, under the signature of Albanian historian Selami Pulaha, contested the Yugoslav thesis that Albanians are late comers in Kosova. The thesis has been used by the Serbs in the past to justify the expulsion of the Kosovars from their homes and land. Pulaha argues that there was a strong Albanian presence in Kosova long before the alleged invasion of the province by Albanians toward the end of the 17th Century. The fact that there are Medieval Serbian churches and monasteries in Kosova is no proof that the population of Kosova has been historically Serbian, just as we cannot say that the presence of mosques in Kosova means that the population of the province was Turkish during the era of Ottoman rule. Pulaha calls the Serbian theses on this issue dogmas that cannot stand up against the latest findings of scientific inquiry. (*Zëri i Popullit*, July2, 1985).

Albanians Abroad Stand By the Kosovars

As in the past, Albanians abroad were steadfast in their support of the demands of the Kosovars. Whether as individuals or through their organizations, they kept up the pressure to break the dangerous impasse in Kosova and initiate action that would eventually bring about a satisfactory settlement in that province.

In the Spring of 1985, representatives of the 35 nations that signed the 1975 Helsinki Act met in Ottawa, Canada to review the Helsinki provisions were being implemented. Taking advantage of the occasion, the New York-based Albanian Kosovar Youth in the Free World, addressed a Memorandum to the assembly of representatives. The Memorandum described the plight of Albanians in Yugoslavia, and urged the representatives to advise the Yugoslav government to respect the rights of its ethnic groups and guarantee them equal treatment under the law. Following are excerpts from the Memorandum:

> "To their great disappointment two million ethnic Albanians, in the S.F.R. of Yugoslavia continue to be specific targets for political persecution, economic neglect, and educational and social discrimination by the Government of Yugoslavia... Today, political killings, massive arrests, torture, unfair trials and heavy jail sentences are part of the daily life of Albanians... Unemployment is very high. Poverty is now a vicious circle stifling the lives of both the young and the old..."

The Memorandum warned that the situation in Kosova is a "classic set-up for an explosion which could threaten the stability and peace of the S.F.R. of Yugoslavia, and not of that country alone!" In September, 1985 the Kosovar Youth organization drafted another Memorandum, this time for the benefit of the United Nations on the occasion of its fortieth anniversary. Signed by Maliq Arifaj, the organization's Executive Secretary, the Memo was presented to UN's

Secretary General, Javier Perez de Cuellar. The Memo summarized in vivid language the sad history of Kosova since the founding of UN, and presented data that illustrate the continuing ordeal of Albanians in Yugoslavia. Among other things, it called attention to the conference of the Association of War Veterans of Yugoslavia where appeals were made to the Federal Government to "intervene militarily in Kosova" and intensify government control of the province.

Far from heeding such pleas, protests and warnings to change policy on Kosova, the Yugoslav leaders sought to make Albania a scape-goat for the problems in that province. An example is the interview the Prime Minister of Yugoslavia, Milka Planinc, gave to the *New York Times* correspondent in Belgrade (May 22, 1985), prior to her departure for Washington, D.C. on a state visit. She said: "Albania is creating problems (in Kosova) because she wants a part of Yugoslavia for herself."

Planinc's visit to Washington and subsequent meeting with President Reagan did not go unnoticed by the Albanians of America. Many of them sent telegrams to Reagan urging him to intervene on behalf of the Kosovars in his talks with Planinc. Following the telegram sent by Dr. Sami Repishti of New York, which said:

> "The persecution (of Albanians) by the Yugoslav government is a blatant violation of their national and human rights. We urge you to raise the question of the two million ethnic Albanians with the Yugoslav Prime Minister as a matter of your commitment to promote respect for human rights and fundamental freedoms wherever they are denied..."

The President also received a telegram from the Albanian Catholic Information Center in Santa Clara, California. The Center's forthright message expressed concern for the Albanians in Yugoslavia who are "oppressed and subjected to national, religious and economic discrimination". The message condemned Yugoslav military and police violence against the Albanian population as "a flagrant violation of the Yugoslav Constitution and of international agreements signed by Yugoslavia". Finally, the message appealed to Reagan to "help our persecuted brothers and sisters in Yugoslavia" who look to the United States for moral support.

In the meantime, Albanian periodicals such as *Dielli* and *Liria* in the United States and *Koha e Jonë* in Paris, continued to publicize the issue of Kosova through reports, articles, commentaries and editorials. In Switzerland Kosovar exiles continued to publish their magazine, *Zëri i Kosovës* (The Voice of Kosova), which has become the nemesis of UDB (the Yugoslav secret police) and Serbian extremists. The magazine represents the militant wing of the Kosovar movement, and is a natural magnet for Albanians who are tired of Yugoslav intransigence on Kosova and are seeking militant solutions to the problem.

Round-Table Discussion on Kosova in New York

Kosova remained an issue of vital interest to scholars and observers of Southeastern Europe. An example is the round-table discussion on Kosova that was held in New York City on October 12, 1985. The setting for the event was the Halloran Hotel. The sponsoring organization was the Kosova Relief Fund, USA, Inc., which is headquartered in Baldwin, New York. Principal organizer for the gathering was Dr. Sami Repishti. He was ably assisted by Sejdi Bitiçi, Tonin Mirakaj and others. The round-table discussion was convened in order to throw light on the situation in Kosova which "has been continuously deteriorating" since the Spring of 1981 and has become a "potentially explosive problem".

The panelists' at the discussions were: Jens Reuter and Dionisio Ghermany, both of them scholars at the Südost Institute in the University of Munich; and Dr. Sami Repishti, an associate of the faculty of Adelphi University in New York.

In his introductory remarks Dr. Repishti said that the problem of Kosova is "neither new nor recent," since its roots can be traced back to the "expansionist policies of the old Serbian bourgeoisie and their dreams of a Great Serbia—a modern version of the medieval Serbian empire". The problem, moreover, is neither insignificant nor dormant, he said. It is actually "an active volcano" fueled by a complex set of forces, including political, economic, social and cultural, all of which need to be elucidated.

Jens Reuter said that a wide gulf separates the views of the two opposing sides in Kosova: the Serbs and the Albanians. Prishtinë is full of policemen and militia men. One has the impression that the city is "under martial law". In spite of what Belgrade authorities say publicly, Reuter said that the Yugoslav government is not inclined to resolve the Kosova question. As a result of the impasse, "new unrest is in the making" there. Reuter doubted that Albanians will ever feel part of a country that calls itself South Slavs.

Dionisio Ghermany discussed the topic in the context of the broader inter-ethnic problems in the Balkan region. He said that for reasons of state, the nations of Southeastern Europe do not feel disposed to involve themselves with the problems of the Kosovars. They have their own nationality problems to contend with. He referred to Rumania as a case in point, a country which is friendly to Albania, yet whose press makes no mention of the problems in Kosova. Like Reuter, Ghermany was pessimistic about the prospects for resolving the Kosova imbroglio.

Despite its generally pessimistic tone, the round-table discussion was a positive development. It kept the Kosova issue before the public, enlarged our understanding of the complex issue, and alerted statesmen and concerned citizens to the seriousness of the problem and the need for action to prevent a new explosion in that troubled region of the Balkans.

Press Coverage in America and Abroad

"Yugoslavia Clamps the Lid on the Troublesome Kosovo" – that was the heading of an article carried by the *Wall Street Journal* (April 30, 1985). Its author was the Albanian scholar, Elez Biberaj, a recent winner of a doctorate in political science from Columbia University. As usual, Biberaj's contribution was an illuminating account of the situation in Kosova. The article was a heavy indictment of the Yugoslav authorities for discriminating against the Kosovars.

Biberaj noted that while Serbian dissidents at a recent trial were sentenced up to two years in prison, on similar charges Kosovars were sentenced to as much as 12 years. He denounced the arbitrary arrests and detention of Albanians, and the "witch hunt that has been initiated against the Albanian elite and intelligencia". Several prominent professors at the University of Prishtinë have been jailed, Biberaj said, and some 40 other distinguished intellectuals have been persecuted in one form or another. He said that the enrollment at the university has been cut back severely over a four-year period since 1980-81, dropping down to 23,000 regular students from a previous high of 35,000. Biberaj summed up his article in these words:

> "The danger to Yugoslavia does not come from the establishment of a
> Kosovo republic but from the free rein given to Serbian nationalism and the official
> toleration and encouragement of anti-Albanian sentiment. But continued Serbian
> colonial subjugation of Kosovo is undermining Yugoslavia's stability, radicalizing
> ethnic Albanians and making it more difficult to manage or contain the conflict...
> No solution short of granting Kosovo the status of a republic is likely to pacify the
> Albanians."

A short but informative article on Kosova appeared in the *London Sunday Times* (June 9, 1985). The influential British paper wrote: "Many prominent Yugoslavs believe that the 'Kosovo problem' is the most serious long-term difficulty facing them, and one which could split the country." The paper said that Albanians make up 80% of Kosova's population, and are now "the third largest of Yugoslavia's seven nations," or ethnic groups. The *Times* article—pointedly headed "Kosovo: the powder keg of Yugoslavia"—had a reference also to the University of Prishtinë, which "has been purged of many of its best professors" and where "the study of Albanian history, literature and culture has been curtailed".

An item in *Le Nouvel Observateur*, under the signature of Gani Azemi, a dissident Albanian poet, told of the practice of torture in

Yugoslavia. The item said that a disproportionate number of those arrested in Yugoslavia since 1980 are Albanians.

Perhaps the most news-worthy article on Yugoslavia to appear in the American press was that of Michael Dobbs, headlined "Without Tito, Yugoslavia Is Falling Apart" (*Washington Post*, Aug. 25, 1985). Dobbs said, "There is a widespread mood of disillusionment and frustration (in Yugoslavia), as if the country is sinking slowly downward". The "collective leadership" left behind by Tito, Dobbs said, is not functioning; it is "almost a recipe for perpetual political stalemate". The people "are losing hope," he said.

Turning to the nationality question, the article noted that the economic difficulties in Yugoslavia have coincided with a "marked resurgence of nationalism" in several parts of the country. Here he touched on the issue of Kosova and the riots in the province, which have "caused a backlash of nationalist feeling among the Serbs." Dobbs then related the bizarre story of a Serb in Kosova named Gjorgje Martinovic, who apparently injured himself severely in May of 1985 and blamed two Kosovar youth for the injury. The incident became the favorite topic of conversation throughout the summer in the "street cafes and restaurants of Belgrade". The incident is an eloquent indicator of the frenzy that has gripped Serbia, and the inability of the Serbs to think rationally and calmly about developments in Kosova.

Another Washington-based publication, *Spotlight*, published an interview (December 24, 1984), by a leading Albanian activist that was strongly critical of the leadership in Belgrade. The interview was given by Ismet Berisha, executive director of the League of Prizren in Exile. Berisha said that "3 million Albanians in Yugoslavia are living as third-class citizens," that they resent being partitioned among three different republics in Yugoslavia—namely, Serbia, Macedonia, and Montenegro —and that they want republican status for Kosova. This is "a categorical imperative of the moment," he said, and "a cause worth fighting for." He added that unless the Yugoslav government satisfies the demand of the Kosovars for a Republic of their own, there will be more unrest and demonstrations in the region.

Scholarly Studies Examine Kosova Question

The repressive policy of Yugoslavia in Kosova attracted attention also in some scholarly quarters. Early in 1985 a study appeared under the title. "Ethnopolitical Conflict in Yugoslavia: Elites in Kosovo, 1912-1982." Its author, Leonard Cohen, is a professor of political science at the Simon Fraser University in Canada. Cohen analyzes in depth the history of Kosova, shows that the grievances of the Kosovars have deep roots, and maintains the Albanians in Yugoslavia have been victims of "internal colonialism". The Serbs and Montenegrins, he argues, have held the most influential positions in Kosova and dominated the province's political and economic life. They represent in fact a "Communist colonial elite." With that as a background, Prof. Cohen believes that Yugoslavia will continue to face grave problems in Kosova. Any solution that does not take into account the vital interests of ethnic Albanians "is not likely to have much success," he writes. We would like to think that his prognosis for Kosova will give the Yugoslav leaders pause for reflection.

Prof. Cohen's study appeared in *Elite Studies and Communist Politics: Essays in Memory of Carl Beck,* Ronald H. Linden and Bert A. Rockman (eds.). The book was published in January, 1985 by the Center for International Studies at the University of Pittsburgh.

Reference to Kosova appeared also in a study by Patrick F.R. Artisien titled, "Albania in the post-Hoxha era," which was published in *The World Today* (June, 1985), a London-based magazine. Commenting on the succession in Albania, Artisien remarks that the appointment of Alia as successor to Hoxha "is certain to appeal to the Kosovo Albanians... Alija's parents were forced to emigrate to Albania to escape from repressive Yugoslav rule in Kosovo before the Second World War, an experience with which many Kosovars can readily identify."

Croatian Input on Kosova

As in the past, Croatians in general supported the Albanians in Yugoslavia. A distinguished contribution to their cause is being made by the Croatian National Congress (CNC), through its publication, the *CNC Report*. The August, 1985 issue of the Report devoted its leading article to Kosova. Written by Dr. Mathew Mestrovic, President of the Croatian National Congress, this article is a valuable document, rich with data and keen observations.

Mestrovic says that developments in Kosova "have created an enormous psychological crisis among the Serbs. They are bewildered, frustrated, angry." And they have reacted with traditional "Balkan brutality and cruelty" toward the Kosovars, because that is "the only policy Yugoslavia is capable of." But military repression and other forms of violence have not broken the spirit of the Kosovars. According to Dr. Mestrovic, the Serbs "cannot muster sufficient repressive force in Kosovo, because others—Slovenia, Croatia, Bosnia, Vojvodina—keep slamming the brakes on the Serbian Steamroller." And they do so mainly because they fear that if the Serbs succeed in crushing the Albanians, they would then move to impose hegemonic rule over the rest of Yugoslavia.

Yugoslavia is faced with a dilemma, Dr. Mestrovic remarks, because "It is a national conglomerate opposed by many of the peoples incorporated into it without their free consent." The federation is having problems not only with the Albanians, but other ethnic groups as well. This explains the undercurrent of sympathy and implicit, and sometimes even explicit support by them of the Kosovar cause. Thus we read in the *CNC Report* that "the Croat press has frequently expressed understanding and sympathy for the Albanian demands and complaints." Slovenia has been even more open in its stand on Kosova. Its leaders have refused to back "excessive repression" there. A development worth noting is the publication in Slovenia of an anthology on Kosova, written by Albanian scholars who advocate republic status for their region. It is reported that this has caused "anger and consternation in Belgrade" (p. 4).

The article on Kosova says that although the Serbs eliminated the Albanian Communist leaders in power at the time of the Spring 1981 outbreaks, the Albanians who have replaced them apparently are not as submissive as the Serbian authorities had expected. At a recent conference in Prishtinë, Kole Siroka (Kolë Shiroka), President of the League of Communists in Kosova, "bluntly blamed decades of Serbian repression and persecution of Yugoslavia's Albanians for their current opposition and resistance." (We might add that Shiroka was educated at the Catholic Diocesan Seminary in Prizren prior to WWII, and is related to Mother Teresa. Indeed, his brother, Gjon Shiroka, was the Yugoslav Ambassador to Sweden in 1979, the year when Mother Teresa received the Nobel Peace Prize).

In another *CNC Report* (December, 1985), the President of CNC makes an interesting comment about the character of the Serbian people. He says:

> "The Serbs are an extraordinary people moved at times by a collective death wish. They are the only people who celebrate as their national day their utter destruction at the hands of the Turks in the battle of Kosovo in 1389. Their history is filled with bloody and sometimes irrational, even self-destructive violence."

This observation helps to explain, in part, the attitude and actions of the Serbs in connection with Kosova.

Human Rights Organizations Report on Kosova

Criticism of Yugoslavia's political, legal, and penal practices came from may groups, among them Amnesty International, a winner of the Nobel Prize for Peace. In its *1984 Report*, it reported that during 1981 and 1982, the number of ethnic Albanians "sentenced for political crimes and minor offenses of a political character in Kosovo had reached the 2,503 figure." The organization noted also that some ethnic

Albanians, convicted of political offenses, had complained of ill-treatment and torture during investigation proceedings.

A more forceful attack on Yugoslavia's violation of the human rights of Albanians came from the New York-based U.S. Helsinki Watch Committee. In a *Special Report on Yugoslavia,* released in September, 1984, the Committee said that it had received reports from Kosova that told of "many violations of human rights," especially in conditions of martial law that prevailed in 1981. "Thousands of Kosovo citizens have been sentenced in summary court trials. Albanian dress [styles], books and songs have been outlawed as 'nationalist provocation.' Each year hundreds of young people in Kosova are convicted of political crimes because of membership in so-called irredentist organizations, or involvement in nationalistic activities," the Report said.

The Helsinki Watch Committee voiced support for the Kosovar demands for "an autonomous republic within the federal state, economic improvements, equality with the other ethnic groups, freedom of the press, and the release of all political prisoners". The Committee called on the Reagan Administration to urge Yugoslavia to abide by the provisions of the Helsinki Final Act and other human rights agreements to which it is a signatory.

Further corroboration of the wrongs suffered by Albanians in Yugoslavia came in February, 1985 when the U.S. Department of State issued its *Country Reports on Human Right Practices in 1984.* The section on Yugoslavia pointed out that Kosova "continues to be troubled by ethnic tension" stemming from "deep-rooted ethnic Serb-Albanian antagonism" (p. 1148). "Arrests on charges relating to 'nationalism' have been especially numerous among ethnic Albanian," the report said. Arrests "on hostile propaganda charges have included citations for participating in demonstrations at which speakers advocated full republic status for Kosovo, passing out leaflets, singing 'nationalist' songs, and writing 'nationalist ' slogans in public places" (p. 1149).

The State Department survey found that some professors in Kosova "who were suspected of propagating Albanian 'nationalism' were dismissed from their positions" (p. 1147), and furthermore the "authorities continue to apply pressure on professors at the Kosovo's Prishtina University," including those who are accused of "failing to oppose" Albanian nationalism (p. 1152). The survey also told of discrimination in Yugoslav courts, "particularly against ethnic Albanians and gypsies" (p. 1157).

We are pleased to see that our government is taking a more objective stand on Yugoslavia and, in keeping with our democratic traditions and professed concern for human rights, is indirectly criticizing the unjust and ultimately self-defeating policy of Belgrade toward ethnic Albanians. We trust that the policy-makers in Belgrade, who have so far ignored the cries of the Kosovars for justice, will heed the State Department's publication which, when read between the lines, implies American dissatisfaction with Yugoslavia's record on human rights.

Instances of oppression and, in many cases, torture of Albanians in Yugoslavia have been documented for a long time in the Albanian press. Now, influential human rights bodies are also expressing concern about this practice by a country that calls itself civilized and democratic. The reports of such bodies perform a useful service in educating world public opinion about the true nature of the Yugoslav state.

We conclude this section with a reference to the International Society for Human Rights, Inc., headquartered in Frankfort-am-Main, West Germany. The U.S. section of the Society, centered in New Jersey, has taken an interest in the case of Adem Demaçi—the Kosovar activist languishing in a Yugoslav prison – and is making efforts to obtain his release. The Society was alerted to Demaçi's plight by the Albanian Catholic Information Center in California. Demaçi, we might add, has been incarcerated on spurious charges for 25 years.

Recent Books on Kosova

Two new books on Kosova were published in the recent past in the United States. Their appearance underscores the lively interest on this subject in certain quarters in the country. The two titles are: *Kosova*, by the Albanian scholar S. S. Juka, and *The Saga of Kosovo*, by A. Dragnich and S. Todorovich. They offer sharply opposing views and interpretations on Kosova. For reviews of them see, *Albanian Catholic Bulletin*, Vol. VI (1985).

Chapter 12:
*An Exposition in Twenty-One Questions and Answers**

(*Note*—The following exposition is in the nature of a commentary on the book, *The Saga of Kosovo—Focus on Serbian-Albanian Relations*, which was published in 1984 in New York. Its authors are Alex N. Dragnich, a professor at Vanderbilt University; and Slavko Todorovich, a former employee of the Voice of America. We shall leave it to the reader to decide how objective they are. But we can say without hesitation that the book has at least the merit, as the Chinese say, of teaching by "negative example." Those who cannot understand the Serbian refusal to consider Albanian demands in Kosova, will find many of the answers in this book. For within the covers of the book the reader can peer into the mind of the Serb, and understand better what motivates, frightens or inspires him. That, at any rate, is our hope and expectation.)

Question No. 1—*What was the nationality of Gjon Kastrioti?*
  Every Albanian school boy or girl knows that Gjon Kastrioti—the authors of this book spell it "John Castriota"—was an Albanian feudal lord and the father of Albania's National Hero, George Scanderbeg (Gjergj Skenderbeu). Correction, say Dragnich and Todorovich. John Castriota was "of Serbian origin" (pg. 21). In saying this, however, they are not original. The Greeks have said it before them. Back in 1968 a Greek "scholar" by the name of John Demus said that Scanderbeg's "father was Greek—Ioannis Kastriotis." It's obvious from his Greek name, he leads the reader to believe. (see, *Balkan studies*, Vol.9, No.2,1968,p.493.) As if it were not enough that Serbs (and Greeks)

---

* Source: *Albanian Catholic Bulletin*, Santa Clara, CA., U.S.A., Vol. VI (1985), pp. 76 – 81. The Article was published anonymously.

appropriated Albanian lands, now they want to appropriate Gjon Kastrioti, as well.

Q.No. 2—*When did the Turks overrun the Balkan Peninsula?*

According to Dragnich and Todorovich, this came about with the demise of the Serbian Despotate in 1459 and the Kingdom of Bosnia in 1463 (p.45). Now, this would certainly be news to an Albanian pupil reading his first book on the history of Albania. For there he learns that Skanderbeg waged one of his greatest battles against a vast Turkish army led by Sultan Mehmed II himself (The Conqueror of Constantinople) in 1466. Reading on, he learns also that the Turks subdued Albania only in 1479, with the fall of Shkoder; in other words, sixteen years later than the date the authors of this book say all resistance to the Turks ceased in the Balkans.

How account for this not-so-insignificant discrepancy? Might we suppose that Dragnich and Todorovich were ignorant of these data? Hardly. It's rather that the authors see Serbia as the center of the Balkans, and therefore all Balkan history naturally revolves about Serbia. Seeing history in that light, they are persuaded that the 25-year long struggle of Scanderbeg against the Turks (1443-1468) was of no consequence. They seem to think that the title "Champion of Christendom" bestowed upon Scanderbeg by Pope Nicholas V was undeserved—the result, shall we say, of an error of judgement on the part of the Vatican.

Q. No. 3—*Were Albanians friends and allies of the Turks?*

No doubt about it, say the authors of *The Saga of Kosovo*. The Albanians in the era of Ottoman dominion in the Balkans received "special treatment from the Turks" and thus "enjoyed a special status" (pp. 55, 56). Unlike the Serbs who looked upon Istanbul as "the center of Serbian oppression," the Albanians regarded it as "the capital of their state" (p. 72).

But as we read on, we find that the Turks had some nasty epithets for the Albanians. According to the authors, they called them "criminals," "brigands," and "murderers" (p. 78). At this point the reader might ask: If the Albanians were friends of the Turks, why did the Turks call them such awful names? After all, people don't talk that way about their friends. The reader's doubts about the Albanians' friendship with the Turks are likely to be strengthened a few pages later, when he learns that in 1830 the Turkish commander, Reshid Pasha, massacred 500 Albanian leaders in Manastir (now Bitolj), to punish them for rebelling against the Sultan (p. 87). We think it will be granted us that this was a very strange friendship. It's bad enough to be called names by your friend, but when you have to pay for that friendship with your life... that's carrying friendship too far.

Q. No. 4—*On whose side were the Albanians in the Greek war of Independence (1821)?*

On the side of the Turks, say Dragnich and Todorovich (p. 87). We wager that this will be news not only to Albanians, but also to the Greeks. For generations they have been told by their parents at home and their teachers in school, that Albanians distinguished themselves in the Greek Revolution. Just last year, the leading daily in Albania wrote: "In the (Greek) revolt of 1821, there took part many Albanians who fought heroically side by side with Greek freedom fighters: and that is why the Greek people have honored, respected, and immortalized them in their history, their songs, etc." (*Zëri i Popullit,* March 24, 1985). Who were these Albanians? The list is long, but the more renowned among them are Bochari, Xhavella, Bubulina, Miauli and Kondurioti.

Again, are we to suppose that the authors of *The Saga of Kosovo* are ignorant of Greek history and the facts cited above? Not likely. A more likely hypothesis is that those facts are filtered into the mind of the Serbs or Serbophiles in such a way that they are distorted or dismissed altogether in favor of some trivial data that are derogatory to the Albanians, and that may serve also to create a split between them and their Greek neighbors. It's a habit of mind that seems ingrained in the mental mechanism of the Serb.

Q. No. 5—*Why did so many Albanians convert to Islam?*

The authors of this book have the answer to this question at their fingertips. It's because, unlike the Serbs, "the Albanians did not have an autocephalous church" (p. 48); and also because the Albanians lacked the individualism that is so characteristic of the Serbian people (p. 49).

True, the Albanians did not have an autocephalous church. But need we remind Dragnich and his colleagues that the Bosnians, too, converted to Islam in large numbers? Are we to conclude then that they did so for the same reason as the Albanians? We doubt that any serious historian would agree. As for individualism, we have the impression that this is a character trait all Balkan peoples have in abundance. I was reading a book recently, titled *The Greeks*, by Stephanos Zotos, which says that the Greeks are "individualists *par excellence*." In fact, the book has an entire chapter on the subject of Greek individualism. The late Albanian scholar and diplomat, Faik Konitza, has said the same thing about his compatriots, only more strongly. He writes that individualism is "the most conspicuous characteristic of the Albanians, and one without the knowledge of which their history remains a mystery" (*Albania: The Rock Garden of Southeastern Europe*. p. 55).

So, it appears that our authors are wrong on both counts on this question. Untroubled by such suspicions, they press their case and go on to say that the phenomenon of Islamization was "the main cause of the estrangement" between the Slavs and the Albanians (p. 52). Well, let us grant, for the moment, that this was the cause of the unfortunate enmity between the Orthodox Serbs and Moslem Albanians. But how explain the even greater enmity of the Serbs (and Montenegrins) toward Catholic Albanians? The authors did not venture to discuss this point.

Q. No. 6—*Who dug out the eyes of Queen Simonis?*

Queen Simonis was the wife of Serbian King Milutin (1281-1321). A lovely image of her was painted in a fresco in the church of Gratchanitsa, a masterpiece of Serbian religious architecture in Kosova. Tragically, however, someone scratched her eyes out, and the Serbs blame the Albanians for the vandalism. Dragnich and Todorovich quote a Serbian poet, Rakich, who cries out: "Oh, pretty image, an Albanian has dug out your eyes" (p. 39).

A very serious charge, indeed, which has contributed not a little to Serb resentment and hatred of Albanians. But was it really an Albanian who committed the crime? Might not the perpetrator have, just as well, been a Kosovar Turk, or Serb-hating Macedonian, or even a crazed Serb? As a matter of fact, there are respected scholars who reject Rakich's accusation, among them Milorad Jankovic, Kosovar writer Mark Krasniqi, and historian S.S. Juka in the United States. Juka says firmly: "...there is irrefutable proof that this act was not committed by any Albanian" (see her book, *Kosova*, pp. 45-46). Krasniqi, for his part, is convinced that Rakich had ulterior motives when he penned those unkind words. He says that the Serbian poet set out purposely to depict Albanians as vandals.

Q. No. 7—*Is the sword the religion of the Albanian people?*

It seems that one of the favorite pastimes of the Serbs is to portray Albanians as a martial, gun-happy race. Hence, we are not surprised to read in *The Saga of Kosovo* that the Albanians have a "famous saying": *Ku është shpata është feja* ("Your faith is where your sword is") (p. 49).

We are to infer from this, apparently, that people who are "fascinated by guns"—to use the authors' phrase—and who make a religion of arms, can easily turn to violence and vandalism, since they have no higher code of conduct to hold their hand, or guide them along a more humane path.

We wish, however, to point out to Dragnich and Todorovich that the Albanians, like the Serbs and the Greeks and others, have numerous other sayings that tell all sorts of things about their beliefs and practices, even some sayings that contradict the one they chose to offer to the reader. For example: *Më mirë të dish se të kesh* (knowledge is better than money; literally, "Better to know than to have"). *Më mirë të të dalë syri, se nami i keq* ("Better to lose an eye than your good name"). *Tek është dashuria, është vetë Perëndia* ("God is where love is"). We ask: Are these sayings any less significant or characteristic of Albanians than the

the one they chose to publicize? Many foreigners who know the Albanian people would answer "No."

Q. No. 8—*Was there an Albanian national uprising against the Turks?*
   In the book under review we are told that there was no such uprising in Albanian history (p. 86). Such an affirmation, it seems to us, is not history but fiction. It is a vain attempt to perpetuate, in our day, the Serbian myth that the Albanians, being in league with the Turks, did not fight to throw off Turkish dominion. But anyone who is familiar with Albanian history, and reads that history objectively, knows that this is not so. For the benefit of Dragnich and Todorovich, we present below a list of Albanian uprisings against the Turks that took place between the death of Scanderbeg (1468), and the founding of the League of Prizren (1878), which marks the beginning of the final phase of resistance against the Turks prior to Albania's independence in 1912.

   1495—Rebellion bursts out in central Albania.
   1509—Uprising in the Highlands of northern Albania.
   1537—Rebellion of the Himariots in southern Albania.
   1701-1704—Rebellion throughout Albania.
   1708—Beginning of a three-year rebellion in central Albania.
   1787-1796—Rebellion of northern Albanians led by Kara Mahmut.
   1811—Uprising of northern Albanians led by Mustafa Pashë Bushatliu.
   1822—Rebellion in southern Albania led by Zylyftar Poda.
   1834—Rebellion in central Albania for the liberation of Berat.
   1835—Rebellion in the north under the leadership of Hamza Kazazi.
   1843-1845—Uprising in Kosova, Shkup, Tetovë and Dibër.
   1847—Rebellion in Kurvelesh engulfs all of southern Albania.
   1854—Rebellion erupts in Shkodër, northern Albania.
   1863-1865—Struggles against Turkish expeditionary forces sent to crush rebels in Shkodër, Kosova, and Dibër.
   1867-1868—Struggles against Turkish expeditionary forces sent to crush rebels in Lumë and Gjakovë in the north.
   1873—Struggle against Turkish expeditionary force sent to crush rebels in the Highlands.
   1876-1877—Rebellion in the Mirditë region in northern Albania.

We end our list here, but in the next three decades there were another dozen uprisings, culminating in the general uprising in the summer of 1912 that ended in a decisive victory for the Albanians.

Q. No. 9—*Was there an Albanian nation in the 19ᵗʰ Century?*
Not according to our authors. Let us refer to their book. In the 19ᵗʰ Century, they say the "Albanian nation…was yet to be formed" (p. 86). Why do they think so? Because, unlike the Slavs and the Greeks, "With three religions, two strikingly different mentalities (Tosk and Gegh), and no common alphabet…or written culture of their own," the Albanians were not in a position "to articulate (their) national identity" (p. 83).

This is another myth the Serbians have energetically diffused abroad, to persuade an unwary world that the Albanians had no clear idea of their nationality, and lacked a common national ideology and goal. It's a myth Europe accepted a century ago—witness the remark of Bismarck at the Congress of Berlin (1878) that "There is no Albanian nation." But the world is much wiser today, and is not likely to accept as genuine coin the anachronistic thesis of Dragnich and Todorovich. It is a pity that they saw fit to resurrect the ghost of the "Iron Chancellor," instead of letting it rest in peace.

We should like to inform them that religiously, the Albanians have a fine record of tolerance and respect for each other's creeds, that northern and southern Albanians (i.e., Tosks and Gheghs) are quite close in their thinking, and although Albanians did not have a common alphabet in the last century, they did have a literary tradition, and an old one at that, reaching as far back as the Middle Ages. The first extant book published in Albanian, *Meshari,* (The Missal) , bears the date 1555. In the centuries that followed other books in Albanian were published by such authors as Pjeter Budi, Frano Bardhi, Pjeter Bogdani, Jul Variboba and others.

We might also add that the Albanian nation is coextensive with the areas populated wholly or largely by Albanians who speak the same language and share a common national and cultural heritage. The authors of the *Saga of Kosovo* confuse the concept of nation with the concept of culture, and a narrow concept at that, as if the culture consists merely of the literary heritage of a people.

Q. No. 10—*Were the Albanians ready for independence in the 19th Century?*

No doubt by now the reader knows what answer to expect from our authors. Still, in the interest of precision, we should like to give their answer in their own words. They say: "With no... centuries-long resistance (to the Turks) to feed their fortitude, Albanians (were)... totally unprepared" for the struggle toward independence (p. 48). Elsewhere they say the Albanians "were not culturally ready" for independence, and furthermore "they had no cadres to do the necessary work" that would lead to independence (p. 83).

As for the charge that the Albanians have an unsatisfactory report card on the subject of resistance to the Turks, we believe we have already clarified that point under Question Number 8. And under 9 we feel we have established that Albanians were, and are a people with a culture of their own, which they cherish no less than the Serbs cherish theirs.

The argument about the lack of cadres is just as flimsy. It's an argument that has a familiar ring to it. We heard it often enough, after the Second World War, from those in the West who opposed granting independence to peoples in Africa, on the grounds that they lacked educated and trained personnel and wouldn't know how to govern themselves. History has already delivered its verdict on the newly-independent African people, and in the case of Albanians it did so much earlier, in the second decade of our century. But apparently Dragnich and Todorovich refuse to accept the verdict, and prefer instead to debate the point, almost as if they thought they could reverse history's verdict.

Q. No. 11—*Were the leaders of the movement for Albanian independence genuine nationalists?*

Certainly not, answer Dragnich and Todorovich. They never tire of making comparisons between Serbian nationalist leaders and their

Albanian counterparts, comparisons that show the Albanians in a very poor light, indeed. They belittle and scorn Albanian patriots as counterfeit nationalists who were alienated from the Albanian masses. We are told that "...they were so remote" from the people, they "could have been Scandinavians" (p. 97). They roamed all over Europe, for the "fragrance of European cities was overpowering for the sheep-herding Albanians" (p. 97).

This is not only bad history, it is gratuitous sarcasm. Besides, what is so disgraceful about the sheep-herding profession? We are of the opinion that Albanian shepherds, like their Serbian counterparts—of whom there were quite a number in the last century—were decent people and honorable patriots.

So enamoured are the authors of Serbia that they present the Serbian national movement as the model which should have guided Albanians, as well, on their road to independence. They seem incensed that the stubborn-headed Albanians chose a different path to independence.

Elsewhere in their book, Dragnich and Todorovich write: "Most of the protagonists of Albanian national awakening lived separated from their homeland... Albanians made history in Constantinople and not in Tirana" (pp. 84-85).

True enough, Albanian nationalists leaders lived abroad, but by necessity, not choice, since their homeland was under Turkish occupation and agitators for independence were severely punished. Albanians made history not only in Constantinople, but in Sofia, Bucharest, Cairo, Italy and the United States—wherever it was possible for them to work for their country. Precisely because they labored abroad under trying circumstances, all the more credit is due them for their fortitude, their discipline, their whole-hearted dedication to the cause of Albania.

Q. No. 12—*Was Kosova liberated or occupied in 1912-13?*

In the introduction to their book, the authors say that they propose to tell the reader "how Serbia... liberated Kosovo in the Balkan wars

(1912)" (p. 3). And they achieve this a hundred pages later, when they relate how Turkey was defeated by the Balkan allies and "Kosovo was free!" (p. 101) . In another passage in the book we are told that a candle was lit in the Serbian Monastery of Dechan in Kosova to mark the liberation of the region.

What the Serbs call liberation is what the Albanians call occupation and annexation of Kosova by Serbia. This annexation amounted to a hefty chunk of the territories that comprised the Albanian nation. Dragnich and Todorovich object, saying that Skoplje (Shkup), Prishtinë, Tetovë and other towns were not "on Albanian territory proper" (p. 87). But if we look at the map of the Balkans at the time, we find that Albania comprised four vilayets: Janina, Manastir, Shkodër, and Shkup, and the latter vilayet included the towns of Shkup, Prishtinë, and Tetovë.

From the Albanian perspective, therefore, the candle in the Monastery of Dechan signified a memorial light over the grave of Kosova, and not its liberation.

Q. No. 13—*What is the meaning of Kosova for the Serbs?*
Our authors tell us that all Serbs "have (Kosova) in their blood. They are born with it... it is a transcendental phenomenon" (p. 4). From the Serbian viewpoint, Kosova is not simply a geographical entity, but a matter of the blood, a phenomenon that defies reason and logic. We need hardly point out that this is not the sort of language one normally finds in the discourse of historians. This is rather the language of irrationalism and mysticism that serves not to enlighten but to confuse and confound the reader. The citation does, however, serve a purpose. It offers insight into the intransigent mentality of the Serbs on the question of Kosova.

Q. No. 14—*Did Yugoslavia attempt to displace Albanians from Kosova?*
In *The Saga of Kosovo* we read that, between World War I and II, "the official policy of the Belgrade government was to encourage... Albanians to leave (Kosova)," and some 40,000 of them did leave (p. 121).

In the quotation above we find a glimmer of objectivity on the part of the authors, which we welcome. But the term "encourage" is hardly the right word to use in speaking of Yugoslavia's policy on Albanian ethnics. For that policy consisted of pressures of the worst sort—intimidation, terror, violence—in order to drive the Albanians out of Kosova. The record shows that in June, 1938 Yugoslavia signed an agreement with Turkey to send over there a quarter of a million Albanians from Kosova (official Yugoslav propaganda organs said the actual number to be expelled was 400,000), and it was only the intervention of World War II that prevented Yugoslavia from carrying out this plan. (See Thomas A. Roth, *Yugoslav (Socialist) Rule in Practice: A Survey of Developments in the Kosovo Region*, M. A. Thesis, Institute of International Studies, University of Oregon, 1970, pp. 23-24.)

Q. No. 15—*Is Dibër a Yugoslav or Albanian city?*
There is an interesting story in this book about Dibër (Debar in Serbo-Croatian). It appears that during WWII (1941), one of Tito's top aides, Svetozar-Tempo Vukmanovich was in Dibër. Reporting on his visit there, he wrote: "…all over the place Albanian flags. One would think that he is somewhere in Albania, not Yugoslavia" (p. 141).
Precisely. Vukmanovich was indeed on Albanian territory, in a town peopled overwhelmingly by Albanians. And what he said about Dibër he could have also said about Kërchovë, Prilep, Prizren, Pejë, Gjakovë, Ulqin—in short, nearly all the towns in Kosova (which, in the Albanian view, includes a large part of Macedonia and Montenegro). It is unfortunate that Vukmanovich and the Tito leadership did not acknowledge this fact when they seized power in Yugoslavia, and allow the Albanians the right of self-determination which, incidentally, they had promised them more than once in the past. Had they done so, the history of postwar Kosova would have been different. Very likely there would be no Kosova problem to worry about today, and the list of international flash-points would have been reduced by one item.

Q. No. 16—*What caused the 1981 riots in Kosova?*

According to the authors, they were caused by "a wild bunch of youth" in the cafeteria of the University of Prishtinë, who "began demolishing everything they could get their hands on" and creating a disturbance, which later took on a political character (p. 165). Earlier in the book the demonstrators are referred to as "people who look upon themselves as Albanians" (p. 1).

We must say that we were not impressed by this explanation. On the contrary, we are astonished that two historians who profess to be objective could offer such an explanation to their readers. This is not a scholarly analyses of the root causes of the bloody riots, but a superficial and unhistorical approach that falls short even of published accounts of the riots by respected journalists.

And what do the authors mean when they refer to the demonstrators as "people who look upon themselves as Albanians"? The whole world knows that they were Albanians, so it is nothing strange that they see themselves as Albanians. Do not the Croatians and the Macedonians and Montenegrins and other ethnics in Yugoslavia do likewise—see themselves as they are, which is to say acknowledge their nationality?

Q. No. 17—*Have the Serbians or the Federal authorities in Yugoslavia intervened in the affairs of Kosova?*

Dragnich and Todorovich would have us believe that the answer is "No". Neither the Serbian nor the federal authorities have intervened in Kosova's affairs, they write, "aside from establishing a military presence" there. (p. 176).

But is it not intervention when a peaceful demonstration by the Kosovars is violently suppressed by armed Yugoslav forces using tanks and helicopters? When Albanians, including teenagers, are arrested, tried and given long prison sentences simply for asking for republican status for Kosova? When numerous books on Albanian history and literature are banned from circulation? When it is considered a crime for Albanians to pay homage to their national figures? The proper term to describe such actions by Serbian and federal authorities is not just "intervention" but persecution and oppression.

Q. No. 18—*Who is responsible for vandalism to Serbian religious shrines in Kosova?*

According to *The Saga of Kosovo*, the culprits are the Albanians. The book's authors dwell at length on this issue that has generated intense emotional feelings—one might even say near-hysteria—on the part of the Serbian public, and great hostility toward the Albanians. At one point they give a two-page long list of acts of aggression and vandalism that were committed, they claim, by Moslem Albanians against Serbian churches and clerics in Kosova over a 13-year period (1969-1882) (pp. 170-171).

Albanians have consistently denied these allegations. Far from damaging or destroying Serbian churches or properties, Moslem Albanians have been the guardians of those churches for centuries. It's a matter of historical record, they claim.

The interesting thing is that Dragnich and Todorovich themselves agree with this, when discussing Serbian holy places in another part of the book. They talk about "respect among Albanians for the Serbian holy places" through the centuries (p. 52), and about Albanians paying visits to Christian homes on Christian holidays and attending Christian weddings and baptismal ceremonies. They note, too, that Albanians provided "guard services to the (Serbian) Patriarchate in Pech and the Dechani Monastery" (p. 52).

One is prompted to ask: Aren't they contradicting themselves here? How do they reconcile this view with their accusation of Albanians as church vandals and muggers of Serbian nuns and priests? Their answer—as implied in the pages of their book—is that Albanians were respectful of Serbian holy places in the past, but that lately they have changed and resorted to violence against those places. This is not a convincing argument. Unless the Serbs are able to document their charges with more credible evidence, we have to conclude that those charges are spurious or so minor as to be insignificant, and as such deserve to be thrown out of court. We have to believe that the evidence of the centuries is more weighty than the allegations of Albanian vandalism over a dozen years.

Q. No. 19—*Are the Albanians in Kosova living in the past?*

Dragnich and his colleague claim that they are. And they grieve that "many Albanian children (are) growing up in an ethnic prison," because of their misguided teachers, as well as the incompetence of Albanian leaders in Kosova (pp. 177-178).

It is ironic to hear this from historians who are steeped psychologically and emotionally in Serbian Medievalism, and who seek through this book to keep alive every vestige of that world—which they affectionately call "Old Serbia"—in the hearts and minds of the Serbs. Overall, it is the Serbs and not the Albanians, it seems to us, who are "living in the past." Do not the authors say that Serbians "have Kosovo in their blood"?

As for Albanian children in Kosovë, we fail to see that teaching them about Albanian history and Albanian national figures and literature and folklore is tantamount to putting them in an "ethnic prison." We ask: Why is it all right for Serbian children to learn about the grandeur of Mediaeval Serbia, but wrong and chauvinistic for Albanian children to learn about their national and cultural heritage? Some Albanian children are, indeed, in prison in Kosova—not however in an ethnic prison, but in grim prisons of stone and steel, put there by Yugoslav authorities because they shouted a slogan or scribbled words on a wall that the government condemns as manifestations of Albanian nationalism.

Q. No. 20—*Will the Serbs "invade" Kosova?*

In the last chapter of their book, titled *The Future*, Dragnich and Todorovich write: "Some ask, can Serbia and Montenegro abandon their nationals to the mercy of the Kosovo Albanians? And, is it possible that one day, Serbia and Montenegro may feel bound to join forces and invade Kosovo, as they did against the Turks in 1912?" (p. 179).

How is the reader to interpret this passage? Well, from the Albanian point of view, the first question in the passage has to be turned the other way around, in order to make sense. For it is not the Serbs (with some possible exceptions), but the Kosovars who are the victims in Kosova. It is they who are at the mercy of the Serbs inasmuch as the Serbs have held the reigns of power there for the better part of a century.

As to the second question, are not the authors guilty, at least, of committing an error in logic here? How, we ask, can a country invade itself? We have been taught that it is an improper use of English to speak in this fashion. Yet, the mere fact that the authors use such language in the passage above, shows the poverty of their thought as far as offering any plausible solutions to the problem in Kosova. It's an indication also of the murderous measures the Serb mind is apparently contemplating as a way of "pacifying" Albanian nationals and "solving" the Kosova problem. Furthermore, what need does Serbia have to invade Kosova? The region is already occupied territory, with some 30,000 Yugoslav army troops stationed there since 1981, ready to open fire on the defenseless population at any given moment.

Q. No. 21—*What has been the role of the Slavs in the Balkans?*

In the far past, that role has been very dubious and open to criticism. We have this on the authority of Dragnich and Todorovich themselves. Writing about the era of Byzantium, they say: "Byzantium had very little reason to cherish the Slavs in the Balkan areas... because they proved to be a nuisance from the time of their arrival" (p. 6). Why were they a nuisance? Because the "Slavs exploited the troubles (of Byzantium) to expand and solidify their positions" (p. 7).

We hasten to commend the authors for their integrity on this point, and only wish they had shown the same integrity on questions dealing with Kosova in our time. Had they done so, they would have to admit, we think that the policy of expansion pursued by the Slavs in the days of Byzantium did not cease with the demise of the Byzantine Empire. It was very much alive in the last century, as it has been in our century as well, and the Albanian nation and people have been among the leading victims of that policy. Is it not time for the Serbs (who have been the chief offenders in this regard) to rethink their role in the Balkans, and revise their policy toward Albanians, particularly those in Kosova?

*   *   *

In summing up, Dragnich and Todorovich had an opportunity to offer a fresh and potentially useful scenario for dealing with the issues in Kosova. Unfortunately they missed that opportunity. Their book is actually a step backward, for it is hardly more than a eulogy of Serbia and a strident justification of Serbian control and dominion in Kosova. The book suffers from corrosive bias and contradictions, and is embittered by sarcasm and contempt for Albanians. Such a work is certain to be welcomed in Belgrade, where anti-Albanian feelings these days are running rampant. But scholars and impartial readers cannot but turn thumbs down on it. A book pervaded by hostility toward an ethnic group, as is *The Saga of Kosovo*, runs counter to the time-honored American tradition of respect and justice for all ethnic groups, and counter also to norms of civilized behavior cherished by all humane beings throughout our planet.

Chapter 13:

*Relationship between Yugoslavia and Albania**

(A publication of the *Review of International Affairs*)

The first thing that occurs to the reader of this book is that it is mistitled, for the book is not primarily about Yugoslav-Albanian relations but about Yugoslav policy on Kosova, home of over two million Albanians in Yugoslavia. One half of the chapters in this 300-page volume, and some two-thirds of the textual mater are devoted exclusively to Kosova, and barely one-third to relations with Albania.

Concern and anxiety over Kosova was the real reason for the publication of this book. Like so many other books published recently in Yugoslavia, this work too is a product of the Spring 1981 demonstrations of Albanian ethnics in Kosova. This is apparent in the Foreword to the book which speaks of "... the causes and consequences of the nationalistic, irredentist and counter-revolutionary events of 1981 in Kosovo."

And what were the causes of that rebellion, which made Kosova and the plight of the Albanians in Yugoslavia a newsworthy issue of world wide scope? Here, in this book, *Relationship Between Yugoslavia and Albania*, we are given the Yugoslav version of the story in its clearest form. We are told that three factors played a role in the events of 1981: One, the rebellion was the work of illegal organizations, linked in most cases with groups abroad that aimed at the "establishment of a so-

---

* Source: *Albanian Catholic Bulletin*, Santa Clara, California, USA, Vol. VII & VIII (1986), pp. 86-89. Published under the pseudonym of "Osumi." – Author's note.

called ethnically pure Kosova and its annexation to …Albania." These organizations sought to coerce Serbs and Montenegrins in Kosova to leave the province, in line with their objective to make Kosova a Republic. A second factor that contributed to the rebellion was "the policy pursued by the political leaders" of Kosova, which objectively encouraged "a nationalistic and separatistic movement" on the part of the Albanian population. Thirdly, Albania itself was "linked in various ways with the irredentist and counter-revolutionary groups in Kosova," in pursuit of its long-cherished design to annex Kosova so as to create "a so-called Greater Albania" (pp. 8-9). The Kosovars and Albania, of course, reject those tenets as false and provocative and tending only to justify the discredited policy of Belgrade on Kosova.

Comprehensive Survey of Kosova

The longest and in many ways the best chapter in the book is the first one, by R. Rajevic, who is identified as "a Serbian judge." This chapter of nearly a hundred pages—one third of the entire book—is a comprehensive survey of Kosova, both past and present. Much research went into the making of this informative chapter. The rest of the chapters and materials on Kosova are largely commentaries and elaborations on the data and analyses presented in this chapter.

Rajevic states a number of important truths about Kosova's past: He notes that the "original inhabitants" of the province were Albanians (p. 13); that the emigration from Kosova in 1690, led by the Serbian Patriarch Arsenius, included not only Serbs but Albanians as well (p. 14); that the Serbs "terrorized… the Albanian population" in 1912-13, causing the victims to rebel (pp. 17-18); that the "agrarian reform" in Kosova during the 1930s was not settled fairly, since land was taken away from the Albanians and given to Serbs and Montenegrins, an injustice that incited the Albanians to rebellion, and "the army had to be called in" to restore order (pp. 20-21); and that the oppression of

Albanian ethnics at the time "went as far as deportation to Turkey" (p. 20).

Rajevic admits that the Serbs and Montenegrins were "a comparatively privileged portion of the population" in Kosova prior to WWII. He blames the oppression of the Kosovars in prewar Yugoslavia on the "greater Serbia bourgeois regime" (p. 38). It is one of the major themes of this book to attribute the deep-seated resentments of the Kosovars to the unjust rule of the Serbian bourgeoisie. That is the reason, Rajevic says, why Albanian ethnics viewed the collapse of Yugoslavia in 1941 as something positive, and the occupation of the country by the Germans and the Italians as liberation "from the Serbian occupying powers." That explains also why comparatively few Albanians (only about 4,000) joined Tito's Partisan forces during WWII (p. 54), and why no more than 15 percent of the members of the Yugoslav Communist Party in Kosova—or Kosmet (*Kos*ova and *Met*ohija, as the region was then called)—were Albanians, even though the Albanians accounted for two-thirds of the population at the time.

According to this book, the majority of the Albanians did not understand Tito's liberation movement, and as a result created "difficult conditions" for the movement in Kosova. Indeed, they did. Rajevic reveals significantly that none of Tito's five battalions and other army detachments that were organized in Kosova—predominantly with Serbians and Montenegrins—were able to operate on the territory of Kosova, so great was the distrust and opposition of most Albanians to the Slav-led communist movement (pp. 50-51). It was not until the last two months of the war in Kosova (Oct.-Nov. 1944), that Tito's National Liberation Army was able to fight on the soil of Kosova, and then only after the arrival of the 3rd and 5th Army Brigades from Albania to assist the Yugoslav Army (p. 52). Yet, even after Kosova was liberated from the Germans in November, 1944, Tito's forces had to fight an army of 10,000 "counter-revolutionary Ballists" (Albanian nationalists) for several months, until April 1945, before taking over control in the region (pp. 53-54, 133). Kosovar elements in exile claim that the Yugoslav army slaughtered about 60,000 Albanians during that operation. Such was the ill-omened beginning of communist Yugoslavia's rule in Kosova.

Bujan Resolution to Join Albanian

We have to say that we are impressed by Rajevic's objective and forthright account of the history of Kosova before WWII. With some exceptions, his account of events in Kosova during the war is likewise valid. He discusses the famous Bujan Resolution of the Albanians in Kosova (Dec. 31, 1943-Jan. 1-2, 1944), in which they expressed their desire "to unite with Albania," and let it be known that they were joining the struggle against the Germans only in the expectation that Kosova would unite with Albania after the war (p. 65). An excerpt of that Resolution is given in this book.

Unfortunately, the moment Rajevic—and other contributors to this volume—begins to discuss postwar Kosova, he switches roles, and is no longer the detached scholar but a partisan writer, using language and logic that is hardly distinguishable from that of a political agitator. He is anxious to convince the reader that, regardless of the Bujan Resolution, Kosova decided in July of 1945 to become a constituent part of the Republic of Serbia, and this action "freely expressed the will of the population" (p. 76). This is another major theme in this book, which echoes through its pages like the pronouncements of a Greek chorus on the stage of classical Greece.

But is this not too much to ask of the reader? Is it reasonable to believe that the Kosovars, after adopting the Bujan Resolution, after rebelling against Tito's takeover of Kosova, and after losing tens of thousands of lives in the rebellion, would freely consent to join their conquerors? We can believe that the Serbs and the Montenegrins in Kosova gave their consent to unite with Serbia, but surely not the majority of the Albanians who made up the overwhelming portion of the population in the region.

It is fairly evident that the thrust of this argument—namely, that the Kosovars joined with Serbia of their own free will—is to discredit the demand of the Albanians in Yugoslavia for a republic of their own, by showing that there is no political, constitutional or legal ground for such a demand. But such an argument cannot carry weight with those who are informed about Kosova, or even with the uninformed who are in possession of their logical faculties.

In fact, the cardinal objective of this book, as we see it, is to bury, under a barrage of words, the claims for a Republic of Kosova. Rajevic, for example, denounces the idea as "an irredentist watchword." Jovan Rajicevic, who has a chapter on the "Greater Albanian Pretensions of Enver Hoxha," calls the idea an "absurdity" and "ill-fated watchword" (p. 244). And Dr. Ivan Kristan, who devotes a whole chapter to the constitutional position of Kosova in Yugoslavia, rejects the idea on the ground that is "only a preliminary step to... the annexation of Kosovo to Albania" (p. 162). He says categorically that "...one cannot expect any basic changes in the constitutional position" of Kosova (p. 168).

Question of National Equality

A chief argument in this book against making Kosova a republic, and in favor of maintaining the *status quo* in the province, is that "the Albanian nationality enjoys complete equality" with the other ethnic groups in Yugoslavia (p. 10). It is an argument that is repeated *ad infinitum*. Indeed, the entire book is in large part an endless legalistic and pedantic discourse on the equality and the human rights that the Albanians allegedly enjoy in Yugoslavia. Rajevic tells us that the Kosovars have "achieved complete affirmation" of their nationality (p. 87), and Dr. Kristan adds that their "national culture is flourishing" (p. 161). In support of this claim, the book offers a stack of statistics to show the achievements of Kosova since the war in economic development, education, health, culture and so on. And it is true that Kosova has made progress, by comparison with prewar conditions in the province. But it is equally true that its rate of development has lagged behind the rest of Yugoslavia, and as a result Kosova is worse off today, in relation to the rest of the federation, than it was in 1945.

Much of the argument for the equality of the Albanians is based on the Constitutions of Yugoslavia, Serbia, and Kosova, all of which guarantee to the Kosovars equal rights with other citizens in the federation. And so they do... on paper, for in theory those constitutions are quite democratic and humane. Indeed, this book would have us believe that the Yugoslav Constitution is the most advanced in the world, superior even to those of France, the United States and other Western societies (p. 182). Concerning the nationality problem, we are told that the Yugoslav solution to this problem is "without precedent in history" and represents "the supreme attainment in social practice... known in the world today" (p. 90). The implication is that the national minorities have no grounds whatsoever for complaints or discontentment in Yugoslavia.

But as the Kosovars can testify, and the findings of Amnesty International make evident—not to mention other human rights groups in the West—the Yugoslav government is in practice dictatorial and repressive, and no amount of academic and legalistic discourse can conceal that fact. Were it not so, why did the Albanians rebel in 1944, 1968, and riot in 1971, and 1974, and 1979, and rebel again in 1981, at the cost of numerous lives? Contented citizens do not risk imprisonment and loss of life and limb without good and sufficient cause.

Perceptions and Remarks on Albania

Not much need be said about Albania in this account since, as we said earlier, this work focuses attention primarily on Kosova. In fact, much of the discussion on Albania, too, relates directly to Kosova.

Perhaps the best of the four chapters on Albania is that of Dr. Ranko Petkovic. His study of the era of friendly relations between Yugoslavia and Albania (1945-1948) is liberally documented and informative. There is considerable data on the diplomatic, political and economic support that Yugoslavia gave to Albania at that time, as for example, at the Paris Peace Conference in 1946, and on the issue of Albania's application for admission to the UN.

Unhappily, Petkovic suffers an abrupt and dramatic loss of perspective when he moves on to a discussion of the post-1948 period in Yugoslav-Albanian relations. He becomes thoroughly defensive regarding Yugoslav policies. It's apparent, at least to us, that this distortion of perspective has its roots in the Yugoslav obsession—for it is really an obsession—with the Kosova question. He claims that the Albanian leadership first allied itself with Stalin, and later with Mao Tse-Tung, to gain support for the plan to create a Great Albania by annexing Kosova (pp. 277, 280). He then goes on to accuse Albania of seeking to destabilize Yugoslavia by "instigating a nationalist-irredentist conspiracy in Kosovo" (p. 284).

This is pretty much the tone and level of discourse adopted in other chapters on Albania. In all of them the late Enver Hoxha, Albania's leader for over 40 years, is the target of bitter attacks. He is denounced as the architect of the 1948 break with Yugoslavia, and the instigator of Albanian nationalist fervor and disorders in Kosova. Elsewhere Albania is attacked as a Stalinist, bureaucratic and dogmatic country, while Yugoslavia is represented as a model socialist country, based on the unique principle of Self-Management. Readers would not be mistaken if they conclude that, on the whole, this book is self-serving, breast-beating, myopic and chauvinistic.

Most of the criticism of Albania, however, is not persuasive, since it amounts to little more that name-calling. It is rather like the pot calling the kettle black, since in most cases the same criticism—such as violations of human rights—can be laid at the door of Yugoslavia, as well. The majority of the contributors to this book hold doctoral degrees. But this is not readily apparent, for the quality of the writing in these pages is uneven, often illogical and simplistic and, in a word, below the standards expected of serious scholars. This is regrettable, but perhaps not so surprising, since the sponsor of this book, the Review of International Affairs, is an information organ of the Yugoslav

Government, whose express mission is to influence public opinion abroad in favor of Yugoslav foreign and domestic policies.

The book, moreover, is defective as a work of printing. There are many errors of dates and names in it, plus word omissions and misprints of words and entire sentences.

Despite the incessant attacks on Albania and the Albanians in Yugoslavia, this book ends with an appeal for friendship and cooperation between Yugoslavia and Albania. That is a sentiment we applaud. But our overall assessment of this work is not favorable. Far from it. We are of the opinion that this book does not serve the cause of peace and justice in Kosova, nor the cause of friendly Yugoslav-Albanian relations. Rather than contribute to the solution of the Kosova problem or the improvement of Yugoslav-Albanian relations, this book tends to cloud the issues and perpetuate the dangerous *status quo* in the area. In essence, it is an *apologia* for Belgrade's intransigence on Kosova and the oppression of the Albanians in Yugoslavia. And as long as that is the case, it is not reasonable to expect a radical or meaningful improvement in the relations between Yugoslavia and Albania.

Chapter 14:

Yugoslavia Continues Oppression of Albanians *

Developments in recent months in Albanian-populated areas of Yugoslavia, known collectively as Kosova, told of continuing persecution of Albanian nationals for alleged political and ideological crimes. Albanians in Yugoslavia, now estimated to number 3 million (about as many as the population of Albania proper), are concentrated in the province of Kosova, which is a constituent part of the Republic of Serbia, and in the two adjacent Republics of Macedonia and Montenegro. Late reports on Kosova emanating from Yugoslavia showed no signs of change in Belgrade's hard-line policy toward Kosovars. On the contrary, they are hounded relentlessly, in open violation of their ethnic and human rights, not only at home but abroad as well, including these United States.

The Case of Pjetër Ivezaj, U.S. Citizen

Pjetër Ivezaj, 30, is an American Citizen of Albanian descent living in Sterling Heights, a suburb of Detroit, Michigan. Born in a town near Titograd, Montenegro, he has been in the U.S. since 1972. He is married and works as a technician in the Detroit Public School system. In the summer of 1986, Ivezaj, accompanied by his pregnant wife and

---

* Source: *Albanian Catholic Bulletin*, Santa Clara, CA., USA, Vol. VII & VIII (1986-87), pp. 73 – 81. The full title in the original text: "Kosova update: Yugoslavia Continues Oppression of Albanians at Home and Abroad."

their daughter, took a trip to Yugoslavia to visit relatives. He arrived there on July 9, was questioned shortly after by the Yugoslav secret police, and arrested and imprisoned on August 19 because he had taken part in a 1981 demonstration in Washington D.C., to protest Yugoslavia's treatment of ethnic Albanians.

Ivezaj's arrest and ordeal was picked up by the media in the U.S. about six weeks later, and created a sensation. Although there have been several other Albanian-Americans from Kosova who have been arrested by Yugoslav authorities when visiting relatives, none of them generated so much interest, or aroused as much concern, as the detainment of Ivezaj. For two weeks, from late September to mid-October, his case made front-page news in the Detroit press, and was widely reported in other major newspapers in Washington, Boston, New York and elsewhere.

Ivezaj's trial began on October 3 in Titograd. He was accused of being a part of an "association that aimed at carrying out hostile activities" against Yugoslavia. On October 8 the court sentenced him to seven years in prison. Citing his involvement in the Washington demonstration, the court said that such demonstrations "were directed against the Yugoslav constitutional order and aimed at overthrowing its communist system," (*Detroit Free Press*, Oct. 4 and 13, 1986). The charge was a clear reference to the demand that Kosova be made a Republic within the Federation of Yugoslavia. U.S. Embassy officials in Belgrade complained that Yugoslav authorities refused to let them see and talk to the prisoner prior to his trial.

Ivezaj's arrest and trial was called "an outrage" by officials in Washington. Rep. William Broomfield of Michigan addressed the House of Representatives, saying; "Mr. Speaker, if you are searching for justice, stear clear of Yugoslavia." He then asked: "Where are the humanitarian concerns of the authorities in that country?" (*Congressional Record*, Vol. 132, No. 133, Oct. 1, '86). Rep. Philip Crane of Illinois said the Yugoslav agents who spy in our country on U.S. citizens are "creeps and slimebags" (*Detroit News*, Oct. 9, '86).

There were threats from lawmakers in Washington to sever U.S. relations with Yugoslavia.

Nor did the lawmakers limit themselves to verbal threats alone. Rep. Broomfield, a member of the House Foreign affairs Committee, supported by Gus Yatron of Pennsylvania and Rep. Gerald Solomon of N. Y., both of whom serve on the House Sub-Committee for Human Rights introduced a bill in Congress to suspend Yugoslavia's "most-favored nation" trade status, if Pjeter Ivezaj were not released forthwith. Their initiative was backed up by 150 of their colleagues in the House. Michigans's Sen. Carl Levin and Sen. Donald Riegle, asked the Senate Foreign Relations Committee to open an investigation into Ivezaj's "deplorable" case. Similarily, Rep. Dennis Jertel of Detroit, together with 15 Congressional colleagues, addressed a letter to President Reagan, urging him to intervene in the matter.

The message U.S. officials were sending got through quickly to Belgrade. One day after being sentenced, Yugoslavia released Ivezaj from prison. Relieved and happy, Ivezaj commented: "I went through a nightmare." He would not give any details while he was still in Yugoslavia, but members of his family in Detroit had said earlier that he had been tortured by the Yugoslav police during his investigation.

Pjeter Ivezaj lived through a terrible ordeal. But his suffering has served, perhaps better than any single incident involving Albanians in Yugoslavia, to educate our leaders in Washington and the American people about the true nature of the Yugoslav regime --one of the most repressive in the world today. If Yugoslavia can abuse an American citizen in this fashion, we leave it to the reader to imagine what it does to the defenseless Kosovars, who are arrested with impunity, and under the cloak of secrecy, hidden from the glare of publicity, are persecuted without mercy, and not just occasionally but routinely, systematically, without letup.

Commentary of a U.S. Congressman on Yugoslavia

The case of Pjeter Ivezaj inspired a most interesting commentary by congressman Jim Courter of N.J., a member of the House Armed Services Committee. The commemtary, titled "Sending Belgrade a Signal," appeared in *The Washington Times* on October 28, 1986. Portions of the commentary are given below.

"Americans must have been ill-prepared for Belgrade's arrest of several U.S. citizens for anti-Yugoslav political activity, especially when the politicking occurred *in America* (emphasis in text).

"Two generations of Western university professors, politicians, and diplomats have so intrigued us with Yugoslavia's break with Stalin and worker management of Yugoslav industries that most Americans view that country as a model of humane Communism, gentle at home and non-aligned abroad. Billions of dollars worth of Western aid and credits have created an unspoken need to preserve the image.

"But sometimes it takes the unwarranted arrest of one of us abroad —one such is Pjeter Ivezaj of Michigan—to make us see a government through the eyes of its subjects.

"As a rule, Belgrade uses the fullness of its police powers, including punishment in psychiatric hospitals, against dissenters. By official admission, hundreds have been sentenced to jail in recent years for political activities.

"Such persecution has never stopped at the Yugoslav borders, and the arrest of an American for joining a demonstration in Washington D.C., six years ago should be less surprising than it was.

"The control the ruling League of Communists holds over the country's centrifugal ethnic and political forces constantly requires reassertion. Denunciation of political opponents as 'fascists' and 'irredentists' has become a commonplace.

"Emigrés who are politically active have become an obsession of the regime, and it appears that the SDS, or Yugoslav secret police, has been deeply involved in killings and intimidations abroad.

"In the United States, there is evidence of extortion, provocation within émigré circles, and even murder. There is still more evidence of violence in Western Europe. Five anti-Communist activists were murdered in Munich during the first half of 1969. A Croation exile, Professor Cizek, was abducted in Yugoslavia a few years ago. Three Serbians...were killed in Sydney, Chicago, and Vienna within a few days this February."

Congressman Courter comments also on Yugoslavia's Libyan connection. He says:

"The Libya/Yugoslavia alliance is something no one in Washington ever talks about. But it lies just below the surface of much of the news.

"Libya has purchased Yugoslav arms, including aircraft and naval vessels. According to a new issue of *Der Spiegel*, Libyan pilots are receiving training in MiG-21s in Yugoslavia as part of an arrangement to pay off the latter's oil debts.

"Little wonder that the journalist and Yugoslav expert Nora Beloff describes Belgade's foreign policy in a new book as 'non-aligned against the West.'"

Congressman Courter ends his commentary with a thought-provoking suggestion.

"Perhaps it's time to take a good hard look."

We agree. Indeed, this is what the Albanians in America have been urging for years, so that our officials in Washington may see Yugoslavia as it is in reality, a dictatorship that has only contempt for the principles on which our country was founded and lives by.

Developments in Kosova and Yugoslavia

Since late 1985 Albanians in Yugoslavia have come increasingly under attack from a four-pronged drive of government authorities, the intellectual establishment, the media, and Serbian activists.

An ominous burst of anti-Albanian feelings occurred in October of 1985, when 2,126 Serbs in Kosova addressed a petition of grievances against the Kosovars to the authorities in Belgrade, urging immediate action against Albanian "chauvinists" and "Fascists". The Serbian petitioners cried out that they were "exposed to violence" by Albanians "unknown to history in peace time in the cradle of our homeland," namely, Kosova; and that "part of Yugoslavia has been occupied" by Albanians who are exerting "brutal pressure" on Serbians and their families, and vandalizing their properties, graveyards and holy places. The petition called for the banning of the Albanian flag in Kosova and charged moreover that 30,000 Serbs in Albania "are exposed to the darkest terror" (The 1979 Albanian census counted a total of 4,163 Slavs in the Country).

The petition is a sad example of Serbian atavistic hostility toward Albanians, and a vivid manifestation of the frenzy that has overtaken Serbia since the Kosovar demonstrations in 1981. Even sadder, however, is that fact that the petition was supported by the Belgrade-based Committee for the Defense of Freedom of Thought and Expression, a group founded in November, 1984 by prominent academics and other public figures. In January, 1986 the committee addressed an appeal to the Federal Assembly expressing total agreement with the Serbian petitioners. The appeal is phrased in such violent language that is difficult to believe that it came from academics dedicated to serving reason and truth. The appeal accused the Albanians of "committing genocide" in Kosova, but offered no evidence to back up the accusation. It noted that "some 200,000 people were moved out of Kosovo" over the past 20 years, falsely implying that the Albanians were responsible for it, instead of deteriorating economic conditions in the province and many others reasons, largely personal in nature. The appeal called for "an end to the internal undermining of Yugoslavia's frontiers" – an indirect attack on the just demand of the Kosovars for a republic of their own within the Federation. Perhaps the most surprising statement in the appeal of the academics is the claim that: "There is no national minority anywhere in the world which enjoys greater constitutional rights (than the Albanians in Yugoslavia)".

Well, let us see how the Albanians are enjoying those constitutional rights. And since no one is better qualified to speak on this point that the Albanians in Yugoslavia themselves, we shall let a Kosovar spokesman take the floor. We shall refer the reader to an interview which the Kosovar scholar, Rexhep Qosja, gave early this year to the Slovenian paper *Delo*. Following are excerpts from the interview of Dr. Qosja:

> "In Macedonia it is now forbidden to give children Albanian names connected with Albanian history and culture, as for example, Kastriot, which is the surname of the renowned Albanian warrior of the 15th century, Scanderbeg. The names Liridon and Liridona (which mean "freedom-lovers" in Albanian – our note) , have also been declared as unsuitable or unlawful, and the reason given is that they express the desire from freedom! This is like forbidding the names of Slobodan or Slobodanka in Serbian or in Croatian, or Libertino in Italian.
>
> "Off limits also are the proper names Viosa and Tomor (names of a river and a mountain in Albania – our note). This is the same as preventing the use of the names Vardarka and Drinka (both proper names deriving from two rivers in Yugoslavia – our note).
>
> "Of 600 Albanian folk songs that have been broadcast until now over radio stations in Macedonia, 570 have been banned because they 'promote Albanian national spirit'. Yet, the majority of those songs are about love and marriage, and about people who go abroad to earn their living.
>
> "At present Albanians in Yugoslavia do not have cultural contacts with Albania (they are not allowed to do so – our note). This is truly an anachronism not only on Europe, but in the entire world. Within a day one can travel, for example from Belgrade or Tirana to Tokio, Sao-Paulo or any other city in the world. Men have even gone to the moon... but they cannot go from Prishtina (the main city in Kosova - our note) to Tirana in Albania, or from Tirana to Prishtina... Scholars in Kosova cannot obtain literature on Albanian studies, books, newspapers or magazines from Albania or, for that matter, from any other country." (The above excerpts were translated from the Alnanian text that was printed in the Albanian daily *Zëri i Popullit*, March 5, 1987).

Such are the "constitutional rights" Albanians enjoy in the Federation of Yugoslavia. The above is but a sample of the daily indignities and suffering to which Albanians are subjected in Yugoslavia. Early in this year reports from Yugoslavia told of bulldozers breaking down scores of walls that surrounded the houses of Albanians living in Macedonia in towns like Tetova, Kerchovë, Gostivar, Stugë, Dibër, Kumanovë and others. Civilized people will no doubt be shocked at this news, but Yugoslav officials have their reasons. We are told that the bulldozers were turned loose by the authorities because they viewed those walls—a traditional architectural feature of Albanian homes—as "divisive symbols and great obstacles to interethnic solidarity". Did the authorities suspect that plots were being hatched behind those walls to undermine the social order in Macedonia and the Federation? The campaign to raze the menacing walls targeted the destruction of 2,716 walls of Albanian homes in the city of Tetova alone (See *Liria* biweekly, Boston, Jan. 15, 1987). One wonders whether there are any limits to the destructive frenzy of anti-Albanian elements in Yugoslavia.

Anti-Albanian Proceedings of Yugoslav Party Congress

In late June of 1986, the Communist League of Yugoslavia (LCY) held its 13th Congress in Belgrade, and a part of the proceedings was devoted to Kosova. Unfortunately, nothing positive, in our view, came out of the deliberations on this question. Basically the congress reiterated ideas that have by now grown stale and proved to be useless and counter-productive.

The congress took note of the "continuing unfavorable trends" in the province, meaning that there is still trouble in Kosova, that the region has not been "pacified" and Kosovar dissent has not been crushed. The congress said that "the sources of Albanian nationalism and irredentism have not been stamped out," which is to say that Kosovars continue to nourish and manifest their Albanian awareness, Albanian consciousness, Albanian spirit and identity. The congress complained that "not enough has been done to eliminate... the indoctrination of young people in Kosovo with Albanian nationalism," which translated means that still harsher measures will be taken to weaken and emasculate, if not eradicate entirely, the teaching of the Albanian language, literature, history and folklore to Albanian children and youth.

The congress let it be known that the "process of ideological-political differentiation" in Kosova has "not been completed," which in plain English means that witch hunts and persecution of Albanians for demanding their ethnic and human rights will be pressed relentlessly, with callous disregard for the suffering of the victims. The congress again rejected the idea for a republic of Kosova, calling this a plot to destabilize and break up the Yugoslav Federation—one of the more prominent myths currently clouding the thinking of the Yugoslav leadership in connection with Kosova. Continuing its tirade against the Albanians, the congress accused Kosovar activists of striving for an "ethnically pure" Kosova, purged of Serbs and Montenegrins, though we have never seen any evidence to support this accusation.

Much was said at the congress about developing Kosova's economy and one of the ways to promote development is "family planning." "Kosovo's population policies must be attuned to the general efforts...in favor of the Province's more rapid development," the congress said. This is Belgrade's convoluted way of saying that Albanian women are giving birth to too many babies, which only aggravates the province's economic woes—a thesis that is far from proved.

The congress was constrained to admit, however, that "of late Serbian and Montenegrin nationalism have intensified" in Kosova, and went on record as opposing those who denounce "the Albanian nationality as such."

The LYC Congress also advocated "strengthening all forms of informational, political and educational work among (Yugoslav) citizens abroad," which properly interpreted means that Yugoslav agents will continue to intimidate and terrorize Kosovar and other opponents of the Yugoslav regime in the U.S. and other countries.

In brief, the congress did not move Yugoslavia a single inch out of the quagmire it has created for itself in Kosova (The proceedings of the LYC Congress were published in the June-July, 1986 issue of *Socialist Thought and Practice*; the sections on Kosova are on pp. XXIX-XXXI, and 172-185).

Serbian Nationalism on the Move

New anti-Albanian actions took place in Yugoslavia throughout 1986 and 1987 encompassing the media, academic conferences, and street rallies and marches. In March of 1986 about one hundred Serbs from Kosova traveled to Belgrade to register complaints against the Kosovars; and in June, 1986 several hundred Serbs from the village of Batuse in Kosova took to the streets to protest "persecution" by Albanians. But the biggest action of this kind to date occurred on April 24, 1987 when a crowd of 10,000 to 15,000 Serbs and Montenegrins staged a rally in Kosovo Polje, a town near Prishtina, to complain about Kosovars to the chief of the Serbian Communist Party who was visiting in town (*New York Times*, Apr. 25 and 26, '87).

Serbian nationalists worked overtime in the drive to arouse public sympathy for their position in Kosova by pointing their finger at the Albanians and yelling "Villains!" But as an old Albanian proverb says "You cannot hide the sun with a sieve." Commenting on the Serbians' charge that Albanians are harassing and driving them out of Kosova, and committing genocide against them, an Albanian observer, Bajram Tonuzi, writes:

> This is the stuff of science fiction; it's an accusation that has no basis in fact, since it is well known that the Serbs have on their side: the local and federal legal apparatus, the police network, the army, the press, the various information media, the chief administrative posts as well as the chief economic and social managerial positions in the region... What they would like us to believe is tantamount to saying that the Germans, during their military occupation of France in 1940-45, were

victims of persecution by the French. Let us admit that this makes no sense at all."
(*Koha e Jonë*, Paris, Jan-March '87. p.28; translated from the French).

The excesses of Serbian activists were too much even for a top-ranking Yugoslav party official. Speaking in Prishtina on November 5,1986 the official, Stipe Suvar, said: "Serbian nationalism has indeed had a finger in what has been going on in Kosovo, encouraging Serbs and Montenegrins to stage protest rallies, to go to Belgrade to seek justice and protection, to emigrate collectively and to propagate ideas to the effect that Albanians are aliens in Kosovo..., that all people in positions of authority in Kosovo are in the service of the irredentist movement of traitors, and so on" *(Socialist Thought and Practice*, Oct-Dec. '86 issue, p.19).

The above remark represents a glimmer of objectivity on Kosova that is all too rare on the part of Yugoslav officialdom. But much more of that sort of realism is needed to check the Serbs, who seem bent on turning the clock back in Kosova. The thesis they defend is, in our view indefensible, for it reverses completely the roles of the victim and the oppressor in Kosova. It reminds us of La Fontaine's fable, "The Wolf and the Lamb." The wolf decided to eat the lamb, but needed an excuse to carry out his dark plan. So he presented himself as a victim of the lamb, and made all kinds of false accusations against him: "You've spoiled my drinking water, your brother or your father has insulted me" and so forth. When the lamb refuted all of his accusations, the wolf stopped "arguing" his case and pounced on the innocent creature.

The fact is, the Serbs are bitter and angry not because they are persecuted by the Albanians, but because they are no longer enjoying the degree of power, prestige and well-being in Kosova that they have been accustomed to for generations. The loss of their former position of absolute supremacy in the province—as in the days of Rankovich, for example—has traumatized and disoriented them. Instead of admitting that the plight of the Albanians in Yugoslavia is real and indeed intolerable, they prefer—as they have done for generations -- to take still harsher measures against them for daring to ask for their rights and seeking to improve their lot.

Reportage and Comment on Kosova in Albania

The Albanian press reacted to the Serbian petition of October, 1985 by calling it "ultra-nationalist" and evidence of hysteria on the part of the Serbs. According to Tirana, the petition aimed to bring back the bygone times of the Serbian monarchs and A. Rankovich, perpetrator of genocidal acts against Albanians in Yugoslavia (*Zëri i Popullit*, Feb. 11, '86). Commenting on the 13th LCY Congress, an editorial in the same paper (dt. July, '86) said the congress demeaned the Kosovars and that "the resolution (it) adopted on Kosova, leaves the two million Albanians in Yugoslavia at the mercy of the Great Serbians," that is, imperialist-minded Serbians striving to expand Serbia's borders and power at the expense of other peoples. The Yugoslav policy toward the Kosovars, the editorial said, is a blind alley that can only aggravate the many problems facing the Federation.

At the 9th Congress of the Albanian Party of Labor, held in Tirana in early November, 1986, a number of delegates made references to the question of Kosova. A woman delegate from Mirdita said: "We are incensed when we hear that the Great Serbians prohibit our sisters, the brave Kosovar mothers, from giving their children the time-honored names of Kastriot, Shqipe, etc. But let them not forget history, for just as no Sultan was able to defeat Kastriot, so no bolt of lightening can shear off the wings of the *shqipe* (eagle)."

The most extensive comments on Kosova at the congress came from Ramiz Alia, leader of Albania. His views on this subject were anxiously awaited by Yugoslav authorities who were eagerly hoping for a change of policy in Albania. Alia however threw cold water on such hopes. He said that "a grave situation has been created in Kosova" by Yugoslavia. The autonomy of the province, he said, is being gradually eroded, the teaching of Albanian is being restricted, and the historical and cultural traditions of the Kosovars are being impaired. The persecution of Albanians in Yugoslavia, is taking on the character of "a true inquisition." "We cannot reconcile ourselves to this situation," he continued. He advised Yugoslav authorities to abandon the use of force in Kosova, and seek instead to solve the problem calmly, through reason, by eliminating the cause of the problem, which are internal in nature and of Yugoslavia's own making, and avoid blaming them on external agents and forces (*Zëri i Popullit*, Nov. 4 '86. p 14).

On December 27, 1986 an ATA (Albanian Telegraphic Agency) dispatch told of a conference of Yugoslav historians in Belgrade at which a Kosovar, Fehmi Pushkolli, complained that history in Yugoslavia is being politicized, and that "everything Albanian, from ancient times to the present, is being presented in a negative light." Even Illyrian rulers, such as King Agron and Queen Teuta, are being dragged into the present conflict and associated, somehow, with "irredentism"—one of the more recent products of the Serbian penchant for myth-making. In early March of this year, Albania observed the centennial of the founding of the first Albanian school. But unlike Greece and Italy, Yugoslavia refused to allow educators and cultural leaders in Kosova and Belgrade to travel to Albania to attend the commemoration (*Zëri i Popullit*, March 5, '87). Referring to the recent events in Kosova Polje, Albanian sources said that foreign observers interpreted those events as a new escalation of Serbian nationalism, orchestrated by Serb activists who are seeking to mobilize all of Yugoslavia in their offensive against Albanians.

Albanians Abroad Demand Justice for Kosova

The unsettled and unsettling question of Kosova continued to engage the attention and energies of Albanians abroad: In America, Canada, West Europe, Turkey, Australia and other countries. In a variety of ways they presented the case of the Kosovars before the court of world public opinion. This was important political work that helped to refute the generally misleading stories given out on Kosova by Belgrade's information agencies.

Demonstration in Detroit and Chicago

On September 7, 1986 a large group of Albanians demonstrated in Detroit against the Yugoslav Festival, heretofore an annual event in that city. The *Detroit Free Press* reported that about 500 people took part in the demonstration, which also included Croatians opposed to the Yugoslav regime. Leaflets handed out at the demonstration said that "almost 3 million Albanians in Yugoslavia are living in conditions similar to those of the Jews under Hitler". The demonstrators accused the Yugoslav government of pushing drugs into the U.S., and facilitating the transportation of illegal aliens into America by way of Mexico. They also called for a national boycott of the "Yugo Car" and a Congressional investigation into the activities of Yugoslav secret agents in the United States.

On April 2, 1987 Albanian-Americans staged another demonstration, this time in front of the Yugoslav Consulate in Chicago. The demonstration, organized by the League of Kosova (*Lidhja Kosovare*) demanded the release of all Albanian political prisoners in Yugoslavia, who number in the thousands, far out of proportion to the Albanian population in Yugoslavia. Those attending the demonstration also heard speeches by Rev. Hafiz Isuf Azemi and Mustafa Henci, top-ranking officials of the league of Kosova.

Activity of "Kosova Watch" groups—Meanwhile Albanian "Kosova Watch" groups continued to give strong support to the Kosovars. In December, 1986, the Albanian patriotic club, "Jusuf Gervalla" in N.Y. drafted a Memorandum denouncing proposals in Yugoslavia to alter the Albanian flag so as to suit the political prejudices of Yugoslavia's leaders—predominately Serb ones –in disregard of the feelings of the Albanian population. The memorandum said: "Hands off the arbitrary proposal to alter our national Flag." Copies of the Memo were sent to the leaders of Yugoslav Federation and the authorities in Kosova and the republics. The issue of the flag prompted another Memorandum by a group that signed itself, The Albanian Communities in the United States and Canada. Dated January 20, 1987, the Memo was addressed to the UN Secretary General, noting that "a member of this organization (Yugoslavia) seeks to destroy the flag of another" and wipe off "the most important symbol of our cultural and ethnic identity and unity." The Memo solicited the aid of the Secretary General to stop Yugoslavia from oppressing "an ancient and proud people."

A press release of the New York based *Albanian League of Prizren* dated September 19, 1986, announced the inauguration of a new radio program in N.Y., called "The Voice of Kosova." The announcement said that the program, scheduled to broadcast weekly for about an hour, intended "to make known...to American public opinion the tragic situation in Kosova."

In keeping with a decade-old tradition, in September, 1986 the Albanian Kosovar Youth in the Free World addressed a Memorandum to the UN Secretary General entitled "On the Persecution and Violation of Human Rights of the Albanian population in Yugoslavia." In the same month, the organization published a small volume, *The Plight of Ethnic Albanians*, containing valuable source material on the history and nature of the Kosova dispute. The volume serves as a useful antidote to the Serb version of the dispute.

The League of Kosova, veteran organization (founded in 1949) and staunch defender of the Kosovars, continued its tireless struggle in the streets of America, in the corridors of diplomats and in the forums of international organizations. In October , 1986 a delegation of the League, headed by Rev. Hafiz Azemi, participated in the congress of the Federation of Minorities in Europe that was held in Klagenfurt, Austria. The delegation presented a Resolution condemning Yugoslavia's repression of Albanian nationals, which was unanimously adopted by the congress. On January 20, 1987, another delegation of the League, this one led by Prof. Luan Gashi, the League's General Secretary, traveled to Washington, D.C. to meet with members of Congress. The delegation had useful talks on Kosova with Sen. Alan Dixon and Sen. Paul Simon (both from Illinois), and Rep. Joseph Dioguardi (N.Y.). Yugoslav officials have become quite nervous about the work of the League of Kosova. Early this year the Prishtina daily attacked the League as a group of extremist exiles hostile to the Yugoslav Federation, proof that that work of the League is effective.

   Albanian press activity—The Albanian press in America and abroad gave wide publicity to the cause of the Kosovars. The list included the newspaper *Dielli* and *Liria* in Boston, the *Vineyard,* organ of the Albanian Orthodox Church in America, which is also published in Boston, and the *Albanian Catholic Bulletin* in Santa Clara, California. Much interesting material appeared in Albanian publications in Europe, among them *Flamuri* in Rome, and *Qindresa Shqiptare* in Paris. The latter carries concise summaries of developments in Kosova. The quarterly *Koha e Jonë*, which is published in Paris featured materials on Kosova in every issue, including the fiery patriotic broadcasts of Hiqmet Ndreu on Radio Melbourne in Australia. In Holm, Sweden, another publication, *Youth* (an "independent Albanian historical-cultural magazine"), printed strongly pro-Kosovar articles in Albanian, Swedish and English.

   Kosova activists in U.S. and Canada —A number of Albanians in America worked conscientiously to secure the rights belonging to Albanian nationals in Yugoslavia. In the forefront of the struggle were the leaders of the League of Kosova, and Dr. Sami Repishti, president of the Kosova Relief Found, U.S.A. In September, 1986 Dr. Repishti met with Vice President of the United States, George Bush, in New York, and had a brief talk with him about Kosova. The Vice-President expressed his appreciation to Repishti for his views and praised his work as a human rights activist. Dr. Repishti also presented a petition to Mr. Bush describing the plight of the Kosovars and proposing ideas for breaking the stalemate in the province. (For the text of the Petition, see *Liria*, Feb 15, '87).

   Other activists were Dr. Elez Biberaj, a senior official with the USIA; Maliq Arifaj, executive secretary of the Albanian Kosovar Youth In the Free World; Tahir Kermaja in N.Y.; Peter James of Jamestown, N.Y., lecturer; Hasan Risila in Philadelphia, Pa.; Prenk Gruda and Ekrem Bardha, Detroit, Michigan; Adrian Gjinaj and Duro Cini in Canada; Ali Gjidiu, an informed and perceptive writer, Zeqir Berisha,

Waterbury, Conn; Zef Shllaku, San Francisco; and Din Kosova in Palm Springs, California. Needless to say, many other Albanian men and women in America and Canada worked energetically behind the scene to help their co-nationals in Yugoslavia.

The intense activity of Albanians abroad on behalf of their suffering compatriots in Yugoslavia has begun to trouble the authorities in Belgrade. It seems they fear the success Albanian activists are having in turning world public opinion around in favor of the down-trodden Kosovars. A TANJUG dispatch from Belgrade (Feb. 11 '87) complained that some West European countries "have not shown understanding for Yugoslav stands" for they "tolerate the subversive propaganda activity of hostile Albanian groups..." This is indeed a cause for concern for Belgrade, for until now Yugoslavia has had a green light in the propaganda battle against Albanians, and as a result managed to lead astray the media, intellectuals and government officials world-wide. Henceforth, it seems, Belgrade will be trodding a bumpy road in its efforts to mislead world public opinion on Kosova.

U.S. and Foreign Press on Kosova

Articles on Yugoslavia and Kosova appeared in the recent past in many publications in America, among them: the *Christian Science Monitor*, the *Washington Post*, the *Wall Street Journal*, and the *New York Times*. Both major papers in Detroit, the *Detroit News* and the *Detroit Free Press* gave excellent coverage to the Pjeter Ivezaj case. Pjeter himself published a letter to the editor of the *Washington Times* in which he said that Yugoslavia is a police state, and the UDBA (the Yugoslav secret police) "did its utmost to recruit me...to spy on Albanian and Croatian dissidents" in the U.S. In Waterbury, Conn., Zeqir Berisha published several letters to the editor in the *Waterbury Democrat* to inform readers about Kosova.

Overseas, the impasse in Kosova made news in the *Frankfurter Allgemeine Zeitung*, in the form of a number of revealing articles by Viktor Meier, an expert on Yugoslav affairs. In an article on December

23, 1986 Meier wrote: "It is suspected that the issue of migration (of Serbs from Kosova) is being used as a political lever to liquidate the autonomy of the province." Elsewhere he wrote that "the tendency of the Serbs to react in an irrational manner" appears to be aggravating existing problems in the province. Developments in Kosova were reported in the pages of the *Spectator* of London, the *Kayham International* of Teharan which criticized Belgrade's treatment of Albanian Moslems, and the Italian paper, *Il Tempo*, which in late June of this year ran a series of articles that showed understanding and sympathy for the Albanian position, in part perhaps because Italy has had its own problems with Yugoslavia over Trieste.

Books and other studies on Kosova —Apart from *The Plight of the Ethnic Albanians* mentioned earlier in this update, a number of other studies explored the issue of Albanians in Yugoslavia. Foremost among these is the book on the *House of Representatives Hearing on Kosova* in October, 1986 (of which more later on). This is a significant publishing event, in the sense that it's the first U.S. Government publication to deal specifically with the violation of human rights by Yugoslavia of its Albanian population. The publication can be obtained from the U.S. Government Printing Office in Washington, D.C. ($2.50 per copy). Interesting, too, is the book, *Human Rights in Yugoslavia*, edited by Gruenwald and Rosenblum-Cale (Irvington Publisher, Inc., N.Y. 1986), which has an enlightening chapter on Yugoslavia's Albanians by Dr. Sami Repishti. Another book on Yugoslavia entitled, *Nationalism and Federalism* in Yugoslavia, 1963-83 (1984), by Dr. Pedro Ramet, has an excellent section on Kosova (pp. 156-171).

The *East European Quarterly* (March '87) carried an article, "Kosovo: A Tragedy In the Making," by Prof. Nicholas J. Costa of the great Hartford Community College. This is a stimulating study based in part on interviews with people like Milovan Djilas, Vukmanovich Tempo, Dr. Elez Biberaj, Anton Logoreci and others. Significant studies on Yugoslavia, with much interesting material on Kosova, appeared in the Spring-Summer, 1986 issue of the *South Slav Journal* (London), an influential scholarly publication. The same journal published a highly favorable review of the book, *Studies on Kosova,* by Pipa and Repishti (eds.), in its Spring, 1987 issue.

Croatian Support for the Kosovars

As in the past, Croatian elements in America and West Europe gave powerful support to the cause of ethnic Albanians in Yugoslavia. News about Kosova accompanied by thoughtful commentary, appeared in almost every issue of the information bulletin, *That's Yugoslavia,* which is published in Hamburg, W. Germany as an English supplement to the Croatian magazine, *Hrvatska Domovina.* Two issues especially relevant to Albanians are those of December, 1986, and April 1987, which discuss Albanian political prisoners in Yugoslavia and the situation in Macedonia where Albanians, numbering at least 400,000, are treated even more harshly than in the province of Kosova.

The *CNC Repor,'* organ of the Croatian National Congress, published numerous reports, news items and analyses on Albanians in Yugoslavia. The April, 1987 issue of the Report carried an account of a speech that Dr. Mathew Mestrovic, CNC President, had given recently in Strasbourg, France, at a convocation of the European Parliament, in which he made several references to the Kosovars. Among other things, he said: " . . . the 2,000,000 Albanians in Yugoslavia must be granted the right to self-determination and republic status" (p. 10). Other Croatian publications such as *Nova Hrvatska* and *Hrvatska Drzava,* which are printed in England and Germany, extensively covered developments in Kosova. Their reporting was sympathetic to the plight of Albanians in Yugoslavia.

Meanwhile, other Croatian human rights activists in the U.S. aligned themselves with the Kosovars. Two of these are Marija Ann Levic, Executive Director of the group, Human Rights in Yugoslavia; and Joseph Vrbich, Coordinating Director of the Northern California Alliance for Justice in Yugoslavia. Both of them wrote excellent letters, in defense of the Albanians in Yugoslavia, to editors of influential papers like the *Washington Times* (July 15, '86), the *Christian Science Monitor* (Dec. 10, '86) and the *San Francisco Chronicle* (Dec.27, '86). Ms. Levic pointed out that "The tragedy of Albanians in Yugoslavia is that they are the victims of Serbian ultranationalism and supremacy". Mr. Vrbich wrote along similar lines.

Congressional Hearing Held on Kosova

We conclude this update on Kosova with an account on an encouraging development in our nation's capital. On Wednesday, October 8, 1986 a hearing was held on Albanians in Yugoslavia before the Sub-Committee for Human Rights in the U.S. House of Representatives, the first time such an event has taken place in Congress. The hearing was chaired by Rep. Gus Yatron of Penna. The immediate cause of the House inquiry was the arrest and detention in Yugoslavia of Pjeter Ivezaj. It appears that the initiative for the hearing was taken by Rep. Williams S. Broomfield of Mich., whose lively concern for justice and readiness to help the victimized Albanians have won the respect and gratitude of Albanians throughout the country.

In addition to Mr. Broomfield, the hearing heard testimony from Rep. Joseph Dioguardi of N.Y., who also introduced a Resolution in the House of Representatives "Condemning the repression of ethnic Albanians by the Government of the Socialist Federated Republic of Yugoslavia." The Resolution is a fine summation of issues in Kosova, which deserves to be framed and hung in the living room of every Albanian home in America, and kept there until the day Kosova has gained its full rights.

Others who testified were Ekrem Bardha, Chairman, Albanian American Republican Clubs of America; Prof. Albert M. Tosches, Salem State College in Mass.; Prof. Sami Repishti of Adelphi University, N.Y.; and Prof. Pedro Ramet, University of Washington in Seattle, Wash., and the Kennan Institute for Advanced Russian Studies, Washington, D.C.

Having in mind the ordeal of Pjeter Ivezaj, Mr. Bardha said in his testimony: "Can the United States permit a foreign communist country to dictate to American citizens which of their constitutional rights (such as the right to demonstrate) they can or cannot exercise?" Prof. Tosches (who it turns out, is an Arbëresh) testified that he did not view the demand for a Republic of Kosova as a threat to the political system of Yugoslavia, but rather as an opportunity for that country to further its goals "for the social and economic and political equality of all her people."

At this point, Rep. Philip Crane of Ill. intervened to make a stinging attack on Yugoslavia, following which the hearing continued with testimony by Prof. Repishti, well-known activist and expert on Kosova. Repishti began by describing in detail the disheartening situation in the Albanian-populated areas if Yugoslavia, and concluded with a proposal that an American Consulate be opened in Prishtina, in the belief that the American presence in Kosova would generate a feeling of security among Albanians, reduce existing tensions and "contribute to the political stability of the region, and consequently of Yugoslavia itself." Prof. Ramet, who has written extensively on Yugoslavia, suggested that the U.S. send impartial consultants to Yugoslavia, with a view to initiating a fruitful dialogue on Kosova. He also endorsed the idea for an American Consulate in Prishtina. (For further details on the hearing, see *Dielli*, Oct. 16, '86 and *Liria*, March 15, '87).

The Albanians of America respectfully commend our government leaders for their support of the brave and unbowed Kosovars. We trust that in the future they will broaden and intensify their support of this ethnic and human rights issue, until the matter is finally resolved to the benefit of all parties concerned: Albanians, Serbs, Montenegrins and others.

*   *   *

We end on a light social note. When Rep. Broomfield returned home to Michigan last October, following Ivezaj's release from prison in Titograd, he was given "a hero's welcome" by the Albanians in the Detroit area. The Congressman was greeted with bouquets of flowers, embraced, applauded, and thanked heartily by members of Ivezaj's family. For over an hour he socialized with several dozen Albanians, eating and drinking in a warm festive atmosphere, with toasts of "Gëzuar!" ("Cheers!") coming to him from every side.

Said Broomfield, "In my 30 years in Congress I've never had such a reception. It is unbelievable." (*Detroit News, Detroit Free Press*, Oct. 12, 1986).

ADDENDUM—Last minute bulletin from Yugoslavia

Just as we were winding up this update on Kosova, it was reported that Branko Mikulic, Premier of Yugoslavia since 1986, has resigned his post. According to the report, Mikulic was driven to that decision by the growing economic crisis in the country (brought on by galloping inflation, labor unrest, and mounting foreign debt), and above all by the impasse in Kosova.

As far as we are aware, this is the first time in the history of the Communist world that a premier of a Communist country has voluntarily resigned his post. It is to be hoped that Mikulic's resignation will have a salutary effect on the future of Kosova.

Chapter 15:
*Position Paper on Kosova**

A proper and potentially useful analysis of the Kosova question suggests:

1. Determining or identifying the root of the problem.
2. Examining the history, aspirations or demands, and present position of the Kosovars.
3. Defining Serbian policy on Kosova.
4. Appraising the role of Albania on Kosova.
5. Taking account of the bearing of world public opinion.

1. Determining the root of the problem:

The root of the problem in Kosova is Serbian control of the province.

The root of the problem is Serbian refusal to grant republican status to Kosova.

The root of the problem is Serbian racism toward Albanians.

The root of the problem is incorporation of Kosova into the Serbian Republic in 1945.

The root of the problem is the severance of Kosova from the Albanian nation in 1913 by the Great Powers of Europe.

Each one of these can be taken as the root cause of the problem in Kosova, for it is the same problem viewed from different perspectives.

---

* This paper was drafted in March of 1988. Afterward it was circulated among a few Albanians intellectuals in the U.S. for comments and criticism. It is being published here for the first time.

Each one of these, therefore, holds the key to the solution of the problem. The resolution of any one of them would mean a resolution of the problem.

2. History, aspirations and positions of the Kosovars:

The history of ethnic Albanians in Yugoslavia is at heart, one of alienation. Being a non-Slavic people, they feel they have little or nothing in common with the Slavs of Yugoslavia. Being Albanians, they identify with their compatriots in Albania historically, culturally and spiritually. This identification is in essence nationalistic in nature, and is bound up with the very existence and continuity of the Albanian nation. This sense of identity and solidarity derives both its force and meaning from the past—and a very long past, at that—and has little or no bearing on the present political system or social order in Albania.

The Kosovars identified with Albania when the country was a monarchy under King Zog in the 1920's and 1930's. And they have, by and large, identified with her in the postwar period: that is to say, with Albania under Stalinist Enver Hoxha. This orientation will in all likelihood persist no matter what government or individual rules Albania at a particular time, for the Kosovars know that governments and political systems come and go, whereas the Albanian nation and people, language and culture, customs and traditions—which express the spirit and essential character of the nation—remain and live on from one generation to the next.

It is quite natural therefore for the Kosovars to formulate policies and undertake actions that are identical with those of their compatriots in Albania. Hence, the adoption by the Kosovars of the unified literary language of Albania in April, 1968. Hence, the adoption by them in early October, 1968 of the Albanian flag as the national symbol of Kosova. Seen from a national frame of reference, these actions were no different than their desire to commemorate Albanian national anniversaries, honor the patriots of the Albanian nation, teach the literature and folklore of the Albanian people, and preserve Albanian customs and traditions—as Albanians do in the home country, and in Albanian settlements abroad, for that matter. All of them are expressions of the spirit and substance of the Albanian national and cultural heritage, which the Kosovars embody and strive to affirm as a distinct ethnic group.

In addition, there are compelling political reasons why the Kosovars turn their eyes toward Albania. Their life in Yugoslavia is a story of oppression, marked by political persecution, economic neglect, social discrimination, and cultural impoverishment. For the Kosovars, therefore, who live in the belly of the beast, Albania stands as a pillar of strength, and is a source of vital moral support in their struggle against their oppressors. In conditions of economic despair and police terror, Albania emerges in their sight as a beacon of light and, yes, freedom— NATIONAL FREEDOM! They are fully conscious that without a sovereign and independent Albania they would have no chance whatsoever of throwing off their shackles. Under the circumstances, Albania's public defense of their position is critical and, indeed, the greatest single source of external support for their cause.

Kosovar intellectuals have been in the forefront of the struggle to obtain ethnic and human rights for Albanian nationals in Yugoslavia. Knowing the risks involved, only deep devotion to their ethnic heritage and great courage could impel them to lead such an enterprise. In our view, they have acted correctly. In our view, no one knows better than they the situation in Kosova and what needs to be done, just as Albanian intellectuals in America can claim that they know best the situation of Albanian-Americans. In our view, the best service we can render to Kosovar intellectuals at this time is to make manifest our solidarity with them. As it is, they have their hands full trying to defend themselves from the brutal attacks of Serbian, Macedonian and Montenegrin intellectuals. They do not need criticism by fellow Albanian intellectuals.

3. Serbian policy on Kosova:

In considering Serbian policy on Kosova, we are guided by the over-riding fact that the Serbs are the oppressors there, while the Albanians are the victims. The initiative therefore for a salutary change on the issue has to come from the oppressors, for it is they who call the tune in Kosova. They are responsible for the conflict, since they created the conditions for it.

Unfortunately, the overall attitude of the Serbs toward Kosova is determined not by logic and dispassionate objectivity, not by the demographic realities in the province, not by human rights considerations, but by frantic passions, antiquated romanticism, myth and Medieval mysticism. This attitude is further perverted by their ingrained racism toward Albanians, and insistence on maintaining political supremacy in the province: in other words, keeping the Albanians underfoot.

It is true that in the last two decades, following the fall of Rankovic, Albanians in Yugoslavia made some gains in the direction of national affirmation. But Tito's policy on nationalities, however sound and democratic on paper, did not alter the Serbs' fundamentally racist and hostile attitude toward Albanians. Events in Kosova since 1981 have made this eloquently clear. The political climate in Kosova today is no different than it was in the days of Rankovic, or Pasic or Karadjorge in prewar Yugoslavia.

The current policy of Yugoslav authorities on Kosova is one of intransigence. It's a policy that rests on force and vindictive persecution of the defenseless Albanians. They have made it clear that:

1. They see Albanian nationalism as the problem in Kosova, rather than Serbian supremacy and control there.

2. They will not grant republican status to Kosova, for they see that as a first step to Kosova's merger with Albania, even though such a fear rests on speculation rather than on hard evidence.

3. They are intent on whittling away the hard-won ethnic rights of Albanians, instead of expanding them and defusing the tense and explosive situation that prevails in the province.

4. They continue to point the finger at Albania as the instigator of the conflict in Kosova, instead of seeing the conflict as the product of internal conditions, above all the constitutional subservience of Kosova to Serbia.

It is our opinion that these positions of Serbian and Yugoslav authorities, being counter-productive, should be reconsidered by Belgrade with a view to altering or abandoning them.

4. The role of Albania on Kosova:

Albania has publicly and consistently supported demands of the Kosovars for ethnic and human rights, claiming that they are legitimate demands, and that in backing the Kosovars she is acting in conformity with the Charter of the United Nations and other international agreements on the rights of minorities. Accordingly, Albania rejects Belgrade's charges of interference in Yugoslavia's internal affairs and complaints that she is the instigator of the unrest and turmoils in Kosova. Albanian authorities have repeatedly disavowed any intentions of seeking to destabilize Yugoslavia and attaching Kosova to Albania.

In our view, Albania's position on Kosova in the last two decades has been marked by restraint, in order not to aggravate relations with Yugoslavia and worsen the situation in Kosova. This is the reason, we believe, why Albania has not raised the issue of Kosova in the United Nations, and other international forums. In view of the Anti-Albanian hysteria in the Yugoslav media, Albania's policy of firm but restrained backing of the Kosovars is understandable and appropriate. Had Albania responded in kind to Belgrade's vehement attacks, Serbian extremists would, in all probability, have flown into a rage and a bloody clash on a massive scale would have already occurred in Kosova. That is just the sort of thing they seem to be looking for to justify a massacre of the Kosovars.

In the decade of the 1970's Albania and Kosova had close cultural exchanges, especially in the academic sphere. These exchanges generated much sympathy for Albania among the Albanians in Yugoslavia, above all among scholars and students. In the aftermath of the 1981 disturbances in Kosova, Yugoslavia charged that Albania took advantage of the cultural exchange program to infiltrate her ideology and politics among the Kosovars. In retaliation, Belgrade cut off all cultural contacts between Kosova and Albania. But this was a mistaken reading of events. In our view, the reaction of the Kosovars toward Albania was but another instance of identification with the Albanian people, rather than with Albanian Stalinism and atheism—except in a minor and unimportant way.

According to a recent report (*That's Yugoslavia*, Hamburg, December, 1987 issue), Tito approved the accelerated cultural exchange program with Albania after being convinced that Yugoslavia was going to emerge as the decisive winner in the exchanges. Tito apparently believed that Kosova could be used as a bridge to propagate Yugoslavia's brand of socialism in Albania. He was persuaded, according to this report, that "Albania would join with Yugoslavia" after Enver Hoxha died. As in previous instances, the Yugoslav leadership did not reckon correctly with the force of Albanian nationalism. As it turned out, Yugoslav socialism made no impact to speak of in Albania, whereas Albanian nationalism stirred the Kosovars to great depths.

We might summarize these observations as follows:

> 1. Whatever mistake she may have made in the past, Albania in recent years and at present is following a correct policy on Kosova.
> 2. Belgrade's accusation that Albania is responsible for the troubles in Kosova has not been documented. Neither has the accusation that she seeks to destabilize Yugoslavia.
> 3. It is a mistake, in our view, to attack Albania's position on Kosova. The cause of the Kosovars would be better served, we believe, if we focused our criticism on the oppressors of the Kosovars.

5. World public opinion and Kosova:

Many factors, both internal and external, determine the outcome of a conflict, and this holds also for Kosova. To some extent, at least, the success or failure of the struggle depends on the extent of support one gets from allies and friends abroad.

The Serbians have known this for a long time, and they have used it with great effect to the detriment of Albanians. Because of the Moslem faith of most Kosovars, they have tried to capitalize on that fact, in their appeals for political support from Christian Europe. They have depicted the Albanians as a divided and fragmented people: regionally, linguistically, religiously, socially, politically and so forth. They have zealously propagated the view abroad that Albanians are a people without culture, without a literary tradition, without a sense of national identity or unity. This campaign of denigration, which began before Albania gained independence in 1912, aimed at convincing public opinion abroad that Albanians are hostile, uncivilized and incapable of ruling themselves. The campaign had a clear political goal: to justify the detachment of Kosova from the Albanian nation in 1913, and prepare the ground for the total partition of the country, if possible.

The Serbian and Yugoslavian public relations department is no less active today in its efforts to conceal or distort the facts on Kosova. Emphasis is placed especially on two or three points: a) That the Kosovars are striving to make Kosova an "ethnically pure" Albanian province. b) That to bring this about they are pressuring the Serbs and Montenegrins to emigrate from Kosova. c) That their final goal is to secede from Yugoslavia and to join Kosova to Albania.

In fact, there is no persuasive evidence for any of these charges. Yet, Yugoslav officials, journalists and academicians have managed to flood the Western media with such claims, and unfortunately have succeeded in misleading numerous people, including diplomats, scholars and media outlets.

It stands to reason that a distorted picture of Kosova benefits Serbian extremists and their allies, and hurts that cause of the Kosovars. Moreover, a distorted picture of Kosova operates as a great stumbling block in the way of settling the conflict peacefully and with justice to all the parties concerned. In the worst case scenario, it can lead to a disastrous and hideous armed conflict in the province.

In the light of these remarks, it is important, in our view, to correct the distorted image of Kosova reality abroad. It is important to plead the case of the victims of Kosova, namely the Albanians, boldly, vigorously and without apologies. It is important to present the case of the Kosovars to the media, government officials, scholars and other parties so as to make their plight still more evident, and rally support for their righteous cause. It is important to show that the Kosovars, far from being aggressors, are in a state of passivity, devoid of real power and ultimate control over their affairs and destiny. In sum, it is important to make the point that *the Kosovars want merely to manage their own affairs, free of Serbian tutelage or supervision.*

Conversely, the fallacy and futility of the oppressor's position ought to be pointed out, as well as the danger it poses to peace and stability in Yugoslavia and the Balkans. The Serbs and their allies have it in their power to initiate an era of harmony and progress in Kosova, and good neighborly relations with Albania, once they banish the ghosts of fear and resentment of Albanians and accept them as equals. They should be encouraged to move in that direction.

In the drama of Kosova, the main actors are the people of Kosova themselves, led by their intellectuals who, in our view, are mature and serious—their scholarly and literary output is evidence of that—and who, moreover, have been tested and tempered by the fire of battle. We feel they can be trusted to chart their own course and choose their own weapons in the struggle to gain respect, equality and freedom in Yugoslavia.

At the same time, we trust that reason, the pressure of world public opinion and an enlightened sense of their own self-interest, will impel the Serbs and their allies to abandon the hard-line policy they have pursued to date, seeing that it has proved barren and holds no hope for the future.

San Diego, California
March, 1988

Chapter 16:
*Ethnic Albanians in a Disintegrating Yugoslavia**

On July 2, 1990, the Albanians of Kosova, Yugoslavia, numbering over two million, proclaimed their province to be a constituent part of Yugoslavia, equal in jurisdiction and status to the other parts of the Federation. The Proclamation amounted to a Declaration of Independence from Serbia, which exercises jurisdiction over Kosova, in opposition to the expressed will of the Albanians, who account for 90% of the population of the province. In effect, the Proclamation made Kosova the seventh republic of the Federation of Yugoslavia.

The Proclamation stunned and enraged Serbia's Communist chief, Slobodan Milosevic. The Serbian Parliament reacted by declaring the Proclamation null and void and dissolving Kosova's Assembly.

The July 2nd event offered the Serbs an excellent opportunity for a dialogue with Albanians, aiming toward a peaceful and amicable resolution of the Kosova question. Regrettably, they missed that opportunity.

Now, a year later, we find Yugoslavia well on the way to disintegration. But the pressures for disintegration did not come from the "secessionist" and "irredentist" Albanians in Kosova, as Serbia has so boisterously claimed for years and decades. They came instead from Croatia and Slovenia. Their cue for action, however, came directly from Kosova. For a decade they watched with growing concern and fear

* Source: ILLYRIA, English-Albanian semi-weekly, Bronx, New York City, N. Y., August 28, 1991 p. 10.

Serbian oppression of ethnic Albanians, and saw that as a preview of what was in store for them. To avoid the tragedy of Kosova, on June 25, last, they declared their independence from the Yugoslav Federation.

The armed conflict among Serbs, Croats, and Slovenes since late June has changed dramatically the political landscape of Yugoslavia. With 70 dead in Slovenia, and over 200 dead in Croatia (as of early August), the Yugoslav Federation has likewise become a casualty of the war. It cannot continue in its present form.

We might ask: Where does that leave the Albanians of Yugoslavia? In our view, events will force them to choose one of two options:

1) Autonomy within Yugoslavia, or
2) Secession from Yugoslavia

Autonomy within Yugoslavia is possible if the country is reconstituted as a Confederation, in which all the ethnic groups will function as self-governing political entities. Practically speaking, they will be independent states, bound loosely in a Confederation. Under such an arrangement, Kosova will be less than a fully sovereign state, but more than a republic—which is all that Albanians have sought up to now. Kosova will be as independent as Slovenia and Croatia are struggling to become, even at the cost of shedding blood, as Albanians have done for decades, though in vain—so far.

But is the first option possible to them? We doubt it. One can hardly expect the Serbs to grant statehood to Albanians, when they dismiss even the idea of a Republic of Kosova. Far from engaging in a dialogue with Albanians to iron out the differences between them, they are moving in the opposite direction. They are creating an apartheid society in Kosova, neatly separating the privileged Serbian minority from the ostracized and suppressed Albanian majority. In short, the Serbs are willy-nilly driving Albanians to the second option—secession from Yugoslavia.

Union with Albania?

Now, secession means union with their mother country of Albania. Until quite recently, the idea of unification of Kosova and Albania was not in the political vocabulary of the Albanians of Yugoslavia. In fact, the idea was considered impractical or undesirable by Albanians, and treasonous by the Serbs. But since communication and negotiations with Milosevic seems out of the question, the idea of unification of the "Two Albanias" is gaining ground.

This bold new concept has begun to circulate lately among respected American journals, as well. A perceptive article on Yugoslavia in *The New Yorker* magazine (March 18, 1991, pp. 58-79), said:

"Since the Kosova Albanians see no prospect whatever of satisfying their nationalist aspirations as a part of Serbia, it appears more and more likely... that a movement for Albanian unification will arise, perhaps very soon." (p. 79).

The movement is already here, and is being helped moreover by the democratic changes going on in Albania. It is not uncommon these days to hear Albanians say: "if the Two Germanys could unite, why should not the Two Albanias?"

This development opens up a new phase in Albanian-Serb relations, full of uncertainties and dangers, but which may also offer a way out of present deadlock. One thing is fairly certain. *If the Croats and Slovenes, who are Slavs, cannot live under the same roof with Serbia, the Albanians, who are not Slavs, have even less reason to do so.*

Chapter 17:
*Toward Statehood**

It was in autumn of 1912, eighty years ago, when the Serbian army overran what was then known as the *vilayet* or province of Kosova. This happened in the context of the Balkan War against the Ottoman Empire, of which Albania was a part. The following year, the Serbian occupation was officially sanctioned by the Great Powers of Europe. With the loss of Kosova (and Chamouria in Greece), one-half of the Albanian population and land was cut off from the body of the Albanian nation.

Kosova had entered the Twilight Zone. Its time of troubles had begun, casting shadows over the province for the better part of a century.

The year that Kosova fell, was also the year when the struggle for its rebirth began. The Kosovars never consented to Serbian or Slav rule. Ever since 1912 they have fought, sometimes with arms, but more often in silence, to emerge from the twilight zone into the light of day. Theirs is a story of unrelenting struggle for freedom and self-determination.

---

* Source: *Albanian Catholic Bulletin*, San Francisco, CA., USA, Vol. XIII (1992), pp. 81 – 85, under the title "Kosova: the struggle for the statehood." Translated in Italian *"Kosovo, la lotta per essere stato "*and published in *POPOLI*, a monthly magazine, Milan, Nr. 5, maggio 1993, pp. 26 – 28.

Historic Steps Toward Statehood

Until recently their drive for self-determination was amorphous and lacking in political sophistication. But the picture changed dramatically in the last two years.

1) The Declaration of Independence

The first milestone occurred on July 2, 1990, when the Assembly of Kosova met in Prishtinë and solemnly proclaimed Kosova a Republic, equal in status and jurisdiction to the other constituent republics of what was then Yugoslavia. The Assembly issued a 5-point Declaration stating that Kosova "is an independent and equal unit of the Federation of Yugoslavia. In effect and *in fact*, the action of the Assembly was a Declaration of Independence from Serbia, much like the American Declaration of Independence from England in 1776.

Item 1 of the Declaration said: "This Declaration expresses and proclaims the political will of the people of Kosova and of this Assembly for self-determination in the context of Yugoslavia."

Item 4 said that henceforth the Kosovars would no longer be bound by the Constitution of the Serbian Republic, nor would they recognize the jurisdiction of Serbia over them.

Item 2 appealed to the "democratic opinion in Yugoslavia" and to "international opinion" for support of the action taken by the Assembly.

The July 2, 1990 Declaration amounted to a giant step in the political awareness of the Albanians of Yugoslavia. But like King George III of England, who paid no heed to the American revolutionary patriots, so also "King" Slobodan Milosevic of Serbia ignored the declaration of the Kosovars. The obtuseness of the Serbian leader obliged the Albanians to take another momentous step on the road to self-determination.

2) The Constitutional Convention

The second milestone was "The Resolution of Kachanik", which was drafted on September 7, 1990. It is so named because of the town Kachanik of Kosova, where the "outlawed" deputies of Kosova convened in secret.

The gathering in Kachanik was nothing less than a Constitutional Convention for the newly-proclaimed Republic of Kosova. The delegates accomplished what they set out to do, in spite of great risks to themselves. They fashioned a Constitution for the Republic.

Unlike the Declaration of Independence in July, 1990, which took as its framework the federation of Yugoslavia, the Constitution of the Republic of Kosova envisioned a new Yugoslavia, organized as a Confederation of independent states. The document was drafted with that assumption in mind. For this reason the document refers to the Republic of Kosova as "a state," with all the symbols and attributes commonly associated with states.

The Resolution of Kachanik notes that, owing to the terroristic regime of Serbia, the Kosovars had no choice but to establish their own sovereign state. The new state is defined in the Constitution as a democratic social order, composed of Albanian nationals and members of other nationalities: Serbs, Moslems, Montenegrins, Croats, Turks, etc. The state guaranties to all citizens equality and all the rights and freedoms common to democratic systems of government. The Kosovar delegates felt confident that by taking this step they were making a contribution to the "democratic processes already in progress in Yugoslavia, and to the integration of Yugoslavia into the democratic European Community."

Like the July, 1990 Declaration, the Constitution of September, 1990 showed the political maturity of the Kosovars, their firm commitment to democracy, and their orientation toward the new Europe.

The Kachanik Resolution might have been seen by Belgrade as a signal that Albanians were not going to be denied their inalienable right to liberty and self-government. But the Serbian leaders only expanded their mechanisms of repression, targeting in particular the Albanian schools and language.

3) Referendum on Independence

A year later, the Kosovars strengthened even more the legality of their claim to govern themselves. They held a Referendum on Independence not only from Serbia (which they proclaimed in the July 2, 1990 Declaration), but from the Yugoslav Federation, as well, just as Slovenia and Croatia had done a few months earlier. The referendum was held over a four-day period, from September 26 to 30, 1991. The vote for independence was decisive—practically 100 percent! (99.87%, to be exact).

This was the third milestone on the Kosovars' road to statehood. Three historic steps within 15 months, leaving no doubt about their political will and the direction in which they want to go.

Commenting on the Referendum, a well-known Serbian intellectual, Dusan Batakovic, warned that it must be taken seriously. "Albanians in Kosova are determined to be independent," he said. They are "very preoccupied with (this)... issue and want it resolved." But his was the voice of reason crying in the Serbian wilderness. The Serbian leaders stuck to their failed hard line, oblivious to the cost in human lives and suffering.

The Three Options of Albanians In Yugoslavia

In June, 1991 war broke out in Yugoslavia, pitting the Serbs against the Slovenes and the Croats. The Federation was beginning to unravel at the seams. In these circumstances, leaders of eleven political parties of Albanians in Yugoslavia, met to deliberate "on the Albanian national question in Yugoslavia" and how to resolve it.

A Coordination Council representing all the parties was formed, with Dr. Ibrahim Rugova, leader of the Democratic League of Kosova, as President. The Democratic League is the largest Albanian political party in Yugoslavia. The other parties represented in the Council were: Farmers Party of Kosova, Parliamentary Party of Kosova, Albanian Demo-Christian Party-Kosova, Party of Albanian National Unity-Kosova, Social Democratic Party of Kosova, Party of Democratic Prosperity-Macedonia, People's Democratic Party-Macedonia, Democratic League in Montenegro, Party of Democratic Action-Serbia, and Albanian Democratic Party-Serbia (The last two are parties of Albanian communities in southern Serbia).

On October 11, 1991 the Council issued a Political Declaration in Prishtine, summarizing first the grim situation of ethnic Albanians, then setting forth options they might consider, depending on how the crisis in Yugoslavia is resolved.

Option One: "If the external and internal borders of Yugoslavia remain unchanged, then Kosova must have the status of a republic as a sovereign and independent state..." This conforms to the Declaration of Independence which said that the Kosovars will no longer recognize nor accept the Serbian jurisdiction over them. They will govern themselves.

Option Two: "If the internal borders between the republics are changed... the Albanian Republic in Yugoslavia (must) be built on the basis of the ethnic and other principles that apply to the Serbs, the Croats, the Slovenes and other peoples of Yugoslavia." The language of this option seems to say that the Albanian Republic would include all ethnic Albanians in Yugoslavia living in compact territories in Kosova, Macedonia, Montenegro and southern Serbia. In other words, Albanians are poised to claim the same rights and powers to organize themselves politically, as the Serbs, Croats and other groups in Yugoslavia.

Option Three: "If the external borders of Yugoslavia are changed, the Albanians in Yugoslavia (would opt for) reunification of

Kosova and other territories in Yugoslavia with Albania..." The reunification would take place through a "plebiscite under international monitoring."

The Political Declaration of October 11, 1991 goes on to say that the "crisis in Yugoslavia began in Kosova... and it cannot be solved without the participation of around 3 million Albanians in Yugoslavia."

The October document served to clarify the position of ethnic Albanians in a disintegrating Yugoslavia. In particular, it laid the groundwork for reunification with Albania, if the other two options are no longer relevant or feasible.

The Drive for Recognition of Kosova

Over the past two years, Kosovar leaders have worked hard to gain recognition for Kosova as a sovereign independent state. The basis of their argument is the demonstrated will of the Albanians in Kosova (who make up 90% percent of its population) for statehood. A government of the Republic of Kosova is in place, but is forced to operate in exile. Its representatives have been busy traveling to numerous countries—such as Turkey, Sweden, Germany, Austria, Belgium, the United States—and conferring with high government officials in a determined drive to win international recognition.

So far, however, only Albania has taken that step. On October 22, 1991 the People's Assembly of Albania issued a declaration saying that it "recognizes the Republic of Kosova as a sovereign and independent state." The Assembly also recognized the provisional government of Kosova, headed by Dr. Bujar Bukoshi. The Assembly's declaration on Kosova won unanimous approval and "was greeted with frantic and prolonged applause," according to a dispatch from Tirane. The Albanian Assembly also appealed to the international community, above all to the member nations of ECSC (European Conference on Security and Cooperation), to accord recognition to Kosova.

As of this writing (April, 1992), Austrian and German officials have taken the lead in putting this question on their diplomatic agendas. Turkish leaders, too, are reported to have said that they were considering recognition.

In the meantime, Albanian communities abroad have been active in raising public awareness on this issue, and appealing to their respective governments to give official backing to the Kosovars' quest for statehood. As a result of such efforts in our country, interest in the question of Albanians in Yugoslavia has grown considerably of late in Washington. One thing that heightened the concern of officials was the annual State Department Report on the situation of human rights in Yugoslavia, which showed that in 1991 Serbia had stepped up its brutal violation of the rights of Albanians.

Beginning in January of this year, a growing number of Senators and Representatives in Congress called publicly on the Bush Administration to recognize Kosova "as an independent state." Over a period of three months, from January through March, 1992, four Resolutions were introduced in Congress urging recognition. Leading the drive for recognition in the Senate were Senators Alphonse D'Amato (N.Y.), Bob Dole (Kansas), Larry Pressler (S.D.), and Claiborne Pell (R.I.). Strong support for recognition in the House came from Representatives Tom Lantos (Cal.), William Broomfield (Mich.), Ben Gilman (N.Y.), and Dick Swett (N.H.). Two other prominent supporters of the Kosovars in Congress are Rep. Susan Molinari (N.Y.) , and Rep. Eliot Engel (N.Y.).

But the laudable efforts of these friends of the Kosovars brought no change in Administration policy on Kosova, despite the fact that our Ambassador in Belgrade, Warren Zimmerman, admitted last March that *"the human rights problem in Kosova is the most serious in all of Europe,"* and that Serbian domination in Kosova is *"a typical colonial situation, in which a subject people is denied its most elementary rights... "* (our emphasis) . (*Illyria* semi-weekly, Bronx, N.Y., March 28, 1992, p. 4). Back in 1920, President Woodrow Wilson saved one-half of the Albanian nation from extinction. Will President George Bush make a serious effort to rescue the other half?

The focus, however, of Kosova's drive for recognition was the Hague, Netherlands, site of the Peace Conference on Yugoslavia. Seated at the conference were representatives of all the republics of what was Yugoslavia, except the Republic of Kosova. Leaders of Kosova, and numerous Albanians the world over, made repeated appeals to British Lord Peter Carrington, the Chief Coordinator of the conference, to grant a seat also to the Kosovars. To date, he had not agreed to such a proposal, although he realized the importance of Kosova in the overall peace scenario for Yugoslavia. He has been quoted as saying: "Kosova's future is one of three key issues that must be resolved, before agreement can be reached on resolving the crisis."

We trust that a representative of Kosova will soon take his rightful seat at the Hague Peace Conference. In the meantime, it would be unrealistic, in our opinion, to pin all hopes on the West for the attainment of Kosova's independence. At a recent meeting with Albanians in the Bronx, N.Y., Adem Demaçi, symbol of Kosovar resistance to Serbian oppression, said that if the Albanians of Yugoslavia are to win independence, they must understand that it will not come as a gift from outside, from foreign powers, rather they must look primarily to themselves, they must organize more effectively, they must heighten the level of resistance to the oppressor.

Words of wisdom from a man whom the European Parliament honored lately with the prestigious Sakharov prize.

Chapter 18:
The Responsibility of Serbian Intellectuals *

The time has come for a ringing denunciation of Serbian intellectuals for the terror and suffering in Kosova, as well as other parts of former Yugoslavia. Serbian intellectuals are an integral part of the problem of Kosova. To date (with rare exceptions), they have shown no realism in dealing with the problem, no compassion for the plight of Kosovars, no willingness to change the oppressor-victim equation.

Instead of seeking to quench the flames in Kosova, they have added fuel to the fire. With their petitions and manifestoes and other public outcries, they aroused millions of Serbs against the Albanians. Their suspicion and contempt for the Albanians reached new heights in the past seven years. Working through the Serbian Academy of Arts & Sciences, the League of Serbian Writers and various public forums, they provided the Serbian chief, Slobodan Milosevic, with the ideological weapon he needed for his savage policy toward the Kosovars.

Consider the January, 1986 Petition on Kosova of 212 Serbian intellectuals, addressed to the Federal Government. That petition might well have been drafted by the notorious V. Çubrilovic himself. The language of that document puts the signatories in the same class as the most vociferous and vulgar anti-Albanian hooligans. We have not seen a more irresponsible political document by a group of intellectuals in the Balkans.

---

* Source: DIELLI (The Sun) Organ of the Pan-Albanian Federation of America, VATRA (The Hearth) , Boston Mass., January-June 1993, p. 9.

It is not merely the Milosevic leadership that is on trial before the court of world public opinion for its brutal policy on Kosova. Serbian intellectuals are also on trial, for they have failed their nation and disgraced their profession.

The intellectuals of a nation are normally the most enlightened, most rational, most democratic and progressive element of society. They have the means to influence the thoughts and conduct of their fellow citizens, shape their culture and world outlook and affect the nation's destiny. In brief, they can wield great power, both for good and ill.

But let us return to Kosova. The responsibility for the conflict there falls on the Serbs, since they created the conditions for it by denying Albanians their lawful rights. In the same manner, they can create the conditions that will lead to a resolution of the conflict.

It is here that the Serbian intellectuals can play a significant and, indeed, historic role. They can turn things around in Kosova. They can change the Serbian people's negative perception of Kosova. They can cure them of their paranoid distrust and fear of Albanians.

True, they cannot do the job alone. But they can be the leading force for change.

If peace and order and a normal life are to come to Kosova, millions of Serbs have to change the way they think and feel, day in and day out, about Albanians. This change has to take place in the hearth of the family, in the classroom, in church pulpits, in the market place, in all the forums that shape public opinion.

Milosevic and his gang are not the least disposed to make peace with the Albanians and let go of Kosova. But if millions of Serbs change their attitude toward Kosova, Milosevic will fall from power like a dry leaf from a tree in autumn.

In our view, the most reliable way to change Belgrade's politics is to change Serbian society. And Serbian intellectuals are the natural locomotive for bringing about such change.

Chapter 19:

Kosovar Albanians in 1996 are the Counterparts of American Patriots in 1776[*]

As I survey American history before the Republic was born, I am impressed by the parallels I find between the condition of the American colonists and the condition of Albanians in Kosova, more than two centuries later. Impressed but not surprised, because both the Americans of that epoch, and the Kosovars of our day are inseparably linked in time by a Common Cause—the struggle for liberty and human dignity! And this struggle is always the same, as vital and irrepressible two centuries ago as it is today.

In 1776 America was a colony of England. Today the province of Kosova, with a 90 percent Albanian population, is a colony of Serbia. It has been a Serbian colony since 1913, when the Great European Powers, ignoring demographic realities and the will of the Albanian inhabitants, detached the province from the body of the Albanian nation and attached it to Serbia.

In 1776 three million Americans were ruled, against their will, by the British Crown in London. Today roughly three million Albanians in Kosova are ruled, against their will, by Serbian authorities in Belgrade. To be ruled against your will is a gross violation of human nature. It is an unbearable yoke. This was the bitter lot of the American colonists in the 18th Century. This has been the bitter lot of the Albanians in Kosova in the 20th Century.

---

[*] Source: DIELLI (The Sun) Organ of the Pan-Albanian Federation of America VATRA (The Hearth), New York, N.Y. October – December 1995, p. 1.

In 1776 Tom Paine, Patrick Henry, Thomas Jefferson and other patriots cried out against the injustices suffered by the American people, and demanded "a redress of their grievances." And when their demands went unheeded, they boldly called for separation of the colonies from England. It was the only realistic road for them to take. Today, President Ibrahim Rugova, Prime Minister Bujar Bukoshi and other Albanian leaders in Kosova, all of them freely elected by the people, are taking the same road. They want an unconditional separation of Kosova from Serbia. Just as the American colonists had an innate right to self-determination, so do also the Albanians in Kosova. It's a right they have asserted with near-perfect unanimity in several elections and referendums since 1990.

In 1776 the American colonists, anxious to break the chains that bound them to King George III, declared their independence from England. A few years later, they won their freedom and the right to govern themselves. They won their freedom by force of arms, under the brilliant leadership of Gen. George Washington. Albanians, too, are anxious to break the chains imposed on them by the Serbs since 1913. They have tried to do so by force of arms through a succession of armed uprisings. They failed not for lack of bravery, but because of the superior might of the Serbs.

Since armed resistance did not bring liberation, as it did to the American patriots, they have opted instead for "peaceful resistance" as the means for achieving their political and national goals.

This noble but bitterly painful path toward liberation from Serbian oppression, is in accord with a basic principle of American foreign policy, namely the peaceful resolution of conflicts. It is in harmony also with the basic political philosophy of the European Union. It makes sense therefore for our Government and the international community to support the Albanians in their peaceful efforts to separate from Serbia and become independent. To oppose separation from Serbia means, in effect, to condone and support Serbian state-sanctioned terror in Kosova.

It is not enough to ask Serbia to grant human rights to Albanians in Kosova. Such rights can be abolished (as they have been abolished in the past) any time it suits the Serbs to do so. To advocate autonomy for Kosova within Serbia, as some diplomats are doing—even in our Department of State—again is not enough. And for the same reason. As long as the Serbs are calling the tune, Albanians would always be at their mercy. Such a policy is as morally wrong today as it was in 1776, when voiced by those Americans who favored maintaining the colonies' ties with England. Autonomy for Kosova is not a realistic option. It never was. It is nothing more than a dangerous pipe dream.

Our Government officials in Washington have it in their power to radically alter the *status quo* in Kosova, and tip the scales in favor of the oppressed. They can be the decisive external factor in the Albanian struggle to break away from Serbia. Following are some of the reasons for giving unconditional support to the Albanian side:

1) Their grievances and goals are essentially the same as those of the Founding Fathers of America.
2) They cannot live with the Serbs, anymore than the Croatians, the Slovenes, and the Bosnians even though they, unlike the Albanians, are Slavs like the Serbs. This argument alone should be sufficient to win the support of all those who truly want to see an end to the Kosova quagmire.
3) They are our political allies in the Balkans. They have demonstrated their commitment to democracy, unlike the ex-Communists who hold power in Belgrade.
4) They are a force for peace and stability in the Balkans.

In a word, Kosovar Albanians today are fighting the same battle, and for the same ideals, for which the American patriots fought in 1776.

(This article is a revised and enlarged version of a tract titled, "Support the Right of Albanians to Separate from Serbia," which I prepared expressly for the March 29, 1995 Albanian demonstration in our nation's capital. – Author's note.*)*

Chapter 20:
*Four Arguments for the Independence of Kosova**

Like people in other countries, Albanians have their differences concerning issues affecting their nation. But on the critical question of Kosova, they are united.

The pacifist Ibrahim Rugova, the militant Adem Demaci, academicians Mark Krasniqi and Rexhep Qosja and others all voice the same demand—independence for Kosova.

Nor is their call for independence merely a rhetorical gesture or an expression of romantic nationalism. The case for Kosova's independence can be seriously argued on historical, demographic, egalitarian and ethnic grounds.

The Historical Argument: The Serbs would like the international community to believe that Albanians are latecomers to Kosova and usurpers of Serbian land. In fact, it is the Serbs who are latecomers to the region. The Albanians are native to the soil. They are heirs to the domains of their Illyrian ancestors, who inhabited Kosova (known in their time as Dardania) centuries before the Slavs set foot in the Balkans around 700 A. D.

This is borne out by Ottoman chroniclers, by West European travelers to the Balkans, and by Catholic missionaries in the region. In our time the historical argument has been strengthened considerably by

* Source: ILLYRIA, semi-weekly newspaper in English and Albanian, New York, N.Y. September 16-18, 1998, p. 5.

the research of historians of Medieval Balkans and the findings of archeologists. Indeed, even some Serb scholars view the Albanians as the original inhabitants of Kosova. It turns out that Albanians hold "original title" to the land in Kosova, while the Serbs rule there not by historical right, but by the force of arms, as colonizers.

The Demographic Argument: One of the fundamental principles of democracy is rule by the majority. This principle lies at the heart of free elections, and the right of the people to choose their rulers. It is the venerable right of self-determination, a right professed by all democratic countries. Now, in Kosova, the Albanians are not merely a simple majority of 51 percent or thereabout, but 90 percent of the population. With such an overwhelming majority, they have an indisputable right to govern themselves as they see fit. By virtue of their numbers alone, they have the right to sever all bonds with Serbia and be independent.

The Serbian claim that the Kosovars have willingly agreed to be governed by Serbia, is not true. They have never consented to be ruled by Serbs at any time: not in 1913, when Kosova was ceded to Serbia by the Great Powers, not in 1920 following World War I, and not in 1945 following World War II, nor later.

Over the past decade, the Serbian 10 percent of the population in Kosova has ruled over the 90 percent Albanian majority, in contemptuous defiance of the expressed political will of the Albanians, who have voted for independence in several elections since 1990. Whoever heard of ten percent of the population in a province or country having the right to rule over the other ninety percent?

The Egalitarian Argument: The doctrine of egalitarianism, which is another name for the democratic principle of non-discrimination, calls for equality of treatment. Applied to the peoples of the former Yugoslavia, this means that Albanians in Kosova are entitled to the same treatment by the international community as the Slovenians, the Croats, the Macedonians and the Bosnians. In recent years all of these ethnic groups broke with Serbia and became independent republics.

The Albanians in Kosova want to do the very same thing—break loose from Serbia. In fact, they have been trying to part ways with Serbia for over four score years! They set out on the road to independence long before the Slovenians and the rest of the newly-independent Slavs in former Yugoslavia. By right they should have been the first ones to be granted independence, not only because they took the lead in the movement for independence, but also because they have suffered the longest.

The Kosova Albanians deserve equal treatment from the international community. And since the international community recognized the independence of the other ethnic groups in former Yugoslavia, how can it deny independence to the Albanians? By what right or logic can it oppose independence for Kosova? In our view, it has no valid grounds for such a stand—not if the Western world truly believes in the democratic principles of equality and fair play that it professes to uphold.

The Ethnic Argument: From the Albanian perspective, this is the strongest argument for severing ties with Serbia. It begins with the fact that the Slovenians, the Croats, the Macedonians and the Bosnians are all Slavs, and brothers under the skin with the Serbs. They share with them the same language and the same ethnic roots.

The Albanians, on the other hand, are not a Slavic people. They are the descendants of the Illyrians, a non-Slavic people, with a long history of struggle against Slav domination and oppression. They do not identify with the Slavs, least of all with the Serbs. And they argue, with iron-clad logic, that if the Slovenians and other Slavs in the former Yugoslavia could not live under the same roof with the Serbs, how can the international community expect them to do so?

These are not the only arguments for an independent republic of Kosova. But perhaps they are sufficient to show that the international community's opposition to independence for Kosova is discriminatory, undemocratic and fundamentally unrealistic.

It is not a prescription for peace and stability in the Balkans.

Chapter 21:
A Summation

In the autumn of 1968, Kosova was in turmoil, as thousands of disgruntled ethnic Albanians took to the streets to demand a "Republic of Kosova." Their peaceful demonstrations were broken up by the armed forces of Yugoslavia and Serbia, using deadly firepower against the demonstrators. Had Tito and Serbian officials in Belgrade reacted with calmness, courage and foresight and heeded the demands of the demonstrators, the question of Kosova would have been resolved thirty years ago. A chance for promoting peace and stability in the Balkans was missed.

Nevertheless, the violence attending the demonstrations alarmed Tito sufficiently to make some concessions to the Albanians, in order to defuse the situation. The most important of these came in 1974, when Tito made Kosova an Autonomous Province of the Federation of Yugoslavia. The upgrading of their political status gave the Kosovars rights and freedoms they had never known before in Yugoslavia. The fatal flaw, however, in Tito's move was to leave Kosova under the jurisdiction of Serbia; in other words, within the borders of the Serbian Republic.

When Tito died in 1980, the restive Albanians saw a chance to throw off the shackles of Serbia. In the spring of 1981, they staged massive peaceful demonstrations in the major towns of Kosova, and renewed calls to Belgrade to make the province a Republic, equal in status to the other six republics in the Federation. But again Belgrade turned a deaf ear to them, and resorted to force to crush the demonstrations. The rulers in Belgrade had missed another chance to solve the problem of Kosova peacefully, and lay the foundations for a new era of harmonious coexistence among the various ethnic groups in Yugoslavia.

With Tito gone, Serbian nationalism reasserted itself vigorously, and became a clear threat to the other ethnic groups in the Federation, above all to the Kosovars. The Serbs never trusted Tito, who was a Croat, and resented his policies on nationalities, which they felt favored the non-Serbs in Yugoslavia, and diminished the power and prestige of Serbia. They resented especially the limited self-rule he granted to the Albanians in 1974, when he made Kosova an Autonomous Province.

After crushing the 1981 demonstrations, Serbian nationalists apparently embarked on a deliberate campaign to deprive the Albanians even of the limited rights they had won under Tito. Albanians now became daily targets of attacks by the Serbian media for alleged crimes they were committing against the Serbs in Kosova. Although these allegations were largely, if not wholly, fabrications, the Serb nationalists succeeded in creating a climate of psychosis throughout Serbia and inflaming the passions of the population.

The Rise of Slobodan Milosevic

The ideological and political groundwork was thus laid, and the stage set for the rise to power of a Serbian extremist who could exploit the polarized situation to Serbia's advantage. That man was Slobodan Milosevic. In the late 1980's he became the leading spokesman for the Serbs in the Yugoslav Federation. As President of the Serbian Republic, Milosevic considered it his mission to restore Serbia to its former commanding position in Yugoslavia.

With regard to the Kosovars, Milosevic had two choices: the path of dialogue and accommodation, or the path of savage repression. He chose the latter. He began by revoking the autonomy of Kosova in 1989, and depriving the Albanians of their ethnic, political and human rights. The draconian move of the Serbian chief augured ill for future Serb-

Albanian relations, and in effect ruled out the peaceful solution of the Kosova problem.

Serb police forces began now to implement a policy of terror in Kosova, with the transparent aim of making life for the Albanians so unbearable that they would abandon their homes and lands and quit the province. Faced with this situation, Albanian leaders in Kosova, headed by Ibrahim Rugova and Bujar Bukoshi, adopted a policy of non-violent resistance to police provocations. This policy contradicted sharply with Albanian tradition. It ran counter to the Albanians' strong sense of personal pride and integrity. But since they lacked the military might necessary to oppose Serb power, a policy of non-violence seemed to be the only realistic option available to them.

The docile and seemingly humiliating policy was not without merit, however. Since it was in line with a basic political doctrine of the European Union and the United Nations, namely, the peaceful resolution of conflicts, it met with approval by the international community. The United States and Western Europe endorsed it and pledged to support the Kosovars in their efforts to secure their legitimate rights.

Breakup of Yugoslavia

In the meantime, war broke out between the Serbs and the separatist republics of Slovenia, Croatia and Bosnia, and in the course of four years (1991-95) the Federation of Yugoslavia disintegrated, and the republics became independent nations. A new realignment of nations and borders had come into being in the former Yugoslavia. In these conditions, independence became the goal also of the Albanians of Kosova. Since the old Yugoslavia had disappeared, the rationale for a Republic of Kosova within the borders of Serbia had also disappeared.

Following the Dayton (Ohio) Accord in 1995, which ended the three-and-a-half-year-long war in Bosnia, attention shifted to Kosova. There tensions were rising steadily, as Serb police forces raided Albanian homes and turned them into shambles, insulted and beat up the residents, robbed and jailed them without cause, all with the intention of creating insecurity and panic to impel them to get out of Kosova. (It is estimated that three to four hundred thousand of them fled abroad, mostly to Western Europe, to escape Serb persecution). The grim reports from the province indicated plainly that unless these tensions were checked, open warfare could erupt between the Serbs and Albanians. That, in turn, could draw into the conflict Macedonia, Albania, Greece, Bulgaria and even Turkey. The flames of war could engulf all of the Balkans.

President Rugova and his underground government of Kosova, kept urging the Western powers to intervene and put a stop to Serbia's terror tactics, but nobody was listening. Commenting on the West's reluctance to intervene, a diplomat said that as far as the international community was concerned, the situation in Kosova was "distasteful, but tolerable". It was not disposed to change the *status quo* in the region.

By 1996-97 patience was running out with Rugova's policy of moderation. Since quiet submission to Serb violence had not brought Kosova a single step closer to freedom and independence, disillusioned Kosovars opted for violence and took to the mountains to fight with arms. These "freedom fighters", as their sympathizers called them, made up what came to be known as the KLA—the Kosova Liberation Army, or *UÇK* in Albanian ("Ushtria Çlirimtare e Kosovës"). The rebel fighters were highly motivated, but disorganized, inadequately trained and poorly equipped for modern warfare.

With the dawn of 1998, the main components of the Kosova question could be described as follows:

One – Within the province itself, the Kosovars were all united strategically, in the sense that all of them wanted an independent state of Kosova, completely separate from Serbia. Politically and tactically, however, they were divided and weak. On one side stood Rugova, with his peaceful approach, while on the other side stood opposing political parties and influential figures like Adem Demaçi, Rexhep Qosja and Mark Krasniqi who rejected or doubted the wisdom of his course. The KLA of course stood the farthest apart from the Rugova leadership.

Two – The international community continued to support Rugova's peaceful policy, but rejected the demand for independence, fearing that a totally sovereign Kosova could bring instability to the Balkans. In place of independence, the U.S. and its allies proposed "Autonomy" within the borders of Serbia, which meant the restoration, more or less, of the rights Albanians enjoyed previously under the 1974 Constitution of the former Yugoslavia.

Three – As for Serbia, strongman Slobodan Milosevic stuck to the position that Kosova was an internal affair of Serbia. In line with this view, he ignored the demands of the Kosovars, and the pressures of American and West European diplomats to settle differences with the Albanians peacefully through negotiations. Serbia's standard line was that Albanian dissidents were in fact "separatists", while the KLA fighters were "terrorists", and the ultimate goal of both was the creation of a "Greater Albania".

Such was the lineup of the forces, at the beginning of the year, involved with the Kosova quagmire. By this time, however, the tensions that had been building up for years, as a result of Serbian oppression, could not be contained. The province was ready to erupt into violence once again, like so many times before, except that this time the whole world was watching.

The Crisis of 1998

The explosion came in February of 1998, when Serbian police, backed up by special forces and army units, cracked down on KLA forces in the Drenice region of Kosova. The sudden Serb offensive cost the lives of over 100 civilians, and leveled a number of villages. Reports of Serb massacres of unarmed civilians caused an uproar in Washington and Western Europe. Envoys of the so-called Contact Group made up of the United States, Russia, Great Britain, Germany, France and Italy, met in London and demanded that Belgrade call a halt to its military offensive. In addition, the Contact Group imposed or rather re-imposed economic sanctions previously in force against Serbia.

Two factors help to explain the international community's high profile involvement in the Kosova crisis. One was the quiet diplomacy of Rugova and his team, who for nearly ten years had presented the case of Kosovars before the leaders of America and the West. The Rugova team challenged the view on Kosova disseminated abroad by Belgrade, and succeeded in quietly internationalizing the problem. The second and undoubtedly the more significant factor was the Kosova Liberation Army. Had not the KLA challenged the Serbs on the battlefield, the Kosova problem almost certainly would have dragged along on its dreary course, and the Albanians would have suffered in silence indefinitely. By injecting itself into the fray, the KLA brought matters to a boiling point and forced the International community to take notice and to act.

Realistically, the rag-tag army of the rebels presented no real threat to Serbian forces. At most, it was a nuisance and something of an embarrassment. But to Milosevic KLA provided the opportunity he was looking for. Its insolent "provocation" gave him the green light to utilize his massive firepower to crush, one and for all, all opposition to Serbia's colonial rule in Kosova, even if this meant the genocide of a two-million strong ethnic group.

Following the angry world reaction to his furious attack on Drenice, Milosevic backed down and halted his military operations, but only temporarily. This became the pattern of his military campaign in the months that followed. He would mount fierce attacks on KLA positions, cause massive destruction of villages, force tens of thousands of terrorized peasants to flee for their lives to the countryside, massacre a few more dozen civilians, then, in each instance, declare before the media that the military campaign had achieved its objectives and was over. But these breaks in the fighting were only breathing spells to prepare for the next offensive.

By spring of 1998, President Clinton and other Western leaders declared that they were not going to let Kosova become another Bosnia.

Milosevic however paid no attention and the war continued. In June NATO threatened to use force against Serbian forces. But again Milosevic was not impressed. The Contact Group made another appeal to Belgrade to abandon the use of force, but this time too there was no response. Serbia's strongman knew that there was a division within the Group, and reluctance on the part of some members to use force against him. Of all the Western powers, the United States was the most willing to use NATO's power to stop Milosevic's war machine, followed by England and Germany. Russia, on the other hand, was strongly opposed to the use of force and warned that NATO airstrikes against the Serbs would strain its relations with the West.

In the weeks that followed NATO repeated its warnings to Belgrade, and human rights organizations condemned Serbian atrocities in Kosova, and still the war continued unabated, except for temporary pauses. Affronted by Serbia's intransigence, in July 1998 the U.S. Senate passed a resolution, introduced by Sen. Alfonse D'Amato, calling Slobodan Milosevic "a war criminal".

Washington's Shuttle Diplomacy

In the meantime, starting in the spring of 1998, Washington set in motion its "shuttle diplomacy" to try to mediate a peace agreement between the Serbs and the Albanians. The diplomats charged with the peace-making mission were Robert Gelbard, Christopher Hill, U.S. Ambassador to Macedonia, and Richard Holbrooke, Washington's top trouble-shooter, and the man who brokered the Dayton Accord in 1995. For several months they shuttled back and forth between Belgrade and Prishtina, talking to Milosevic and the Kosovar leaders in hope of finding some common ground in their respective positions, on which to build peace. But Milosevic was not serious about negotiations. He made numerous promises and commitments to seek a political solution to the differences with the Kosovars, yet did not honor them. His lack of integrity drove President Bill Clinton to remark that "Balkan graveyards are filled with President Milosevic's broken promises."

The problem was that the Serbia's President seemed convinced that NATO was only bluffing when it threatened to use force against him. And as long as he believed that, he was not going to stop the war.

In the meantime, alarming reports kept coming back from Kosova about the ravages the war was causing. By September of 1998 stories of new atrocities filled the media, scores of villages had been destroyed and the number of refugees had climbed to an estimated 250,000 to 300,000. With winter approaching it was feared that the exposed refugees faced certain catastrophe.

The concerns about the civilian victims of the war, reached a turning point on September 30, 1998 when the *New York Times* published a graphic front-page article titled, "New Massacres by Serb Forces in Kosovo Villages". The news made headlines in newspapers all over the country. Film footage of the atrocity hit the TV screens morning and night. The UN Security Council promptly condemned the atrocity, and demanded that Belgrade honor a previous Security Council resolution, dated September 23, 1998 which called on Serbia to stop the war and withdraw its armed forces from Kosova. Momentum was gathering quickly for NATO to go into action in Kosova.

The pace of Talks between Holbrooke and Milosevic intensified. Finally, feeling the pressure from Washington, the UN, the Contact Group and especially the credible threat from NATO, Milosevic capitulated and on October 12, 1998 reached agreement with Holbrooke. The agreement called for: 1) A cease-fire; 2) An immediate withdrawal of Serbian armed forces from Kosova; 3) Safe access for humanitarian workers helping the refugees; 4) Safe access for 2,000 international observers who were to be sent to the province to verify Serbian compliance with the terms of the agreement. In addition, the agreement included a pledge by the Serbian leader to negotiate a political settlement with the Kosovars over the next three years.

After signing the agreement, however, Milosevic dragged his feet on compliance. It required a personal visit to Belgrade and face-to-face

talks with Milosevic by Javier Solana, NATO's Secretary General, and
Gen. Wesley Clark, NATO Commander in Europe, to prod him into
action. One day before the NATO deadline, set for October 27, 1998
Serbia started to withdraw at least some of its forces, including tanks and
other heavy weapons—enough to avert NATO airstrikes.

After eight months of bloodshed and untold human misery, the
latest drama in the tortured land of Kosova came to an end. But the
future of the province is still clouded. It is too early to tell whether the
dramatic events of 1998 will make this a watershed year. Much depends
on how well the peace agreement is implemented by both sides.

San Diego, California
November, 1998

II.

Correspondence On Kosova

(Including Replies from Some Recipients)

Letters:
1. TO U.S. PUBLIC OFFICIALS
   - The White House and Department of State
   - Senators
   - Congressmen
2. TO U.N. OFFICIALS
3. TO YUGOSLAV OFFICIALS
4. TO THE MEDIA

1. Letters To US Public Officials

- The White House and Department of State

San Diego, Ca.
December 22, 1982

Director
Office of Eastern European Affairs
Department of State
Washington, D.C. 20520

Dear Sir:

Yugoslav authorities are carrying out a ruthless policy of persecution of Albanian ethnics in Kosova and elsewhere in Yugoslavia. The violations of the human and ethnic rights of Albanians have been amply documented by scholars, and by much of the world press, particularly in Western Europe.

Our country rightly proclaims its concerns for human rights and freedoms in the world. But to this day, no voice has been raised in Washington to condemn Yugoslav violation of the rights of Albanian ethnics.

I appeal to you to end this anomaly. Let our government officials in Washington speak out against the persecution of Albanians in Yugoslavia. Let them call on the Yugoslav government to grant to the Albanians the rights to which they are entitled by the Yugoslav Constitution, and in particular the right to have a Republic of their own.

Such a course of action, I am convinced, will serve the true national interest of Yugoslavia, as well as the cause of peace in the Balkans.

Enclosed is some material relative to this issue, which may be of interest to you.

Respectfully yours,

Peter R. Prifti

Language Consultant, University of Cal., at San Diego
Author, *Socialist Albania Since 1944* (MIT Press, 1978)

Philadelphia, Pa.
June 22, 1986

President Ronald Reagan
The White House
Washington, D.C. 20500

Mr. President:

The subject of this Petition is the United States policy toward Yugoslavia, as it affects the more than two million Albanian nationals in that country. That policy was enunciated with particular clarity by the Department of State in a broadcast on April 5, 1985 over the Voice of America. The declaration by the Department of State affirmed support for Yugoslavia's domestic policy, and implicitly ignored the just demands of Albanian nationals.[1]

Mr. President, we are greatly distressed by declarations of that nature, for we consider them to be misguided, unfortunate, and potentially harmful to the interest of all parties concerned, including those of our country, the United States of America.

The Albanian people have traditionally been friends of the American people, respectful of American ideals of justice and freedom, and admirers of America in general. To this day they speak with pride and gratitude of President Wilson's efforts in 1918-1920 to secure Albania's independence and sovereignty. Those attitudes and feelings are shared to an even greater degree by the tens of thousands of Albanian immigrants in America, who bear witness daily to America's greatness and reap the full benefits of her bounty and priceless freedoms at their place of work or study, and in the hearths of their homes.

But while we live in freedom here, Albanians in Yugoslavia are suffering from deepening poverty, rampant unemployment, social discrimination, and ruthless cultural and political oppression. There is no need to dwell on this point. Their miserable condition has been amply documented by scholars and the media in the West, as well as the statistical evidence from official sources within Yugoslavia.

The root cause of this situation has likewise been established. It is Serbian domination and control over their lives. To condone this situation is morally wrong and politically shortsighted.

Seven decades ago America, led by Wilson, wrote a golden chapter in the history of Albanian-American relations. Our country has it in its power to repeat that

---

[1] This letter was drafted at the request of an Albanian-American activist in Philadelphia, Pa.

historic act in our time, by publicly declaring its support for the legitimate demands of the Albanians in Yugoslavia, including the demand for a Republic of Kosova.

Mr. President, we appeal to you to issue a declaration which affirms unequivocally the right of Albanian nationals to take charge of their lives and manage their own affairs, in the same manner as other nationality groups in Yugoslavia. We believe that such a declaration will break the current dangerous stalemate in Kosova and create the necessary conditions for a genuine resolution of the conflict. Your initiative in this direction will be applauded by the seven million Albanians world-wide, and by all men and women who fear that the present trend of affairs in Kosova will inevitably destabilize Yugoslavia and invite chaos in the Balkans.

We trust, Mr. President, that you will give our petition your earnest attention.

Sincerely yours

The Albanian Community of Philadelphia, Pennsylvania

San Diego, Ca.
October 23, 1988

The Honorable George P. Shultz
Secretary of State
Department of State
2201 C Street, NW
Washington, DC 20520

Dear Mr. Secretary:

The tensions in Yugoslavia have grown to alarming proportions. Especially acute is the Serb-Albanian conflict over Kosova. This conflict has now reached the powder keg stage. And the Serbs, driven by racist hatred of Albanians, appear determined to light the fuse.

The recent call of Serbian mobs in Kragujevac for war against Albania is the latest step in that dangerous road. It is not surprising that their leader, Milosevic, has been compared with Mussolini. This rash rabble rouser is feeding the appetite of the Serbs for aggression against the Albanians and war in the Balkans.

In this critical situation our government can play a significant and perhaps decisive role. It can do so, I believe, by releasing a firm public rebuke of Milosevic and his drive to place Kosova and Vojvodina completely under Serbia's control.

The Serbians are no friends of democracy and the West. In times of crises, they and the Montenegrins have historically turned to the Russians for support. I am of the opinion that they will do so again, if hostilities break out in Yugoslavia and the Balkans and they find themselves pressed. Already some Serbs have publicly identified themselves not only with the Soviet Union, but with Stalin, to boot.

Sincerely yours,

Prof. Peter R. Prifti

San Diego, Ca.
July 16, 1990

Mr. James A. Baker 3d
Secretary of State
Department of State
2201 C St. NW
Washington, DC 20520

Dear Mr. Secretary:

I understand that Serbia's leader, Slobodan Milosevic, is coming to Washington on an official visit next week.

Considering that he has gone a long way toward wrecking the Federation of Yugoslavia, principally because of his callous violation of the rights of ethnic Albanians in Kosova, I think it is entirely appropriate to ask him:

1. "Why do you deny the Albanians the democratic right of free expression?"
2. "Why do you deny them the democratic right of free elections?"
3. "Why do you deny them the democratic right of self-government?"

Then, I suggest you advise Mr. Milosevic that unless Serbia abandons her anti-democratic rule, and therefore illegitimate rule over Kosova, our country, being bound by conscience and tradition to oppose anti-democratic rule, shall withhold all economic and financial aid and credits to Serbia and Yugoslavia.

A strong message, to be sure, but I believe the situation warrants it, to disperse the gathering clouds of civil war in the province and the rest of Yugoslavia.

Respectfully yours,

Prof. Peter R. Prifti

Copies to:
Sen. Bob Dole
Rep. Dante Fascell
Dr. Elez Biberaj
Prenk Gruda

San Diego, Cal.
May 22, 1991

Richard Schifter
Assistant Secretary, Human Rights and Humanitarian Affairs
Department of State
2201 C St., N.W.
Washington, D.C. 20520

Dear Mr. Schifter:

Yesterday, in the *LOS ANGELES TIMES*, I noted with great relief and satisfaction the announcement by the Department of State that our government has "*suspended economic assistance to Yugoslavia,* because of the conduct of the Serbia republic leadership, which is exercising severe repression in the Kosovo province." This is an appropriate and laudable stand, under the circumstances, and I congratulate you for it.

The Serbian leaders have tried our patience far too long. Despite our most generous assistance to Belgrade over the years, they have persisted in their brutal, anti-democratic policy in Kosovo, fracturing the unity of the Federation, and bringing the country to the brink of civil war.

I trust this wise action by our country will erode support for S. Milosevic (and V. Draskovic, whose policy toward Albanians is even more savage than that of Milosevic), and bring about a radical change of course on Kosovo by Serbia, so as to enable Albanians to exercise their inalienable democratic right of self-government.

Respectfully yours,

Prof. Peter R. Prifti

Copies to:
Sen. Bob Dole
Sen. Don Nickles
Rep. Tom Lantos
Rep. Dante B. Fascell
Hon. Joe DioGuardi

- *Letters to Senators*

San Diego, Ca.
September 15, 1987

The Honorable Senator
Robert Dole
United States Senate
Washington D. C. 20510

Dear Senator Dole:

I wish to commend you on the Resolution on Kosova which you introduced in the Senate last July, with Sen. Paul Simon of Illinois as co-sponsor.

This was a wise and timely step, in view of the troubling situation in Kosova.[1] The Serbs have so far shown a curious inability to think rationally and objectively on the question of Kosova. Indeed, the spirit of anti-Albanian hostility has been growing steadily among the Serbs since 1981, and poses a clear threat to peace and stability in that region.

Hence, the significance of your Resolution on Kosova. I feel confident that it will help to restrain the Serbian momentum toward a bloodbath in the province of Kosova.

I also believe that your statesman-like action will have a positive effect in Albania and contribute to better U. S.-Albanian relations.

Enclosed is a copy of a letter I sent to the *New York Times*, regarding your resolution, to which I respectfully invite your attention.

Sincerely yours

Peter R. Prifti

---

[1] Two other letters to the Senator about the Kosova problem dated May 16, 1990 and November 25, 1990 expressed thanks and gratitude for his powerful support of ethnic Albanians in Yugoslavia.

San Diego, Ca.
October 2, 1987

The Honorable
Senator Alan Cranston
1250 24ᵗʰ Str., N. W. Suite 300
Washington , D. C. 20077

Dear Senator Cranston:

I wish to commend you for coming out in opposition to the nomination of Judge Bork for a seat in the U. S. Supreme Court.

My main reason for writing, however, is the question of Kosova in Yugoslavia.[1] This is a matter that concerns over two million ethnic Albanians in Yugoslavia, who are repressed by the government of that country, above all by the Serbs. It's a matter of critical importance for the future of Yugoslavia, and very likely the peace and stability of the Balkan Peninsula.

Recognizing the seriousness of this situation, a group of 57 Representatives in the House (7 of them from our own state of California) submitted a House Concurrent Resolution (162) on July 15, 1987, "expressing concern over the conditions of ethnic Albanians" in Yugoslavia. This was a timely and wise move, which, it is hoped, will help to influence Yugoslav policy on Kosova in the direction of a peaceful and equitable solution of the problem.

Last July, Sen. Robert Dole of Kansas, and Sen. Paul Simon of Illinois, co-sponsored a Senate Resolution asserting that the Albanians in Yugoslavia are being persecuted. This is a sound initiative-- indeed, an act of statesmanship that serves the cause of peace and democracy. Trusting that you and I are in accord on this point, I would be very pleased to learn that you support the Resolution. Strong support of this Resolution by the Senate is certain, I believe, to make the Yugoslav leadership sit up and take notice.

To acquaint you further with the facts on Kosova, I am enclosing herewith an article I published recently titled, "The Plight of Ethnic Albanians In Yugoslavia". Please look at it.

Sincerely yours,

Peter R. Prifti

---

[1] Three other letters on Kosova to the Senator, are dated: December 22, 1982, May 2, 1988 and October 9, 1989.

San Diego, Ca.
November 2, 1988

The Honorable Senator
Larry Pressler
United States Senate
Washington, D. C. 20510

Dear Senator Pressler:

I have just read the text of the colloquy you held on Yugoslavia with your distinguished colleagues, Senator Paul Simon of Illinois and Senator Alfonse D'Amato of New York. I also read your speech headed, "Yugoslavia Must Avoid Civil War" (as per *Congressional Record*, dt. Wed., Oct. 12, 1988).

I applaud warmly the comments made by you and your colleagues, which are strongly supportive of ethnic Albanians in Yugoslavia, for decades the victims of Serbian oppression (as well as Montenegrin and Macedonian oppression).[1]

In my view, friction and turmoil in Kosova will not cease as long as Serbia insists on having the upper hand there, maintaining what amounts to colonial rule over Albanians, and ignoring their petitions to be allowed to manage their own affairs (indeed, punishing them cruelly for daring to voice such sentiments!).

The leaders of Yugoslavia, and especially those of Serbia, will do well to pay attention to your remarks, and those of your colleagues, which clearly point the way to ending the current crisis, and laying the foundation for a just solution of the problem.

Sincerely yours,

Peter R. Prifti

---

[1] Another letter, sent to the Senator on May 16, 1990, congratulated him for his co-sponsorship of the Senate Concurrent Resolution no. 124, dated April 26, '90 which lashes out at Yugoslavia and the Republic of Serbia for persecuting the two-million-plus ethnic Albanians.

San Diego, Ca.
November 2, 1988

The Honorable Senator
Alfonse D'Amato
United States Senate
Washington. D. C. 20510

Dear Senator D'Amato:

I wish to congratulate you on the splendid support you gave to the Albanians[1] in Yugoslavia in the colloquy with Senator Pressler and Senator Simon on October 12, '88.

You spoke with the voice of a statesman, and a man of conscience who is rightly outraged over the oppression of ethnic Albanians by the Serb majority in Yugoslavia.

I am confident that the Albanians of America, who are the proud heirs of a culture that values integrity and straight talk, applaud and respect you for championing the just cause of their co-nationals in Yugoslavia in their hour of need.

Respectfully yours,

Prof. Peter R. Prifti

---

[1] Two other letters sent to Senator D'Amato, the first one on May 16, 1990, and the last one on November 25, 1990 congratulate him for his splendid support to the Albanians in Yugoslavia.

San Diego, Ca.
October 9, 1989

Senator Pete Wilson
U.S. Senate
Washington D. C. 20510

Dear Senator Wilson:

Permit me to invite your attention to the plight of nearly three million ethnic Albanians in Yugoslavia. Concentrated mostly in the province of Kosova, these Albanians are cruelly repressed by the Republic of Serbia which has jurisdiction over the province. An especially vicious manifestation of such repression took place in Kosova last March, when Yugoslav police and army units killed and wounded hundreds of Albanians, merely for exercising their lawful right to protest against the drastic curbing of the autonomy of their province by Serbia.[1]

The brutal crackdown sent shivers throughout Europe, drawing criticism by Amnesty International and many other human rights organizations. Our own Congress, as you know, was shocked to the point that it approved Amendments condemning Yugoslavia for gross human rights violations against her ethnic Albanian population.

I trust, Honorable Senator, that you will strongly endorse the language of these Amendments when the Foreign Aid Bill comes up for a vote. Such endorsement by the Congress will send a clear message to the Yugoslav authorities that we expect them to cease and desist their brutal persecution of ethnic Albanians. In my view the endorsement of the language would be both a reaffirmation of our country's adherence to the ideals of liberty and justice, and a concrete contribution to the stability and welfare of the Yugoslav Federation.

Sincerely yours,

Peter R. Prifti

---

[1] Another letter, sent to Senator Pete Wilson on May 18, 1990, congratulated him on signing, along with twelve other Senators, a letter that was addressed to Secretary of State, James Baker, regarding Albanians in Kosova.

PETE WILSON   **UNITED STATES SENATE**   COMMITTEES :
CALIFORNIA   Washington D. C. 20510   ARMED SERVICES
                                              AGRICULTURE, NUTRITION AND
                                                      FORESTRY.
                                              SPECIAL COMMITTEE ON AGING
                                              JOINT ECONOMIC COMMITTEE

January 19, 1990

Mr. Peter R. Prifti
P.O. Box 4441
San Diego, California 92104

Dear Mr. Prifti

Thank you for contacting me regarding resolutions introduced in Congress
concerning the abuses of human rights in both Yugoslavia and Albania.

I agree with the view that some of these resolutions narrowly focused on real or
alleged persecutions of specific minority populations while ignoring the suppression
of basic religious and political freedoms in other communities of southeastern
Europe. Most of my colleagues on the House and Senate Foreign Relations
Committee also recognized this problem, and as a result, the final version of the FY
1990 State Department Authorization Bill did dot contain any provisions addressing
the human rights records of either the Yugoslavian or Albanian governments.

Congress, however, must continue to take a leading role in condemning systematic
tyranny and ethnic discrimination in all areas of the world where men and women do
not enjoy the right to exercise self-determination. Towards this end, please rest
assured of my ongoing commitment as a U. S. Senator to strongly condemn human
rights abuses by any regime that does not govern with the consent of its people.

Thank you once again for making me aware of your views on this important
moral issue.

                         Sincerely,

                         PETE WILSON

PW : pm

San Diego, Ca.
May 16, 1990

Senator Richard Luger
United States Senate
Washington, D. C. 20510

Honorable Sen. Luger:

I am gratified to learn that you were one of some dozen Senators who recently addressed a letter to Secretary of State, James Baker, regarding Albanians in Kosova who are "suffering extreme oppression at the hands of Serbian authorities."

It is hard to believe, but the fact is that Serbian racism and violence against Albanians is fed by the very segment of the Serbian population that should be the light of reason, understanding, tolerance and restraint; namely the Serbian intellectuals, writers and artists. The hostile declarations of the Serb Academy of Sciences and Arts toward Albanians is clear proof of this. We probably will not see a significant, long-term change in Serbian policy on Kosova, until we see a radical change of attitude toward Albanians by the Serbian intelligentsia.

Please accept my best wishes in all your endeavors, and especially those that affect the lives and fortunes of Albanians in the pitiful Federation of Yugoslavia.

Respectfully yours,

Prof. Peter R. Prifti

San Diego, Ca.
May 16, 1990

Senator Claiborne Pell
United States Senate
Washington, D. C. 20510

Honorable Senator:

Please accept my warm appreciation for all that you are doing to help the downtrodden Albanians in Yugoslavia, and especially in Kosova, where the Serbian chief Slobodan Milosevic, is riding roughshod over them. In particular, I wish to thank you for your sponsorship of Senate Concurrent Resolution 124 last month, which speaks out boldly in condemnation of the policies of Serbia and Yugoslavia that deny Albanians their right to live as equals and as free men and women, like other ethnic groups in that country.

Milosevic is the culmination of Serbian efforts in our day to humiliate, de-humanize and de-nationalize ethnic Albanians. That is why, his fall from power -- when it comes, as it should -- may well signal a turning point in the history of Serbia; a shift from racist, dictatorial, irrational and violent politics, to the politics of reason, justice, equality and true brotherhood.

I do believe that your work in Congress, in behalf of the Albanian minority, is contributing to the process of democratization in Yugoslavia, including Serbia, where it is needed the most.

Respectfully yours,

Peter R. Prifti

San Diego, Ca.
May 16, 1990

Senator George Mitchell
United States Senate
Washington, D. C. 20510

Honorable Sen. Mitchell:

I am writing to commend you and to thank you for supporting the demands of ethnic Albanians in Yugoslavia for equality and democracy.

I am of the opinion that your continued support of the oppressed Albanians, together with the support of your colleagues in Congress, will one day crack the wall of Serbian intransigence and induce Belgrade to seek a peaceful and democratic solution to the conflict in Kosova.

Respectfully yours,

Peter R. Prifti

George J. Mitchell
Senator
COMMITTEES:

UNITED STATES SENATE

Washington D. C. 2051   FINANCE
                                    ENVIRONMENT AND
                                    PUBLIC WORKS
                                    VETERANS' AFFAIRS

June 8, 1990

Professor Peter R. Prifti
P.O. Box 4441
San Diego, California 92104

Dear Professor Prifti:

Thank you for contacting me to express your views on matters of interest and concern to you. I appreciate hearing from you.

Since becoming Senate Majority Leader, I have been pleased that a large number of people like yourself, from all over the country, have taken the time to write to me. Unfortunately, however because the volume of mail I receive in my office is sometimes very large, I have found that I am not always able to respond to every letter in as much detail as I would like. Nevertheless, I want you to know that your correspondence has been received, and your views noted. Our system works best when people stay involved and concerned with the action of their elected officials, and when those elected officials have the views of informed citizens on hand. I hope you will continue to make your views known.

With best wishes.

Sincerely,

George J. Mitchell

San Diego, Ca.
May 17, 1990

Senator Paul Simon
United States Senate
Washington, D. C. 20510

Honorable Sen. Simon:

I am writing to you again to thank you warmly for your ceaseless efforts in behalf of the oppressed ethnic Albanians in Kosova and other parts of Yugoslavia.

It is my considered judgement that Serbian leader, Slobodan Milosevic, is a political dinosaur, an anachronism, a throw - back to the Middle Ages. He has shown to be an "expert" in Medieval statecraft, seeing how he has manipulated and fed the sentiments and yearnings of the Serbian people for the long - gone Serbian Medieval Empire. But he is not a politician for our time.

As far as the question of Kosova is concerned, he has been a disaster.[1] And he is proving to be a disaster to the rest of Yugoslavia, for he has gone a long way toward wrecking the federation. Truly, the sooner he falls, the better.

Please know that I value deeply your work to help the defenseless Albanians in Yugoslavia, in their hour of need.

Respectfully yours,

Peter R. Prifti

---

[1] A previous letter to Senator Simon on September 15, 1987 congratulated him on a Resolution on Kosova presented in the U.S. Senate. Another letter, dated Nov. 2, 1988 thanked him for his ceaseless efforts in behalf of the oppressed ethnic Albanians in Yugoslavia.

Paul Simon
COMMITTEES :
Illinois
RESOURCES

LABOR AND HUMAN

JUDICIARY
FOREIGN RELATIONS
BUDGET

UNITED STATES SENATE
Washington D. C. 20510

June 5, 1990

Prof. Peter R. Prifti
P.O. Box 4441
San Diego, California 92104

Dear Professor Prifti:

That you for contacting my office.

It is good to know my efforts in the Senate are appreciated, and it was very thoughtful of you to take the time to write.

Thanks again for letting me hear from you.

My best wishes.

Cordially,

Paul Simon
U. S. Senator

PS/vas

San Diego, Ca.
May 17, 1990

Senator Daniel Patrick Moynihan
United States Senate
Washington, D. C. 20510

Honorable Sen. Moynihan:

I am writing to compliment and thank you for adding your signature to the letter addressed recently to Secretary of State, James Baker, regarding Albanians in Kosova who (to quote from the letter) are "suffering extreme oppression at the hands of Serbian authorities". This was a statesman-like act which has been warmly welcomed by Albanian Americans throughout our country.

Rather than seek to negotiate an equitable and honorable settlement of the Kosova problem, where most of the two-million-plus Albanians in Yugoslavia live, Slobodan Milosevic of Serbia has chosen to rely on brute force to keep Albanians down. He has thus made enemies of Albanians, and not only Albanians, but Slovenians and Croatians as well, because they sympathize with the plight of Albanians. The record shows that Milosevic is not a builder, but a wrecker. He is tearing down in four years what the late Tito built in 40! The sooner, therefore, he is booted out of office, the better!

Respectfully yours,

Peter R. Prifti

DANIEL P. MOYNIHAN
New York

UNITED STATES SENATE
Washington D. C. 20510

October 5, 1990

Prof. Peter R. Prifti
P.O. Box 4441
San Diego, California 92104

Dear Prof. Prifti:

I apologize for the delay in responding to your letter. While I am pleased that an extraordinary number of New Yorkers have taken the time to contact my office recently, this increasing volume prevents me from responding to you as promptly as you deserve.

Thank you for contacting me to express your thoughts on the unfortunate events taking place in the Serbian province of Kosova in Yugoslavia.

The situation in Kosova is tragic indeed. Ethnic Albanians have suffered greatly in this on-going conflict, and the Yugoslavian government has been unable -- or unwilling -- to suggest any constructive course of action. Moreover many Serbians disapprove of the policies of their Serbian rulers as well as with those of the central Yugoslavian government. These individuals have also suffered.

It is time for Yugoslavia to join its Eastern European neighbors in moving to guarantee fundamental liberties for all its citizens, including those living in Kosovo. And we, here, in the United States should encourage positive steps toward that end.

Please be assured that I will monitor closely the situation in Kosovo and give serious consideration to any bills or resolutions concerning both Kosovo and Yugoslavia that come before the Senate.

Again, I do thank you for contacting me. Please do not hesitate to do so again in the future.

Sincerely,

Daniel Patrick Moynihan

San Diego, Ca.
May 17, 1990

Senator Jesse Helms
United States Senate
Washington D. C. 20510

Honorable Sen. Helms:

I have noted with satisfaction your support over the years of the cause of Albanians in Yugoslavia. This is a matter of great concern to the tens of thousands of Albanian Americans, and your consistent stand in this matter is greatly appreciated.

It is comforting indeed to see our leaders in Congress fight for the human rights of the downtrodden Albanians in Kosova. I trust you will continue your support of them in the times to come.

Respectfully your,

Peter R. Prifti

San Diego, Ca.
May 17, 1990

Senator Joseph Lieberman
United States Senate
Washington, D. C. 20510

Honorable Sen. Lieberman:

I am writing to thank you for signing, along with a dozen colleagues of yours in the Senate, a letter sent recently to the Secretary of State, James Baker, regarding Albanians in Kosova who, as the letter put it, are "suffering extreme oppression at the hands of Serbian authorities."

As far as Albanians are concerned, Serbia is de facto the most Stalinist political body in Yugoslavia. And in view of the rapid pace of liberalization in neighboring Albania, Serbia may soon be the only Stalinist "state" in the Balkans. Yet, at a deeper level, Serbian Stalinism has its roots in Serbian political culture, which has been aggressive and expansionist for generations, especially toward Albanians.

I trust you shall continue to help the Albanians in Kosova, Macedonia and Montenegro to throw off the shackles of their oppressors.

Respectfully yours,

Peter R. Prifti

San Diego, Ca.
May 17, 1990

Senator Malcolm Wallop
United States Senate
Washington, D.C. 20510

Honorable Sen. Wallop:

I am writing to express my pleasure and thanks to you for the letter which you, and a dozen colleagues of yours in the Senate, addressed recently to Secretary of State, James Baker, regarding Albanians in Kosova, Yugoslavia, who are "suffering extreme oppression at the hands of Serbian authorities"--to quote from the letter.

Serbia is trying hard to convince the world that the conflict in Kosova is religious in character; or, at least, that religion is a major component of the conflict. It is telling people that the conflict is between Christian Serbs and Moslem Albanians. This is but one of many Serbian myths about Kosova. For the fact is that the conflict in Kosova is political, not religious. Albanians in Yugoslavia are fighting for their political rights; they have no religious ax to grind. Truly, when this Serbian myth is laid to rest -- it has actually been around for generations -- the forces of freedom and democracy will have won another victory for Kosova and Yugoslavia!

Respectfully yours,

Peter R. Prifti

San Diego, Ca.
May 17, 1990

Senator Chris Dodd
United States Senate
Washington, D. C. 20510

Honorable Sen. Dodd:

I am writing to commend you for your endorsement of the recent letter (signed by 12 other colleagues of yours in the Senate) to Secretary of State, James Baker, regarding Albanians in Kosova who are indeed "suffering extreme oppression at the hands of Serbian authorities."

Another step which would contribute, I believe, to a just resolution of the conflict in Kosova, is for United States officials, including Senators and Representatives, to make regular and frequent visits to Kosova and Belgrade, so as to obtain first-hand data on the situation of ethnic Albanians in that country. This is vitally necessary, in my view, seeing that Serbian authorities are doing their utmost to conceal the truth about Kosova and mislead world public opinion into believing that "all is right" with the Albanians in Yugoslavia.

Respectfully yours,

Peter R. Prifti

San Diego, Ca.
May 17, 1990

Senator Frank Lautenberg
United States Senate
Washington, D. C. 20510

Honorable Sen. Lautenberg :

I am writing to compliment you on your support of the just cause of ethnic Albanians in Kosova, Yugoslavia.[1] In saying this, I am confident that I speak not only for myself, but for the Albanian community in our country, as well -- all the way from Maine and New Jersey to California and Washington state.

I take this occasion to also appeal to you to support initiatives in Congress to establish an "institutional United States presence" in Kosova, such as a consulate or a U.S.I.A. service. Such a presence would make it possible to monitor closely developments in that troubled area, provide direct access to the Albanian community, and at the same time would tend to inhibit Serbian violence against Albanians.

Respectfully yours,

Prof. Peter R. Prifti

---

[1] Another letter sent to Senator Lautenberg on November 25, '90 expressed delight and warm thanks for his efforts to bring relief to the embattled ethnic Albanians in Kosova, Yugoslavia.

San Diego, Ca.
May 17, 1990

Senator Joseph Biden
United States Senate
Washington, D. C. 20510

Honorable Sen. Biden:

This letter comes to you with my warm thanks for your support of the Albanians in Yugoslavia, who suffer constant humiliation and deprivation at the hands of the Serbs and their Macedonian and Montenegrin allies.

Serbia has tried hard to paint Albanians as the aggressors in Kosova, accusing them of poisoning Serbian water wells, setting fire to Serbian religious shrines, destroying Serbian properties, and raping Serbian women. But when asked to produce evidence for such accusations, Serbian authorities and their media find themselves in a tough spot. They cannot back up their charges.

The Serbian propaganda machine is rapidly going bankrupt, as far as the Kosova issue is concerned. And it is no wonder. As an Albanian proverb has it, "You cannot hide the sun with a sieve."

Please continue your laudable efforts to secure democratic and human rights for ethnic Albanians in Yugoslavia.

Respectfully yours,

Peter R. Prifti

San Diego, Ca.
May 18, 1990

Senator Robert Byrd
United States Senate
Washington, D. C. 20510

Honorable Sen. Byrd:

I am writing to commend you for endorsing the letter which you, and a dozen other Senators, addressed recently to Secretary of State, James Baker, concerning Albanians in Kosova, Yugoslavia, who, as the letter put it, are "suffering extreme oppression at the hands of Serbian authorities". Heaven knows, Albanians in that country are in great need of such sympathy and support as you have given them.

After fomenting a vicious anti-Albanian campaign in Yugoslavia, Serbian authorities are trying to do the same thing abroad. Instead of seeking to defuse the conflict through open talks with the Albanians, they have carried the struggle to these United States. Working through the media, churches, civic groups, academic institutions and our government, they are hard at work to create an anti-Albanian climate in our country. For example, a friend of mine here in San Diego recently attended a folk fair sponsored by the local Serbian Orthodox Church. There he picked up some of the literature that was prepared for the visitors, and was shocked to see that a great deal of it was full of Serbian polemics against Albanians! Truly, the arrogance and ambition for power of Milosevic and his cohorts have no bounds...

Trusting that you will continue your support of ethnic Albanians in Yugoslavia, I am,

Respectfully yours,

Prof. Peter R. Prifti

San Diego, Ca.
May 18, 1990

Senator Charles Grassley
United States Senate
Washington, D. C. 20510

Honorable Senator Grassley:

I have learned recently, with pleasure, that you are one of thirteen Senators who addressed a letter to Secretary of State, James Baker, regarding Albanians in Kosova, Yugoslavia who (to quote from the letter) are "suffering extreme oppression at the hands of Serbian authorities." Please accept my warm thanks for what you have done.

The Serb-Albanian conflict in Kosova has deep roots, but it can be settled. Outside pressure on Belgrade, especially economic pressure by our country, will go a long way to bring about the result.

However, for a long-term solution, what is needed, I believe, is a turnabout of opinions and attitudes toward Albanians within Serbia itself. A radical change is necessary in what is taught about Albanians in the schools, what is said about them from church pulpits, what is printed about them in the press, what authors write about them in books, and what government officials say about them in their speeches. When that change occurs, we can confidently expect freedom and democracy to come to Kosova, and peaceful, friendly and fruitful relations between Serbs and Albanians.

Respectfully yours,

Prof. Peter R. Prifti

San Diego, Ca.
May 18, 1990

Senator Phil Gramm
United States Senate
Washington, D. C. 20510

Honorable Sen. Gramm:

I am writing to commend you for your support of Albanians in Kosova in their conflict with Serbia. Specifically I am referring to the letter which you, and twelve colleagues of yours in the Senate, addressed recently to the Secretary of State, James Baker, in connection with Albanians in Kosova, who (as the letter correctly put it) are "suffering extreme oppression at the hands of Serbian authorities."

It is sad but true, nevertheless, that the Serbs have a curious psychological hang-up about Albanians. Because most of the Albanians in Yugoslavia are Moslems, they tend to identify them with the Turks, their former oppressors. This is a pathological condition whose roots go far back into the Middle Ages, when the Turks crushed the Serbian Medieval Kingdom at the Battle of Kosova in 1389. One of the reasons why the Serbs have been persecuting the Albanians since the 1870s is to "settle old scores," as they put it -- old scores, that is, against their old Moslem "enemy." They simply ignore the fact (for expedient political reasons) that Albanians fought the Turks tooth and nail for over five centuries, longer and apparently more fiercely than any other Balkan peoples, until they freed themselves from the Ottoman Empire in 1912.

Trusting that you will continue your laudable support for the just cause of ethnic Albanians in Yugoslavia, I am,

Respectfully yours,

Prof. Peter R. Prifti

- Letters to Congressmen

San Diego, Ca
September 17, 1987

The Honorable John Miller
U. S. House of Representatives
Washington, D. C. 20515

Dear Congressman Miller:

I wish to commend you for your support of the Concurrent Resolution (H. Con. Res. 162, 100th Congress, 1st Session, dt. July 15, 1987) , "expressing concern over the conditions of ethnic Albanians living in the Socialist Federal Republic of Yugoslavia."

Your co-sponsorship of this Resolution is timely and an act of statesmanship that is especially meaningful on this, the 200th Anniversary of the signing of our Constitution. Your open public support of the just cause of Albanians in Yugoslavia is welcomed by Albanian-Americans not only as an act of political realism, but also as an expression of the spirit of freedom and democracy that our Constitution embodies and symbolizes.

The situation in Kosova [1] remains tense and ominous, owing to the frenzied Serbian drive to deprive Albanians even of the limited rights they have won since World War II, and reduce them to their prewar status of total powerlessness and subjugation to Serbia. This short-sighted policy is leading Kosova toward a bloody Serb-Albanian confrontation, with incalculable consequences for peace and stability in the Balkans.

Hence the importance of the House Resolution on Kosova. I feel confident that the action you and your colleagues have taken will help to restrain the irrational Serbian momentum toward disaster in that area of the world, and promote initiatives toward a peaceful and just settlement of the issue.

Respectfully yours,

---

[1] The author also sent a letter to Honorable Congressmen Gary Ackerman and another to Honorable Gerald Solomon to express his thanks for their support of the Concurrent Resolution about the situation in Kosova.

Peter R. Prifti

TOM LANTOS
CALIFORNIA

FOREIGN AFFAIRS COMMITTEE
GOVERNMENT OPERATIONS COMMITTEE
SELECT COMMITTEE ON AGING

CONGRESS OF THE UNITED STATES
House of Representatives

Washington, D.C. 20515

October 5, 1987

Mr. Peter Prifti
P.O. Box 4441
San Diego, California 92104

Dear Mr. Prifti

Thank you very much for taking the time to share your thoughts with me about H. Con. Res 162, a bill expressing concern over Albanians in Yugoslavia.[1]

I very much appreciate the fact that you are supporting my position on this issue. You can be assured that when the appropriate legislation comes before the House, my vote will reflect your opinions.

Thanks again for contacting me. Please continue to keep me informed of your views on other issues of concern to you.

Cordially,

Tom Lantos
Member of Congress

---

[1] *Note* - The letter sent by the author to Congressman Lantos is not available.

San Diego, Ca
November 17, 1987

The Honorable Jim Bates
U. S. House of Representatives
Washington, D. C. 20515

Dear Congressman Bates:

Thank you for your recent communication, dated November 12, 1987. I appreciate your concern and efforts to reduce the federal budget and trade deficits, and I wish you success at it.

Permit me to alert you to another issue, connected with foreign affairs which, although geographically distant, is nevertheless important, in my opinion. I am referring to the plight of the ethnic Albanians in Yugoslavia, who inhabit the region of Kosova[1] and number over two million. On July 15, 1987 Rep. Joe DioGuardi (N. Y.) and 56 of his colleagues in the House submitted a Concurrent Resolution (H. Con. Res. 162, 100th Congress, 1st Session) to the House Foreign Affairs Committee "expressing concern over the conditions of ethnic Albanians living in the Socialist Federal Republic of Yugoslavia." (A similar Resolution was introduced a couple of days later in the Senate by Sen. Robert Dole and Sen. Paul Simon.)

Among the co-sponsors of the House Resolutions were seven Congressmen from our state of California, which I welcomed. The situation in Kosova is deteriorating in the direction of a violent Serb-Albanian confrontation. Hence any influence the United States can exert in Belgrade to reverse the trend would serve the interest of peace and stability in Yugoslavia and the Balkans, as well as advance the cause of ethnic and human rights with regard to the oppressed Albanian in Yugoslavia.

Looking forward to your future communications, I remain

Sincerely yours,

Peter R. Prifti

---

[1] A similar letter was sent to Honorable Congressman Guy V. Molinari for his support of the Concurrent Resolution over the conditions of ethnic Albanians in Yugoslavia.

San Diego, Ca
October 28, 1988

The Honorable Joe DioGuardi
U. S. House of Representatives
Washington, D. C. 20515

Dear Mr. DioGuardi:

I thank you heartily for your understanding of the plight of ethnic Albanians in Yugoslavia, [1] and your laudable support of their struggle to gain their lawful rights in that country.

Next year, I believe, will be a watershed in Serb-Albanian relation. In June of 1989 the Serbs will commemorate the 600th anniversary of the Battle of Kosova. Being in the grip of chauvinistic frenzy, they will do their utmost to deprive Kosova of her autonomous status and melt her into the Republic of Serbia. If need be, they will resort to genocide to get what they want. They will take up arms against the defenseless Albanian population, and slaughter them by the tens of thousands. Their thinking, no doubt, is "It's now, or never!"

Already they have threatened to do just that in recent street demonstrations. Their cries: "Give us arms," "We want blood," "Let's wipe out the Albanians" are proof of their savage intentions.

But 1989 can also be a year of opportunity. Wise and courageous statesmanship can deal a decisive blow to Slobodan Milosevic and his warmongering Serb fanatics. It's an imperative of the times, I believe, to stop him, if Yugoslavia is to avoid bloody inter-ethnic strife, chaos and collapse.

Sincerely yours,

Prof. Peter R. Prifti

---

[1] A previous letter on the issue of Kosova was sent to Honorable J. DioGuardi on September 22, 1987 and another on November 25, 1990.

JOSEPH J. DIOGUARDI
20th DISTRICT, NEW YORK

CONGRESS OF THE UNITED STATES
House of Representatives
Washington, D.C. 20515

November 2, 1988

Mr. Peter R. Prifti
P.O. Box 4441
San Diego, California 92104

Dear Mr. Prifti:

Thank you for taking the time and effort to contact me and enclose a copy of your letter to Secretary of State Shultz. It was good to hear from you and I appreciate your thoughtfulness.

It was good to hear your kind words of support for my efforts on behalf of ethnic Albanians in Yugoslavia. Your letter makes some very good points. You can be assured of my continuing efforts on behalf of all victims of ethnic strife in that region.

Again, it was good to hear from you and if I can ever be of further assistance, please do not hesitate to contact me.

Sincerely,

Josef J. DioGuardi
Member of Congress

JJD/kas

San Diego, Ca
October 28, 1988

The Honorable Tom Lantos
U. S. House of Representatives
Washington, D. C. 20515

Dear Mr. Lantos:

I wish to express my thanks and gratitude to you for your sympathy for, and support of the Albanians in Yugoslavia, in their struggle for equal treatment in that country.

The Serbs live in the same country with ethnic Albanians, but not in the same world. Temporally they live in the 20th Century but emotionally and spiritually they are mired in the Middle Ages. They long for the long-lost Medieval Serbian Empire with its seat in Kosova.

Unfortunately, instead of facing reality, they are regressing. Their recent behavior indicates that they are on the move to recapture (after a fashion) the glory of their vanished empire by swallowing up Kosova. Then Vojvodina. Then other parts of Yugoslavia. Then...

This quixotic drive, I feel, will reach very dangerous levels next year when the Serbs commemorate the 600th anniversary of the Battle of Kosova, (June 28). On that occasion, the chauvinistic passions of Serbian mobs will no doubt reach fever-pitch excitement. And the Albanians will be the primary target of those murderous passions.[1]

I am gratified to know that you, Honorable Lantos, along with other colleagues in Congress, are active in opposing Serbia's misguided policy in Kosova, and are striving to get the Yugoslav leaders to reverse that policy, and deal with the problem of Kosova from a rational, realistic and democratic perspective.

Sincerely yours,

Prof. Peter R. Prifti

---

[1] Three other letters expressing the author's concern about Kosova were sent to Congressman of California Tom Lantos, on October 8, '89, May 20, '90 and November 26, '90.

San Diego, Ca
November 1, 1988

The Honorable Wm. Broomfield
U. S. House of Representatives
Washington, D. C. 20515

Dear Mr. Broomfield:

Allow me to express once again my warm thanks for your consistent defense of the downtrodden ethnic Albanian population in Yugoslavia.

Your position on this issue is laudable and statesman-like. You are upholding cherished humanitarian and democratic principles that are sorely needed in the authoritarian state of Yugoslavia, above all in the republic of Serbia, which is aiming to strangle Kosova completely as a political body, and turn the clock back to the dark days of prewar Yugoslavia.

Time is running out on Yugoslavia for a peaceful and democratic solution to the Kosova problem. The rise of Slobodan Milosevic is no accident. He is a natural product of the anti-Albanian psychosis in Serbia, which has been building up steadily since 1981, but whose roots in fact extend far back into the past.

In my view, the light at the end of the Kosova tunnel will appear only with the fall of Milosevic and his Fascist followers.

Sincerely yours,

Prof. Peter R. Prifti

Enc. - Copy of letter to Secretary of State George Shultz.

San Diego, Ca
November 1, 1988

The Honorable Benjamin Gilman
U. S. House of Representatives
Washington, D. C. 20515

Dear Mr. Gilman:

It is a great pleasure and comfort for me to compliment and thank you for your vigorous support of the just cause of ethnic Albanians in Yugoslavia.

As you know, the nationality question in Yugoslavia continues to fester. And the question is most acute with regard to relations between the Serbs and the Albanians in the province of Kosova and other parts of Yugoslavia.

At present (as in past decades), Kosova represents the most extreme case of the abuse of political authority in the Yugoslav Federation. And the root cause of this abuse is the Republic of Serbia. The result is a callous suppression of the legitimate, democratic yearnings of Albanians for self-expression and affirmation of their ethnicity. They are denied their natural right to be masters in the territories they inhabit in overwhelming numbers, and to run their affairs as they see fit, free of Serbia's veto power.

It is in Kosova, in my view, where the need to promote democracy in that country is greatest. Were Serbia to be persuaded, or pressured if need be, to relinquish control over Kosova, the nationality question would be solved, as far as the ethnic Albanians are concerned. Such a development would be a dramatic breakthrough, which could subsequently serve as a powerful example and catalyst for resolving the nationality question in general in the Yugoslav Federation.

Sincerely yours,

Prof. Peter R. Prifti

Enc. - Copy of letter to Secretary George Shultz.

San Diego, Ca
September 28, 1989

The Honorable Dante B. Fascell
Chairman
Committee on Foreign Affairs
House of Representatives
Washington, D. C. 20515

Dear Mr. Fascell:

It was most gratifying to receive your letter regarding the Kosova issue in Yugoslavia. Please rest assured that the delay in my reply does not diminish my appreciation of your fine letter; specifically, your Committee's "concern for human rights violations in Kosovo," and the amendment passed by the House "criticizing Yugoslavia for recent actions in Kosovo."

The action taken by the House and later by the Senate have been warmly welcomed by Albanians in America, and also reported with approval by the official press in Albania -- which marks a new development in that country's attitude toward our government. The new attitude may have favorable repercussions in future U. S. - Albanian relations.

But getting back to Kosova, I have been disappointed by the official reaction in Belgrade to the actions of our Congress. Instead of stopping to review and revise the policy on Kosova, the Yugoslav authorities reacted with barely concealed anger and sense of hurt.

After 20 years of study of the Kosova question, I am convinced that the core of the problem is Serbian racist hatred of Albanians. It is this blind hatred that makes them persecute the Albanians without letup or feelings of remorse. The same aberration has made the Serbs extremely arrogant toward Albanians and prevented them from questioning their Kosova policy, admitting their errors and initiating a democratic dialogue with ethnic Albanians in order to bring about a just resolution of the problem.

Please accept my warm thanks for the persistent efforts of your Committee to defend the victimized Albanians in Yugoslavia, and encourage democratic and humane practices in that frightful Communist dictatorship.

Sincerely yours,

Prof. Peter R. Prifti

San Diego, Ca
May 21, 1990

The Honorable John Porter
U. S. House of Representatives
Washington, D. C. 20515

Dear Congressman Porter:

I am writing to commend you for co-sponsoring the recent Resolution in the House of Representatives, denouncing Serbian and Yugoslav oppression of ethnic Albanians in Kosova. I applaud your efforts to bring sanity to Belgrade politics and end the long nightmare of over two million Albanians in Yugoslavia.

Driven by irrational hatred of Albanians, the Serbs go so far as to deny that Albanians have a "right of domain" in Kosova, arguing speciously that they are usurpers of the land they live on. This is one of the arguments they used to justify the expulsion from Yugoslavia of hundreds of thousands of Albanians, both before and after World War II. In reality, the Serbian argument is a crude revision of history, for the Albanians in Kosova have a far stronger claim to the land than the Serbs. The Slavic ancestors of the Serbs came to the Balkan peninsula only in the 6th and 7th centuries A.D., whereas the ancestors of Albanians, known as Illyrians, inhabited the Balkans, including the land of Dardania (ancient Kosova) at least one thousand years prior to the Slavs.

The Serbs' perverse misreading, or misrepresentation, of the history of Albanians in Kosova, is one of the obstacles to a correct and speedy resolution of the festering conflict in that region.

Respectfully yours,

Prof. Peter R. Prifti

San Diego, Ca
May 21, 1990

The Honorable Robert Lagomarsino
U. S. House of Representatives
Washington, D. C. 20515

Dear Congressman Lagomarsino:

This letter is addressed to you in recognition and appreciation of your work in Congress in behalf of the oppressed Albanians in Kosova and elsewhere in Yugoslavia.

Truly, those Albanians are in need of outside support, especially from our powerful country, which is in a better position to help them than perhaps any other country. The knowledge that we sympathize with their plight and are working to end their persecution by Serbia and the government of Yugoslavia, gives them more strength to endure their bitter fate, and hope that one day they shall be masters in their own land, instead of servants of the Serbs and their allies.

I trust you will continue your commendable efforts to bring to the Albanians of Yugoslavia the fruits of democracy, peace and prosperity. They have been deprived of them far too long.

Respectfully yours,

Prof. Peter R. Prifti

San Diego, Ca
May 21, 1990

The Honorable Gus Yatron
U. S. House of Representatives
Washington, D. C. 20515

Dear Congressman Yatron :

I am writing to compliment and to thank you for your noble international and humanitarian work, in response to the plight of the Albanians in Kosova, Yugoslavia. I, along with tens of thousands of Albanians in America, applaud your efforts.

Last year, or the year before, Serbia had another opportunity to end its interference into the affairs of Kosova, or to put it more exactly, to end its semi-colonial rule in that province. But instead of expanding the rights and powers of the province and granting it the status of a Republic, Serbia effectively wiped out its autonomy status, and now maintains almost total control in Kosova. Instead of defusing the conflict in Kosova, the Serbs and the Yugoslav government have aggravated it.

In these circumstances, much work remains to be done to bring Belgrade to its senses, and agree to a political settlement of the Kosova problem by entering into a dialogue with Albanian leaders, and respecting the wishes and aspirations of the Albanian people in Yugoslavia.

Respectfully yours,

Prof. Peter R. Prifti

San Diego, Ca
May 21, 1990

The Honorable Lee Hamilton
U. S. House of Representatives
Washington, D. C. 20515

Dear Congressman Hamilton:

Please accept my warm thanks for your support of ethnic Albanians in Yugoslavia, in their painful struggle for human rights and the opportunity to live decent lives in peace and freedom. With your stand on this issue that affects the lives and fortunes of millions of Albanians in Yugoslavia, you have won the gratitude of Albanians throughout our country.

Instead of embracing the future-oriented political trends in Europe, based on tolerance, understanding and cooperation, the Serbs are looking backward. They are mired in the discredited Balkan politics of the past; that is to say, the politics of force, violence and expansionism. Their adherence to, and practice of such wrong-headed politics is best shown in Kosova, where they have assumed almost total control over Albanians inhabitants, and persecute them with impunity.

Truly, Milosevic is out of step with the time. And the sooner the Serbs abandon him and attune themselves to the "new vision of the Balkans" that is slowly evolving right before our eyes, the better it will be for them, for Albanians and the rest of the people of Yugoslavia.

Respectfully yours,

Prof. Peter R. Prifti

DANTE B. FASCELL, FLORIDA
CHAIRMAN

CONGRESS OF THE UNITED STATES
Committee on Foreign Affairs

House of Representatives

Washington, D.C. 20515

June 19, 1990

Prof. Peter R. Prifti
P.O. Box 4441
San Diego, Ca 92104

Dear Prof. Prifti

Thank you for you recent letter expressing concern for the fate of ethnic Albanians in the Autonomous Province of Kosovo in Yugoslavia.

The Committee on Foreign Affairs is closely monitoring the delicate situation in Kosovo and has informed the Embassy of Yugoslavia here in Washington of its concerns for human rights violations in Kosovo. In addition, the House of Representatives has recently passed an amendment to legislation on foreign assistance criticizing Yugoslavia for recent actions in Kosovo which have resulted in several deaths, and the arrest, imprisonment and isolation of hundreds of others.

You may be assured that the Committee on Foreign Affairs will continue to press Yugoslavia to bring its human rights practices in line with its obligations under the U. N. Charts, the Helsinki Final Act and other international documents.

Best wishes

Sincerely yours,

DANTE B. FASCELL
Chairman

DBF:msb

2. Letters to UN Officials

San Diego, Cal.
Jan. 24, 1992

The Honorable Cyrus Vance
Personal Envoy of the U.N. Secretary General
425 Lexington Ave.
New York, N.Y. 10017

Honorable Sir:

I am writing in reference to the crisis in Kosova, in the Republic of Serbia.

In the middle of the night, Serbian police cordon off Albanian villages and fire their weapons wildly into the air. The startled people rush to the doors and windows. The police immediately rush into the houses and start searching supposedly for hidden weapons. They turn the house upside down, breaking up the furniture, robbing the members of the household of their money and valuables and beating them up without mercy, beating some of them unconscious, while abusing them with vile language, and threatening to wipe them out.

Sir, I am convinced that the threats of the Serbs are not to be taken lightly. They spring from irrational racist hatred of Albanians,, and could easily explode into wanton slaughter of the Albanian population.

I implore you, Sir, to act promptly to prevent the impending genocide of an innocent and defenseless people.

Please urge the Security Council of the United Nations to send Peacekeeping Forces to Kosova without delay. Prompt action by the UN is needed to forestall tragedy. Such action would also go a long way toward resolving the conflict between Serbians and Albanians in that troubled region.

Respectfully yours,

Prof. Peter R. Prifti

425 LEXINGTON AVENUE
NEW YORK, N. Y. 10017 - 3909

January 31, 1992

Professor Peter R. Prifti
Post Office Box 4441
San Diego, California 92104

Dear Professor Prifti:

Cyrus Vance has asked me to reply to your letter, just received, concerning his efforts in Yugoslavia and, in particular, the situation in Kosova. Given the current situation in Yugoslavia, with the Geneva agreement of November 23rd still not being implemented, Mr. Vance at present cannot recommend to the Secretary-General the deployment of a peacekeeping operation.

With respect to Kosova, Mr. Vance has raised the issue directly with Serbian leaders on several occasions. Additionally, he has brought the situation to the attention of the Secretary - General of the United Nations and, through him, to the Security Council, stressing that human rights are indivisible and must be recognized everywhere.

Sincerely yours,

Ambassador Herbert S. Okun
Special Adviser to Mr. Vance

San Diego, Ca.
February 5, 1992

Ambassador Herbert S. Okun
Special Adviser to Cyrus Vance
Personal Envoy of U. N. Secretary General
425 Lexington Ave.
New York, N. Y. 10017

Dear Ambassador:

I wish to thank you for your kind letter of January 31, 1992. It is gratifying to learn of the efforts of Mr. Vance to engage the United Nations to come to the aid of Kosova.

In *The New York Review of Books* issue of January 30, 1992. BBC correspondent, Misha Glenny writes: "After reporting for more than a year on the reborn Chetnik movement in Serbia I have found its most striking characteristic to be its obsession with violence. Its members apparently take pleasure in torturing and mutilating civilian and military opponents alike."(p. 30).

The Albanians in Kosova have known this tragic truth for decades, from the Rankovic era down to the Milosevic era of our days. Bands of Chetniks, armed to the teeth, are roaming wildly throughout Kosova, stopping innocent Albanians on the road or bursting into their homes without provocation, and indulging their sadistic passion for violence in whatever way it strikes their perverted fancy.

Sir, the Chetniks and their allies are terrorizing the Albanians of Kosova at will. They are making life unbearable for them.

The savagery of the Serbs towards Albanians (and others) must be checked, for it is a cancer in the body of the Balkans. It should also be an intolerable burden on the conscience of the Europe of our time.

Respectfully yours,

Prof. Peter Prifti

San Diego, Ca.
February 13, 1992

The Honorable Cyrus Vance
Personal Envoy of the U.N. Secretary General
425 Lexington Ave.
New York, N.Y. 10017

Honorable Sir:

I am taking this opportunity to write to you again about Kosova, and respectfully invite your attention to the following:

Even as I write, contingents of hundreds of armed Serbian police are using brutal force to prevent nearly half a million Albanian pupils in Kosova from entering school buildings and attending classes in Albanian. This is a calculated policy of the Serbs to deny Albanians the right to an education. It is not hard to understand the motive of the Serbs. They believe that by denying Albanians the opportunity to be taught in their own language, eventually they will lose their Albanian consciousness and become assimilated into Serbian society.

Sir, the goal of Serbia in Kosova is obvious. It is the genocide of ethnic Albanians -- by violence, if necessary (and they are daily creating the conditions for that), or by the slow death of their culture, or a combination of the two.

Since both of those courses are abhorrent and unacceptable to men of decency and civilized societies, I entreat you, Sir, to use your great influence at the U.N. to negate Serbia's current policy and long-range plan in Kosova. A good start would be to send U.N. Peacekeeping Forces to the region, as soon as possible.

Respectfully yours,

Prof. Peter R. Prifti

3. Letters to Yugoslav Officials

San Diego, California (U.S.A.)
20 March 1987

Mr. Svetislav Dolasevich
Chairman,
Presidency of the SAP of Kosova
Prishtina, Yugoslavia

Dear Mr. Dolasevich:

This letter is in reference to Professor Ali Hadri, formerly Director of the Institute of History in Kosova, and presently a member of the Academy of Science and Arts in Kosova.

It has come to my attention that Prof. Hadri has been accused of committing a legal offense in connection with his retirement, for which he was to be tried in court.

Prof. Hadri is a distinguished scholar and intellectual, who is widely recognized in the United States for his contributions to the advancement of learning and education in Kosova and Yugoslavia. He has brought honor to his profession and to the country where he lives. Both as a scholar and as a man of integrity, he has won the respect and affection of numerous people in the United States.

I appeal to you, therefore, to dismiss all charges against Prof. Ali Hadri, and let him live and work in peace. He is a man who deserves to be honored, not persecuted.

Sincerely yours,

Prof. Peter R. Prifti
P.O. Box 4441, San Diego, Ca. 92104, U.S.A.

Prof. Peter R. Prifti
P.O. Box 4441
San Diego, Ca. 92104
U.S. of America

October 7, 1987

The Honorable Lazar Moisov
President
Presidency of the S.F.R. of Yugoslavia
2, ul. Lenin
Belgrade, Yugoslavia

Dear Mr. President,

This letter[1] is in reference to the incident on September 3, 1987 at the military barracks of Paracin, which resulted in the death of five military men and the wounding of several others.

I grieve for those who lost their lives, as well as for the wounded, and I extend my sympathies to the families of the victim. I do this without regard to the ethnic backgrounds of the persons involved, for pain and suffering and death do not recognize ethnic boundaries. Before the great realities of existence we are all the same: not Serbs or Bosnians or Turks or Albanians, but human beings, equally frail, equally fallible, equally in need of understanding, respect, dignity and help.

Tragic incidents like this, and far worse, happen in America rather frequently. But they do not get out of hand to inflame the passions, to aggravate relations between one ethnic group and another, to become a festering wound in the body of the society and a destabilizing force in the body politic. An impartial, fair, open-minded investigation of the incident is launched by governmental authorities with the aim of discovering the facts of the matter, not hurling accusations springing from ignorance and prejudice. Social and medical experts inquire into the possible motives that drove the individual to kill or cause injury to other people, not condemn him outright or claim that he was a part of a conspiracy orchestrated by a particular ethnic group, political party or foreign power.

I do not know the details of the tragic incident of September 3. I do know that the soldier who did the shooting, Aziz Kelmendi, happened to be an Albanian citizen of Yugoslavia. And because he was Albanian the incident has been blown out of

---

[1] Source: THE SOUTH SLAV JOURNAL, London, Winter 1987-88, p. 69-70.

proportion by the media and, what is worse, by social groups and governmental authorities. Not only the Albanian who pulled the trigger, but his family and indeed *all* Albanians in Yugoslavia are being reviled and blamed somehow for what happened.

This is clearly an abnormal and irrational reaction. The Albanian soldier, like certain unfortunate members of any ethnic group, may have been mentally disturbed. Or it may be, as I have heard, that he was infuriated because one or more of his fellow soldiers insulted him brutally, causing him to react in a violent manner. I believe that a Serbian or Montenegrin soldier in the same situation would have behaved in the same manner.

The loss of life in the incident was a tragedy. But a greater tragedy, surely, in the manner in which the media and the authorities in Yugoslavia have been handling the matter—in effect, pouring fuel into the fire, instead of *quenching the flames and closing the incident,* before the flames consume both the accused and the accusers! It does not take a political genius to see that the course that is being followed, which resembles the action of a lawless mob, can only lead to disaster for the Albanians, the Serbs, the Macedonians and all the people of Yugoslavia.

Is it not time to turn around before reaching the precipice? Where are the political realists, the statesmen, the voices of reason in Belgrade? It is time for them to step forward boldly and take the reins away from the hands of anti-Albanian extremists.

Respectfully yours,

Peter R. Prifti

P.S. My apologies for writing in English. I do not know Serbo-Croatian.

4. Letters to the Media

San Diego, California
January 19 1983

Hana Umlauf Lane
Editor
The World Almanac & Book of Facts 1983
Newspaper Enterprise Association, Inc.
200 Park Avenue, New York, N.Y. 10166

Dear Ms. Lane:

I have just purchased a copy of your Almanac for 1983. It is a valuable reference work. I find it helpful in many ways.

Permit me, however, to point out an error in your article on Yugoslavia (p. 579). With regard to ethnic groups in that country, the percentage given for Albanians (namely 2%) is wrong.

According to the latest (1981) national census in Yugoslavia (results were released by Yugoslav information agencies in March, 1982) , the total population of the country is 22,411,000. The breakdown on the leading ethnic groups was as follows:

Serbs	8,137,000
Croats	4,428,000
Moslems	1,999,000
Slovenes	1,753,000
Albanians	1,730,000
Macedonians	1,341,000
Montenegrins	577,000

That means that Albanians account for 7.7% of the total population.

Also, the reference to Serbia's "annexation of Old Serbia" (bottom of p. 579) is misleading. What the Serbs call Old Serbia is actually the northeastern part of the Albanian nation that was ceded to Yugoslavia by the Great Powers in 1913, in the wake of the collapse of the Ottoman Empire. It is the area known as Kosova, where most of the Albanians (1,223,000) in Yugoslavia live at present.

I am pleased to make this information available to you, in the interest of greater accuracy and value for your very useful publication.

Respectfully yours,

Peter R. Prifti
Author, *Socialist Albania since1944* (MIT Press,1978)

San Diego, U.S.A.
February 25, 1986

Sergiu Grossu
Editor

Catacombes

B.P. 98 - 92405 Courbevoie
Paris, FRANCE

Dear Editor:

I have just read the article "L'Histoire des religieuses des Kosovo," [1] by Dragoljub Golubovic in the *Catacombes* (November - December 1985 issue), and I must say I was quite disappointed. Permit me to explain.

The Serbs have embarked on a campaign to discredit the Albanians in Kosova before world public opinion. The two main pillars on which that campaign rests are: 1. The accusation that Albanians in Kosova are striving for an "ethnically pure" province; 2. The accusation that Albanians are doing violence to Serbian religious shrines and religious personnel in the province.

Neither of those accusations is true. The Albanians have never claimed that they want the Serbs or other non- Albanians to move out of Kosova. And far from being hostile to Serbian churches and clerics, they have been respectful of them. Indeed, they have been their guardians over the centuries to protect them from the Turks and other dangers. This is a fact that even some Serbian historians admit publicly.

This is not the first time that Yugoslavs, headed by the Serbs, have mounted a campaign to discredit the Albanians. They have done this many time before, particularly at the time of the Congress of Berlin (1878), and during the Balkan War (1912). In the past they claimed that Albanians were really Turks, and that they were an ignorant and savage people. Unfortunately, many uninformed people in the West, including some diplomats and heads of state, believed those allegations and as a consequence Albanian national interest were severely damaged.

But world public opinion is wiser in our day. People are becoming increasingly aware about the actual situation in Kosova, and they are no longer accepting the Serbian version of developments there without reservations or questioning.

The article by Golubovic is misleading and destructive. It does not serve truth, and therefore does not throw light on the problem of Kosova. It does not contribute to efforts to resolve the

---

[1] *History of Nuns of Kosova.*

complex question of Kosova. On the contrary, it fans the flames of discord between the Serbs and the Albanians.

It is most regrettable that you saw fit to publish such an article in *Catacombes*.

Sincerely yours,

Peter R. Prifti
P.O. Box 4441, San Diego, California 92104 U.S. of America

San Diego, Ca.
October 22, 1988

Editor
Time
Time & Life Bldg.
New York, NY 10020

Dear Editor:

This letter is in reference to your informative and interesting report on Yugoslavia (Oct. 24, '88, p. 46).

"Sinister," "demagogue," "dangerous" are apt terms with which to describe Serbia's party leader, Milosevic. He has rightly been compared with Mussolini. I would go a step further and compare him with Hitler. His racist attacks on the Albanian population in Yugoslavia are a page borrowed from Hitler when he lashed out against the Jews.

Serbian charges that they are being persecuted by Albanians are both groundless and ludicrous. The charges make sense only when they are reversed.

For decades Albanians have been the victims of oppression by the Serbian majority. They still are. Yugoslav jails are full of them. They live in a climate of insecurity and fear. Three times since the war (in 1945, 1968, and 1981) they have rebelled to throw off Serbian oppression. Three times their attempt was bloodily suppressed.

Now, Milosevic is creating a situation that could easily lead to a blood bath in Kosova, tear Yugoslavia apart, provoke war with Albania and bring the Soviets into Yugoslavia. Far from being the bold leader who can cure Yugoslavia's ills, Slobodan Milosevic is a rash rabble rouser who could deal her the death blow.

Sincerely yours,

Prof. Peter R. Prifti

San Diego, Ca.
October 22, 1988

Editor
NEWSWEEK
1150 15ᵗʰ St., N. W.
Washington. DC 20071

Dear Editor:

I am writing in reference to the article on Yugoslavia in this week's issue of *Newsweek* (Oct. 24, '88, p. 33).

You hit the nail right on the head when you questioned the veracity of Serb charges of Albanian crimes against them in Kosovo. Actually, it's the other way around.

Ever since the Congress of Berlin in 1878, and especially since World War I, the Albanians have been incessantly under attack by the Serbs and their allies. It was only in the last years of Tito's rule that they enjoyed a measure of freedom and security in Yugoslavia.

Since 1981 they have been the target of Serb persecution across the board. They risk arrest even for so innocuous an act as singing an Albanian song or reciting an Albanian poem. The jails are full of them, including children, and the sentences they receive are the heaviest of any ethnic group in Yugoslavia.

The attempt of Slobodan Milosevic to portray the Serbs as victims of Albanians is like that fable of La Fontaine, in which the wolf accuses the lamb of muddying up his drinking water, so as to have an excuse to pounce on the innocent creature.

Sincerely yours,

Prof. Peter R. Prifti

San Diego, Ca.
October 26, 1988

Foreign News Editor
The San Francisco Chronicle
925 Mission Street
San Francisco, Ca. 94103

Dear Editor:

I am writing in reference to your very interesting "calendar of anniversaries" in East Europe ("Issues & Ideas," Wed., Oct. 19, '88).

You do well to draw attention to the anniversaries the Serbs plan to commemorate this coming December and next June.

Following the death of Tito in 1980, the Serbs bid good-bye to his mandate to shun chauvinism and cultivate fraternal relations with all ethnic groups in Yugoslavia. Although publicly they still pay lip service to Tito, in fact they yearn for the restoration of Serbian dominance in Yugoslavia, a goal which the late Yugoslav leader, of course, opposed. Hence their eagerness to commemorate the Kingdom of the Serbs, Croats and Slovenes that was proclaimed on December 1, 1918. They are doing this in defiance of the feelings of Croats, Slovenians, Albanians and others who oppose such a commemoration.

The commemoration next June of the 600th anniversary of the Battle of Kosova (1389), which marked the destruction of the Serbian medieval state by the Turks, bears close watching. In view of the Serbs' racist hatred of Albanians in Kosova, who at present make up over 80 percent of the population there, the commemoration could easily turn violent and bring disaster to Yugoslavia and war in the Balkans. In my view, the chances of that scenario becoming a reality are better than 50-50, unless the Serbs, led by the demagogue, Milosevic, abandon their inane drive to put Kosova (and Vojvodina) totally under Serbia's control, and deny Albanians (and Hungarian ethnics) the right to rule themselves in their own territories.

Sincerely yours,

Prof. Peter R. Prifti

San Diego, Ca.
October 27, 1988

To the Editor of the
Los Angeles Times

Dear Sir:

I am writing to compliment your Belgrade correspondent, Charles T. Powers, on his fine reportage on developments in Yugoslavia.

Powers is right on target when he refers to Serbian party leader, Milosevic, as a "renegade." He is that and more -- a Serbian chauvinist demagogue who has built his career on racist hatred of Albanians in Yugoslavia.

Milosevic is correct when he says there is terror in Kosova (*TIMES,* Oct. 18, p. 9), but it is the Albanians, not the Serbs, who are living in terror. That has been their bitter lot there for generations. Serbian officials and media are making feverish efforts to hide the truth on the Kosova issue, but happily fewer and fewer people abroad are buying their story.

Sincerely yours,

Prof. Peter R. Prifti

San Diego, Ca.
October 27, 1988

Editor
U.S. NEWS & WORLD REPORT
2400 N Street, N.W.
Washington, DC 20037

Dear Editor:

I wish to compliment you on the excellent report on Yugoslavia by your Belgrade correspondent, David Lawday (*U.S.N.& W.R.*, Oct. 24, p. 50).

Lawday is right when he speaks of "a ruthless, demagogic side" in the strategy of the Serbian party leader, Milosevic. This man has shown himself to be a clever rabble rouser, who has attained notoriety and power by feeding Serbian racist hatred of ethnic Albanians in Yugoslavia.

It is not the Serbs but the Albanians who are persecuted in Kosova. They have been living in a climate of insecurity and terror there for generations. Serbian charges that they are being victimized by Albanians are, in reality, a ploy to maintain Serbian supremacy in Kosova, and reduce the two million or so Albanians to a state of semi-serfdom, as they were, in fact, in the days of Rankovic and prewar Yugoslavia.

Lawday correctly notes that the "Serbs may turn Kosovo into an ethnic battlefield." My hunch is that they will, unless they and their ambitious leader, Milosevic, are checked and turned back decisively.

Sincerely yours,

Prof. Peter R. Prifti

San Diego, Ca.
October 31, 1988

V. Rev. Leonid Kishkovsky
Editor
THE ORTHODOX CHURCH
P.O. Box 675, Route 25 - A
Syosset, N.Y. 11791

Dear Editor:

Looking at the October issue of *The Orthodox Church*, my attention was attracted by the report, "Serbian Church Brings Problem to Govt. Attention" (p. 4).

In this report the Serbian Church makes some serious accusations against Albanians in Yugoslavia. It is alleged that Albanians in the Kosova province have perpetrated acts of "cruelty and violence" against the Serbs and their "holy objects." According to my information, such accusations are not well founded.

It is not true that ethnic Albanians vandalize and desecrate Serbian holy objects. Albanians have traditionally been the guardians of Serbian shrines and monuments in Kosova. This is avowed even by some Serbian writers.

It is not true that "200,000 ethnic Serbians and Montenegrins" have been pressured by Albanians to migrate from Kosova. First of all, the figure is closer to 20,000 rather than 200,000, according to official Yugoslav sources. Second, reports from Kosova's daily *Rilindja*, affirm that Serbian and Montenegrins who have emigrated have done so, in almost all cases, for economic and personal reasons, rather than pressure from Albanians.

The accusations of the Serbian Church, unfortunately, are part and parcel of a sustained effort by Serbian leaders and media to discredit ethnic Albanians by portraying them as immoral, incompetent, backward, fierce and so on. Wittingly or unwittingly the church has been politicized. And while it is not inherently improper for a religious institution to support the policies of a political institution, in this instance, the support by the Serbian Church of Serbia's anti- Albanian policies in Kosova is misguided, I feel, and quite harmful to inter-ethnic relations in Yugoslavia.

Sincerely yours,

Prof. Peter R. Prifti

San Diego, Ca.
November 11, 1988

Foreign News Editor
SAN FRANCISCO CHRONICLE

Dear Editor:

May I invite your attention again [1] to the escalating Serb-Albanian conflict in the province of Kosova, Yugoslavia?

For several years now Serbian leaders and media have been waging a furious anti- Albanian crusade. They have flooded the world with horror tales of "persecution of the Serbs" in Kosova by the Albanians, alleging that they vandalize Serbian properties, desecrate Serbian graveyards, rape Serbian women and so forth.

In reality such tales either have no foundation at all, or are irresponsibly blown up out of proportion. The object is to portray the Albanians as oppressors and the Serbs as victims, when in fact the opposite is true -- and has been for generations!

It might be asked: What is the motive for such a crusade? The answer is that the Serbs want to put Albanians totally under the control of the Republic of Serbia, either through political maneuvers and intimidation, or outright violence and genocide, if necessary.

Yet, the solution to the Kosova conflict is not the abolition of the few ethnic rights Albanians presently enjoy, but granting them full rights, including the right to have their own Republic of Kosova, thereby admitting them to full citizenship in the Yugoslav Federation.

Fortunately, we have leaders in Congress who are informed about the true situation in Kosova, and have boldly denounced Yugoslavia's outrageous repression of ethnic Albanians. Senators Larry Pressler (Rep., S. D.) Paul Simon (Dem. Ill.), and Alfonse D'Amato (Rep., N. Y.), are three of those leaders.

I take the liberty herewith of enclosing a couple of excerpts from the *Congressional Record* (Oct.12, 1988), which contain their views on this subject. Please take a look at them.

Sincerely yours

Prof. Peter R. Prifti

---

[1] Letters identical to this one, were sent to LOS ANGELES TIMES and   SAN DIEGO UNION.

San Diego, Ca.
November 28, 1988

To the Editor of the
San Diego Union

I wish to compliment you on the broad coverage you have given lately to the serious Serb- Albanian conflict over Kosova. Of special interest was the extensive and perceptive report from Belgrade by your correspondent Ruth E. Gruber (*S. D. Union*, Nov. 20, p. 1, pt I).

One point, however, in Gruber's report is debatable, namely that ethnic Albanians in Kosova moved in there from Albania. This is an old and by now threadbare argument of the Serbian propaganda arsenal. The aim apparently is to persuade the world that Albanians in Yugoslavia are not indigenous to the land, but usurpers of Serbian territory. That is why Serbs are presently shouting slogans such as "Kosovo Is Serbia," and "Albanians Out."

But in fact the presence of Albanians in Kosova is as old as recorded history. Their Illyrian ancestors were there centuries before the Serbs set foot in the Balkans in the 7th Century A. D. Albanians have not always been as numerous in Kosova as they are at present (over 80%), but they have been there in respectable numbers at all times.

To set the record straight, it is the Serbs rather than Albanians who moved into Kosova, either as invaders or as colonizers. Yet, Albanians are not shouting "Serbs Go Home" and the like. They are willing to live side by side with them -- but as equals, not as subordinates of the Serbs.

Sincerely yours,

Prof. Peter R. Prifti

San Diego, Ca
April 23, 1989

Editor
THE MILWAUKEE JOURNAL
333 W. State Street
Milwaukee, WI 53201

Dear Editor:

This letter is in reference to the article, "Tito's grand plan blamed for turmoil" (*MJ*, Apr. 9, 1989, p. 3).

Prof. Vojtislav Seselj, whom your staff writer, Tim Cuprisin, identifies as "a strong Serbian nationalist," is mistaken about the cause of the recent bloody turmoil in the province of Kosova, home of more than two million ethnic Albanians in Yugoslavia.

The true cause of the turmoil was none other than Serbian nationalism, whose ideology and politics Prof. Seselj embraces, and is currently seeking to popularize in his lecture tour up and down our country. What he calls "Albanian separatism" is in reality a Serbian myth to rationalize the century-old domination and oppression of Albanians in Yugoslavia. The massive March 23-28 demonstrations of Albanians in Kosova marked only their most recent desperate attempt to throw off the Serbian yoke. As in the past, this time, too, the Serbs and their allies crushed their bid for justice and equality with army units firing automatic weapons into crowds of unarmed Albanians, killing scores of them, including several children.

Prof. Seselj tries hard to portray the Serbian- Albanian confrontation as a religious conflict, with Christian Serbs on one side, and Albanian Moslems on the other side. This accounts, according to him, for the support of the Albanians in Yugoslavia by Moslem countries in the Middle East. A neat theory, only it won't wash.

The problem in Kosova is not religious, but political. It is not Moslem Albanians vs. Orthodox Serbs, but Albanians demanding the ethnic, democratic and human rights to which they are entitled. Their demands, being just, are supported not only by Moslem countries, but by many people in Christian countries, such as Greece, Italy, Austria, West Germany, Great Britain and others.

The recent turmoil in Yugoslavia cannot be blamed either on Albanians, or the late Tito. But a large measure of it can certainly be blamed on Serbian intellectuals like

Prof. Seselj, whose ultra-nationalist passions prevent them from understanding the true nature of the Kosova problem.

Sincerely yours,

Peter R. Prifti

San Diego, Ca
April 4, 1991

Editor
INSIGHT weekly
3600 New York Ave., N.E.
Washington, D.C. 20002

Dear Editor:

This letter is in reference to the article on Yugoslavia in your April 8, 1991 issue (p. 35).

Please do not refer to the two provinces of the Yugoslav Federation as "autonomous." Kosova and Vojvodina were, at best, semi-autonomous prior to 1988-89. But in 1989, Serbia's communist chief, S. Milosevic, in disregard of the 1974 Federal Constitution, revised the constitution of the Serbian republic, and effectively deprived Kosova and Vojvodina of even the limited autonomy they had under the Federal Constitution. They are now under strict Serbian control.

The two provinces are "autonomous" in name only, not in fact. It is therefore misleading to refer to them as autonomous.

Respectfully yours,

Prof. Peter R. Prifti

San Diego, Ca.
April 8, 1991

The New York Review Of Books
250 West 57 St.
New York, N.Y. 10107

To the Editors:

I wish to commend and thank *The New York Review Of Books* for publishing the collective letter on "The Plight of Kosovo" (issue of April 11, '91, p. 61).

The brutal suppression of ethnic Albanians by Serbia is indeed intolerable, and deserves to be exposed and condemned until it is destroyed root and branch. There cannot be peace and democracy in Yugoslavia as long as Albanians are denied human and democratic rights, are denied the right of self-determination, and are treated with less respect and sensitivity than that shown animals.

Respectfully,

Prof. Peter R. Prifti

P.S. -I am taking the liberty to include here also a copy of a letter I wrote to Secretary James Baker on this issue. The copy is slightly abbreviated.

P.R.P.

Enc. - (1)

San Diego, Ca
April 12, '91

Editor
The Milwaukee Sentinel
333 W. State St.
Milwaukee, Wis. 53201

Dear Editor:

This letter is prompted by the article on Yugoslavia and the graphic data on that country that appeared recently in *The Milwaukee Sentinel* (Sat. March 30, '91, p. 2, pt. 1).

The article gave a misleading account of the Albanians in the province of Kosova. It erred on two counts: their number, and their language and alphabet. At present, ethnic Albanians make up not 77 percent of the population in Kosova, but 90 percent. This is the estimate that has been given almost universally by the media in the last two years. The 77 percent figure is taken from the 1981 Yugoslav census, and is clearly out-of-date.

The article was off-track also in saying that the language spoken in Kosova is Serbo-Croatian, and the alphabet is Russian. Since the Albanians of Kosova have their own language, which is quite distinct from Slavic, ninety percent of the population of Kosova speaks Albanian, and only about ten percent (Serbian and Montenegrins) speak Serbo-Croatian. Also, the Albanian language uses the Latin alphabet, unlike Serbo-Croatian which uses the Cyrillic alphabet.

Respectfully yours,

Prof. Peter R. Prifti

San Diego, Ca.
July 20, 1991

The Santa Barbara News-Press
715 Anacapa St.
Santa Barbara, Ca.

To the Editor:

Question: What's wrong with the enclosed cartoon-map of Yugoslavia (published in your paper last Monday, July 15, p. A7)?

Answer: Plenty. It left out the entire province of Kosova, which is to say, the region of ethnic Albanians, currently the third largest ethnic group in Yugoslavia, after the Serbs and the Croats.

Kosova and Vojvodina are both provinces of the Republic of Serbia. Yet, while Vojvodina figures in the "map", Kosova does not. It has been completely ignored. This, despite the fact that the Hungarians of Vojvodina number less than half a million (420,000), and make up only 46 percent of the total population of that province; whereas the Albanians of Kosova number well over two million, and account for 90 percent of the population in their province.

As a matter of fact, the Albanians were the first to demonstrate *en masse* in 1981 (less than a year after Tito died) against Serbian domination and oppression. They were the first because they have suffered the most from Serbian oppression.

Don't you think they deserved better of your cartoonist?

Respectfully yours,

Prof. Peter R. Prifti

Enc. - cartoon-map.

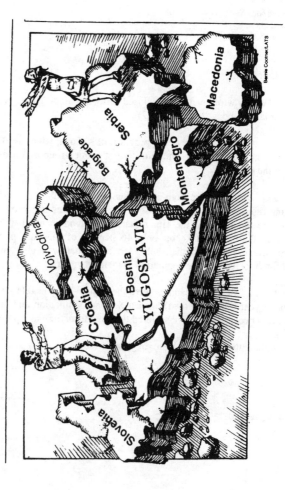

Bernie Cooner/LATS

Postscript

After the signing of the October 12, 1998 cease-fire accord by the U.S. special envoy Richard Holbrooke, and Serbian strongman Slobodan Milosevic, a relative calm set in over the province of Kosova. The fragile peace prevailed for the most part through the warning weeks of 1998.

With the arrival of the New Year, however, the accord suffered a severe setback when Serbian security forces attacked the village of Racak ("Reçak" in Albanian) on January 15, 1999 killing 45 ethnic Albanian civilians. The massacre shocked U.S. officials and public opinion. William Walker, U.S. head of the multinational team of peace monitors in Kosova, set up by OSCE (Organization for Security and Cooperation in Europe), called the killings " an unspeakable atrocity" and "a crime against humanity." He put the blame bluntly on the Serbs. Belgrade retaliated by ordering Walker to get out of Yugoslavia within 48 hours, but later relented and did not enforce the order. The incident added new strains to relations between the Yugoslav government and the United Stated.

Two weeks later, on January 29, Serbian forces committed another massacre when they slaughtered 24 ethnic Albanians in the village of Rogovo. The new atrocity, plus armed attacks on Serb forces by the KLA (Kosova Liberation Army), impelled the U. S. and its allies to order both the Serbs and Kosovar Albanians to settle their differences through negotiations within three weeks; i.e., by February 19, or face punishment by NATO. The ultimatum was issued by the foreign ministers of the Contact Group (U.S., Britain, France, Germany, Italy, and Russia) on January 30, and was delivered personally in Belgrade and Prishtina by British Foreign Secretary Robin Cook, chairman of the Contact Group. The warring parties were expected to sign a peace plan which envisioned broad autonomy for the Albanians, within the borders of Serbia.

For the Albanians, the "invitation" to take part on an equal footing, at a peace conference organized by the international community, was a notable diplomatic victory, without precedent in the history of their relations with the Great Powers. For the first time, the "Albanian Question" in the Balkans had taken center stage and became the focus of world attention.

Among themselves the Kosovars were divided over tactics for achieving independence, but they managed to paper over their differences and craft a common negotiating position, just prior to the opening of the talks. To accommodate the Contact Group, they agreed to accept autonomy under the protection of NATO forces, provided that at the end of three years, a Referendum on Independence would be held in Kosova. The Albanian delegation of 16 included Ibrahim Rugova, President of the Kosova shadow government, and four KLA members, led by the insurgents' political director Jakup Krasniqi. For the KLA, participation in the talks was a double victory: first, because it gained admittance to the conference over strong objections by Belgrade; second, because one of their delegates, Hashim Thaçi, was chosen as head of the Albanian delegation.

Reluctantly, the Serb leadership also agreed to hold talks with the Kosovars, and by so doing tacitly abandoned its previous position that Kosova was an "internal affair" of Serbia.

The peace conference began in France on February 6, 1999 in an historic 45-room chateau in the little town of Rambouillet, close to Paris. The basis for the talks was a peace plan drafted by the U.S. Ambassador in Macedonia, Christopher Hill. Co-hosts and managers of the conference were the French Foreign Minister Hubert Vedrine, and British Foreign Secretary Robin Cook. Among other things, the peace plan called for the deployment of 28,000 NATO troops in Kosova, including 4,000 Americans, to guarantee compliance with the provisions of the proposed peace accord, by both parties to the dispute.

When the February 19 deadline arrived, the two sides were deadlocked and the talks were extended another three days. The Serb delegation at one point said it accepted the political part of the peace plan, but rejected the military part, namely the deployment of NATO troops, on the grounds that their presence in Kosova would amount to occupation of Yugoslav territory by foreign powers. The Albanian delegation was disposed to sign, but drew back when the provision for a referendum was suddenly dropped from the peace plan. The talks collapsed on February 23, although the Albanians indicated that they accepted the draft "in principle," but needed to return home to consult with their people, before signing the document.

The organizers of the Rambouillet Conference then decided to give the conference more time to study the plan, and set March 15 as the date for a second round of talks. On the given date, the Kosovar delegation returned to Paris and signed the accord. The Albanian signatories were: Hashim Thaçi, Ibrahim Rugova, Veton Surroi and Rexhep Qosja, while Ambassador Hill signed for the mediators, with the Russian mediator abstaining. Upon its return to Paris, the Serb delegation was more intransigent than before, and rejected even the political part of the peace plan, which formerly it had accepted. In retrospect, it was clear that the Serbs were not serious about the conference from the start. Four days later, the Rambouillet peace initiative foundered. In a last-minute attempt to save the talks, Richard Holbrooke had intensive discussions with Milosevic in Belgrade (March 22-23) , but was unable to obtain his consent to the peace plan.

On March 24, 1999 NATO launched airstrikes against Serbia, using both missiles and planes. The NATO powers felt compelled to use force for several reasons. Their year-long efforts to persuade Milosevic to resolve the conflict peacefully had come to naught. Secondly, according to NATO officials, Belgrade took advantage of the three-week interval in the peace talks (February 23-March 15), and built up its forces in and around Kosova to 40,000 troops—a clear sign that Serbs planned to launch a massive military offensive against the Kosovars. Lastly, NATO was constrained to act to save its credibility. After threatening to use force against Serbia several times before, if Milosevic did not rein in his army, the growing pressure on it to make good on its threats, could no longer be ignored.

Serbia reacted to the airstrikes by breaking off relations with NATO countries, and declaring Yugoslavia to be "in state of war." The pro-West government of Montenegro, however, which is the smaller republic of Yugoslavia, abstained from following in Serbia's footsteps.

The airstrikes were denounced by Russia, as well as China, both of whom had consistently opposed the use of force contemplated by NATO. Yet, neither of them had raised their voice against the violence of the Serbian military machine in Kosova, nor did they appreciate the patient efforts of the U.S. and its NATO partners to reason with Milosevic and resolve the conflict by diplomatic means.

The airstrikes triggered demonstrations against the United States in Greece, Macedonia, Moscow, Toronto and elsewhere. Demonstrations erupted also in towns in America with Serbian communities. The demonstrators accused America of violating the sovereignty of an independent country and harboring imperialistic designs on the Balkans. Counter-demonstrations mounted by Albanians and their sympathizers in America and abroad defended U.S. policy, arguing that America and her NATO allies were merely reacting to the violence unleashed by Yugoslavia's President against a defenseless and oppressed people. In their view, human rights—the foundation stone of the United Nations— took precedence over state sovereignty. Rather than denounce America, they said, she should be applauded and supported for coming to the aid of the victims of Serb aggression.

After the OSCE monitors left Kosova, following the breakdown of the talks, NATO's top commander, Gen. Wesley Clark, said that the Serb forces were poised for "a vast and violent onslaught." [1] Albanians in Kosova were aware that if NATO were to drop bombs on Serbia, the Serbs would retaliate against them in revenge. Even so, they were convinced that NATO's intervention was their only hope of salvation.

As one of them put it, "It's better to bomb because otherwise we cannot survive." [2]

President Bill Clinton defended the airstrikes, saying they were necessary: 1), To prevent a human catastrophe that was certain to happen, if NATO did not act; 2), To prevent a widening of the war in the Balkans.

However, within days after the bombing began, it became clear that the first objective was not going to be achieved. A human catastrophe began to unfold, as tens of thousands of Albanian refugees streamed out Kosova and sought shelter in neighboring Macedonia, Albania, Montenegro, and Bosnia. They brought with them tales of horror, cruelty and depravity. The refugees, most of them women, children and old men, told the same story. They left Kosova not because of the NATO bombings, but because they were forcibly deported by armed Serbian troops wearing masks, who broke into their homes and told them to flee or be killed. Prior to leaving, they were robbed of their money and jewelry, and deprived of passports and other personal documents, even the license plates of their cars, so as to obliterate their identity and prevent them from returning to their homes. There were gruesome reports of young women raped and murdered. Scenes of refugees packed like cattle into trains bound for the border of Macedonia, brought back memories of the Holocaust in World War II.

By the end of the second week of the "ethnic cleansing" by Serbian forces, about 900,000 Kosovars, or one-half of the Albanian population of Kosova (1.8 million), had been displaced, some of them within the province. The numerical breakdown for the refugees abroad was as follows: Albania - 290,000; Macedonia - 140,000; Montenegro - 60,000; Bosnia - 11,000. Shocking as these figures were, they were expected to increase dramatically within a short time. Indeed, it was feared that, if the Serbs were not stopped quickly, Kosova could be emptied of its Albanian population altogether. Officials of the United Nations High Commissioner for Refugees (UNHCR) called the plight of the refugees the worst humanitarian tragedy in postwar Europe. A Reuters dispatch quoted U.N. Secretary General Kofi Annan as saying:

The brutal persecution the refugees and displaced persons are suffering, the loss of their family members, their homes and even documentation of their identities, underline the urgency of their plight. [3]

As reports of atrocities piled up, officials of the UN War Crimes Tribunal for Yugoslavia in the Hague, headed by Judge Louise Arbour, began collecting evidence for possible indictment of Serbs guilty of committing crimes against humanity in Kosova. Indeed, the notorious Serb, Zeljko Raznjatovic, known as "Arkan", leader of a band of terrorists called The Tigers, was officially indicted recently as a war criminal and was liable for arrest.

Although criticism of NATO airstrikes continued in some quarters, public opinion polls showed that a large majority of Americans supported the bombings, especially after the Serbs captured three American soldiers serving with the U.N. peacekeeping mission in Macedonia. Most people in the major NATO countries, including England, France, and Germany, also backed the continuation of the air war.

With the public behind them, President Clinton and leaders of NATO said repeatedly that they were determined to press the bombing campaign until Milosevic met their demands for peace. These included: 1) a cease-fire by the Serbian forces, 2) withdrawal of Serbian military, police and paramilitary forces from Kosova, 3) deployment of an international security force in Kosova, with NATO as a core, 4) return of all refugees to their homes, 5) drawing up a political framework for the province, based on the Rambouillet peace plan.

Some observers noted, however, that in the view of the violence against ethnic Albanians in recent weeks, coexistence between them and the Serbs was no longer possible. They argued that the option of autonomy had been bypassed by events, and that a more practical alternative was to make Kosova an international protectorate.

Much to the surprise of NATO officials, by mid-April, 1999 (the third week of the bombing), Milosevic seemed unmoved and unbending, despite the widespread destruction visited upon Serbia by NATO's airpower. Indeed, the bombing increased Serbian public support of him, even from the ranks of the democratic opposition, all of whom professed to back him for patriotic reasons. In any event, the international community made it clear that Serbia's hold on Kosova by force was unacceptable. In the words of Javier Solana, Secretary General of NATO:

> Peace, stability and justice in the Balkan is a crucial interest of all peoples of the Euro-Atlantic region. Success will require patience, perseverance and the continuing unity and determination of the alliance. But let there be no doubt: Justice will prevail and ethnic cleansing will be reversed.[4]

* * *

To Albanians the war that engulfed Kosova came as no surprise. This was but the latest phase of a long saga that has cost the Kosovars great losses in lives and property. Most assuredly, the humanitarian catastrophe that took center stage since March 1999 was not the result of NATO airstrikes on Serbia. The seeds for the catastrophe, which impelled the 19-nations NATO allies to intervene militarily in a campaign dubbed "Operation Allied Force," were sown long before Slobodan Milosevic took power in Serbia in the late 1980's. To understand Serbian policy on Kosova at a deeper level, it is necessary to digress briefly and go back more than a hundred years, when Serbia was not yet a fully sovereign nation.[5]

The "founding father" of modern Serbia, who is credited with crafting its national ideology, was Ilija Garashanin, its foreign minister in mid-19th century. In 1844 he drafted a paper titled *Naçertanije*, meaning "Project." This document has had the greatest influence in shaping the political thought of the Serbian people. In essence *Naçertanije* inspired and rationalized a politics of expansionism for Serbia, whose goal was to unify all the Serbs and Slavs in the Balkans.

Garashanin viewed Serbia as the direct heir of the Medieval Kingdom of Tsar Stefan Dushan, and believed that it was the historical mission of the Serbs to restore the kingdom that was crushed by the Turks in 1389 in the Battle of Kosova. This supposedly enlightened statesman, whom Serb historians rank with Talleyrand and Metternich, [6] had a mean regard for Albanians. He thought Albanians were people who could neither read nor write and were "a big nuisance." [7] Garashanin's hostile view tainted the Serbian popular image of Albanians, and fed Serbia's expansionist policy at the expense of the Albanian nation.

The first instance of Serbia's aggressive politics in Kosova occurred in 1877, when the Serbs seized a number of mostly Albanian-populated towns, in the wake of the Russian-Turkish War of 1877-78. Among such towns were Nish, Leskovac and Prokuplje. But this was merely a prelude to a more ambitious plan to occupy all of Kosova at a later date, when the times were more propitious.

To advance this process, beginning with the Congress of Berlin (1878) and continuing until the Balkan Wars (1912-13), Serbia engaged in a deliberate campaign to demonize the Albanians, so as to convince the European powers that they were too primitive to have their own state and unfit to rule themselves. Accordingly, they were painted in the darkest colors: they were illiterate, dirty and vengeful, people who have no word for "love" in their language, a fierce lot who were closer to the beasts in the forests than to human beings. The campaign reached its zenith in 1912-13, with a volley of books that pressed this negative view of Albanians. The most notorious of these was a book of Vladan Djordjevic, a former Prime Minister of Serbia. In this work, titled *Les Albanais et les Grandes Puissances* (The Albanians and the Great Powers), which he published in 1913, Djordjevic had the temerity to write that "as late as the 19th century" there were Albanians with tails in their rear. [8] Crude and callous as this publicity blitz was, it succeeded in its objective. With the consent of the Great Powers, Serbia in 1913 took control of all of Kosova. With this victory, Serbia realized what I would call "Phase One" of its overall strategy, namely acquiring full territorial possession of the province.

Serbian leaders now turned their attention to "Phase Two" of the strategy: finding ways to eliminate the Albanian majority in Kosova through assimilation, changing the demographic composition of the province through massive settlements of Slavs, or by deporting the Albanians.

The first two options were tried, but failed for the most part. Albanians resisted assimilation, and attempts to colonize the region with Slavs proved inconclusive. Attention then shifted increasingly to option three—deportations.

According to Albanian sources in Kosova, between World War I and World War II, the Yugoslav Government (which was dominated by the Serbs) deported "hundreds of thousands" of ethnic Albanians to Turkey. [9] Preoccupation with the deportation option crystallized in the late thirties in the cogitations of a Yugoslav academician, Dr. Vaso (or Vasa) Cubrilovic. It was he who gave the clearest expression to the concept of deportation, as the "final solution" for the Albanian problem. He set forth his ideas in a 10,000-word Memorandum titled, "The expulsion of the Arnauts,"—"Arnaut" being the Turkish word for "Albanian", which he submitted to the Yugoslav Government in 1937. The Memo is a chilling prescription for driving the Albanians out of Kosova by making life unbearable for them. It is the Master Plan for the ethnic cleansing of the Kosovars, and the ideological basis of Milosevic's war in Kosova. Following are excerpts from the Memo:

> The law must be enforced to the letter, so as to make staying unbearable for the Albanians: fines and imprisonment, the ruthless application of all police dispositions, such as ... cutting forests, leaving dogs unchained, compulsory labor and any other measure that an experienced police force can contrive.
> ... The refusal to recognize land deeds (of Albanians) , the ruthless collection of taxes... withdrawal of permits to exercise a profession, dismissal from state, private and communal offices... the ill-treatment of their clergy, the destruction of their cemeteries.

Dr. Cubrilovic also recommended "secretly burning down Albanian villages and city quarters."

Agreements signed between Yugoslavia and Turkey prior to WWII envisioned the deportation of as many as 400,000 Albanians from Yugoslavia. However, they were not implemented, owing to the outbreak of general war in Europe. The deportation resumed after the war, during the communist regime of the late Marshal Tito. The man chiefly responsible for the persecution of Kosovars in Tito's time, was his heir-designate and Vice-President of Yugoslavia, Aleksandar Rankovic, a hard-line Serb who nourished a deep resentment of ethnic Albanians. Reportedly, over 350,000 Albanians were forced to migrate to Turkey during the Rankovic years.[10]

Since Milosevic rose to power a dozen years ago, the banner of ethnic cleansing first held aloft by Cubrilovic passed on to Voislav Seselj, the current Deputy Prime Minister of Serbia. In October of 1995, Seselj published a draft-plan for the deportation of Albanians that bears an eerie resemblance to the Cubrilovic Memo, both in spirit and in substance. [11] Seselj advocates taking away from Albanians their property deeds, citizenship documents and other personal papers, and destroying their intellectual and political leadership through contrived scandals, accidents and other means. He notes ominously: "If we have to fight a war to defend Kosovo... it should be fought with all possible means, and have it finished as soon as possible." [12]

From the foregoing, one can see that the deportation of Albanians from Kosova in the spring of 1999 was inevitable under the circumstances. The mass exodus was the culmination of Serbian expansionist politics, first enunciated by Garashinin in the *Naçertanije* document back in 1844. There is a direct line from Garashinin to Djordjevic, Cubrilovic, Rankovic, down to Seselj and Milosevic. Until the current crisis, previous Serbian nationalists had attempted to clear the Kosovars out of the province, but never succeeded. It remained for Slobodan Milosevic to set aside all inhibitions and make an all-out attempt, however cynical and brutal, to carry out the Cubrilovic Memo to the letter. His policy of "ethnic cleansing" came as a shock to most people. But in fact it had been going on quietly for ten years prior, ever since he revoked the autonomy of Kosova in 1989. Hidden from the glare of the world media, Serbian police had put such pressure on the Kosovars that tens of thousands of them had fled the province before the massive deportation of recent weeks.

As of this writing, however, it is too early to tell whether or not Milosevic has succeeded. NATO seems determined to spoil his scheme, insisting that all refugees must be allowed to return to their homes.

The final year of our century seems to be shaping up as the "Year of Decision" for Kosova, which will determine its political status for years to come. But it's not likely that any lasting change for the better will occur, short of a radical change in the nature of both Serbian and Kosovar societies. To become part of the new Europe, both Serbs and Albanians have to define themselves less by the past and more by the future that lies ahead. They need to let go of inter-ethnic hatreds and long memories of past wrongs and injuries, and focus instead on building a future based on deep respect for human rights, and fulfillment of common human needs and aspirations.

San Diego, California
April, 1999

Notes

[1] *Los Angeles Times*, March 20, 1999, p. A9.

[2] *Ibid.*

[3] *Illyria*, Albanian-American semi-weekly, Bronx, N.Y. , April 7-9, 1999, p. 8.

[4] *Los Angeles Times*, April 13, 1999, p. B7.

[5] Serbia was established as an independent country in 1878.

[6] Alex N. Dragnich, Slavko Todorovich, *The Saga of Kosovo*, New York, 1984, p. 81.

[7] *Ibid.*, p. 81.

[8] s.s. juka, *Kosova - The Albanians in Yugoslavia in Light of Historical Documents*, New York, 1984, p. 15.

[9] *Perparimi* (Progress) , Albanian review in Prishtina, Jan.- Feb., 1974, p. 127.

[10] *The Struggle of the Kosovars*, July, 1974; *Flamuri* (The Flag) , August, 1974; both periodicals of Albanian emigres.

[11] *Velika Serbija*, The Greater Serbia journal, Belgrade, October 14, 1995.

[12] *Ibid.*